Justin Huntly McCarthy

The French Revolution

Justin Huntly McCarthy

The French Revolution

ISBN/EAN: 9783337229719

Printed in Europe, USA, Canada, Australia, Japan

Cover: Foto ©ninafisch / pixelio.de

More available books at **www.hansebooks.com**

THE
FRENCH REVOLUTION

BY

JUSTIN H. McCARTHY, M.P.

IN FOUR VOLUMES

VOL. II.

London
CHATTO & WINDUS, PICCADILLY
1890

CONTENTS

OF

THE SECOND VOLUME

CHAPTER		PAGE
XXII.	PARIS	1
XXIII.	THE PEOPLE OF PARIS	39
XXIV.	THE ELECTIONS	66
XXV.	THE SPRING OF '89	80
XXVI.	THE ROW AT RÉVEILLON'S	87
XXVII.	STATES-GENERAL AT LAST	99
XXVIII.	THE PLAY BEGINS	105
XXIX.	THE WILD GABRIEL HONORÉ	112
XXX.	THE MAN FROM ARRAS	159
XXXI.	SOME MINOR CHARACTERS	181
XXXII.	PEOPLE IN THE STREETS	196
XXXIII.	THE OVERTURE ENDS	211
XXXIV.	THE EIGHT WEEKS	215
XXXV.	SLOW AND SURE	240
XXXVI.	ON AND ON	250
XXXVII.	DRIFTING	263
XXXVIII.	THE TENTH OF JUNE	272
XXXIX.	THE SEVENTEENTH OF JUNE	279
XL.	TENNIS	289
XLI.	PARIS AND VERSAILLES	315
XLII.	CAMILLE DESMOULINS	330
XLIII.	TWELFTH AND THIRTEENTH OF JULY	338
XLIV.	THE BASTILLE	351
XLV.	AFTERMATH	386
XLVI.	THE STONES OF THE BASTILLE	395

THE
FRENCH REVOLUTION

CHAPTER XXII

PARIS

In the month of October of the year 1783 the hero of a certain famous or infamous fiction entered Paris for the first time by the Faubourg Saint-Marceau. 'I sought,' he says, 'that stately city of which I had read such wonderful accounts. I found but high and squalid tenements, long and ludicrously narrow streets, poor wretches everywhere clothed with rags, a crowd of well-nigh naked children; I beheld a dense population, and appalling poverty. I asked my father if that was indeed Paris; he answered coldly that it was certainly not the finest quarter; on the morrow we should have time to see another.' These sentences, almost the opening sentences of the once renowned romance of 'Faublas,' make a strangely appropriate text for any study of or any speculation upon the French Revolution. As we think of those two riders entering Paris in the gathering gloom of the dying day, the haughty, sombre man to whom Paris and all its ways were long familiar and the eager excited youth who enters for the first time the enchanted palace and finds it dust and ashes, we are half inclined to forgive Louvet all the follies of his life for that single picture which seems to bring pre-revolutionary Paris nearer to us than any other picture in pen or pencil known to us.

Neither Faublas the fictitious nor Louvet his maker would seem to have learnt any lesson from the rags, the hunger, and the agony which the one saw and the other recorded. And yet when the book in which those words appear was first printed the old world was drifting with awful swiftness to its destruction. No one can read such a story as 'Faublas' without seeing that in such corruption the germs of Revolution must be inevitably hidden; no one can read 'Faublas' without feeling that the society and the civilization which it not unfaithfully, and most certainly not satirically, described called for some cataclysm to sweep it out of existence. Listen to Louvet once again, speaking this time in his own proper person in the preface to a concluding portion of his romance, published, of all odd times in the century, in the month of July 1789. He is boasting of his book and of its hero. 'I have striven,' he says, 'that Faublas, frivolous and gallant as the nation for which and by which he was made, should have, as it were, a French physiognomy. I have striven that in the midst of his defects the world should recognise in him the tone, the language, and the manners of the young men of my country. It is in France, and it is only in France I believe, that we must seek the other types of whom I have too easily designed the copies—husbands at the same time so libertine, so jealous, so facile, and so foolish, beauties so seductive, so deceived, and so deceitful.' With the crash of the greatest fall in Christendom ringing in the ears of Europe, Louvet de Couvray makes his bow to mankind, and begs them to accept that estimate of his countrymen and countrywomen. Revolution was sorely needed when the nobility of France could find such a panegyrist.

Yet there are worse books than 'Faublas,' and worse writers than Citizen Louvet, ci-devant Louvet de Couvray. Mr. Carlyle speaks wild and whirling words about the book; calls it happily enough a 'wretched cloaca of a book,' but asks unhappily enough 'what picture of French society is here?' and answers yet more unhappily his own question, 'picture properly of nothing.' The picture is unfortunately true enough. It is not an exhaustive picture. All the France of 1789 is not encompassed in its pages, but what it does present is sufficiently veracious. Autobiographical, fictitious Faublas is a gentleman and a moralist compared with autobiographical, real Casanova. A society which could tolerate and even idolize a Richelieu and a de Fronsac, damnable father and yet more damnable son, can hardly complain of being travestied in the pages of poor, sensual, not all unmanly or all uncourageous Louvet. Madame Roland, the high-minded, the beautiful Girondist, can speak, and speak seriously, of Louvet's 'pretty stories.' Not all the praise of all the Girondists who ever perished on the guillotine could make us of to-day think the adventures of Faublas a 'pretty story.' But Madame Roland's words could make us and do make us see very distinctly that the book which an ardent revolutionary and patriot can describe in such nursery terms can hardly be a very highly coloured picture of the society it delineates.

It is one of the blessings of the historian that fortune is pleased every now and then to inspire individuals here and there with the ardent desire to describe for the benefit of posterity the familiar scenes of their everyday theatre. A Petronius gives us a presentment of Cæsarian Rome, which we could scarcely piece together from the grave historians and the gay poets. A Brown or a Ward can almost re-create for us the little London of Queen Anne. A Mercier does his best to present us with a faithful picture of what Paris was like before the Revolution, and a no less faithful picture of its changed condition after the Revolution was accomplished. Citizen Mercier was a wonderful man, and his 'Picture of Paris' is a wonderful book. He began it when Paris was to all appearance the tranquil city of a stately and secure dynasty; he brought it to a close just a year before Saint-Antoine shook itself from sleep, and shook the house of Capet into chaos. The first volume of the 'Picture of Paris' was published anonymously. The Parisian police disliked it, and sniffed for the author; Mercier coolly avowed himself—he never wanted courage—and stalked off into voluntary exile in pleasant Neuchatel, where he finished his task in peace. What a debt we owe to the solitary, sturdy, indefatigable man! It is very much to be feared that nobody or next to nobody reads the 'Tableau de Paris' nowadays, and yet nobody can thoroughly hope to understand the Paris of 1789 who has not studied it.

Mercier himself said of his book that he wrote it with his legs, and the quaint phrase is in itself the highest endorsement of its merit. Mercier loved his Paris as a cultured American citizen loves his London; he explored every inch of it patiently, pertinaciously. Wherever his legs could carry him, he went; whatever his ears could hear, whatever his eyes could see, whatever his tongue could ask, he noted, garnered, and gave as his gains to the world. As we read the book, we seem for the moment, like the councillor in Hans Andersen's delightful story, who slipped his feet into the goloshes of fortune, to be transported across the chasm of time and to live again in that earlier age. Nothing practically is left of that old Paris. It would be as easy to discover the Alexandria of Jerome and of Hypatia in the half-Oriental, half-Parisian sea-city of the Khedive; it would be as easy to conjure up ancient Athens from a lounge down Hermes Street, or to call up

Corinth from a survey of the half a dozen Doric pillars which are all that remain of it, as to re-create the Paris of Mercier's picture in the Paris of the Third Republic. Directory and consulate, empire and monarchy, kingship of France and kingship of the French, republic and prince-presidentship and empire again, and yet again republic, have rolled in wave upon wave of change over that old Paris of Mercier's and swept it away far out upon the sea of time. Much of it was already changed when Mercier, in the days of the Directory, set to work upon his 'New Paris.' What would Mercier's shade think of his new Paris now, so Haussmannized and Boule-vardized out of ghostly recognition?

Mercier was fond of saying in his later days with a cheery self-complacency that he was the prophet of the Revolution. It is a noteworthy fact that whenever a great political event takes place, some person whom nobody suspects of prophetic powers gets up and declares himself to have predicted the prodigy. If he sticks to his text sturdily enough he will probably be accepted in his prophet part, and no doubt Mercier found his believers. But it is difficult to discover any trace of the prophecy. A certain unconscious prophecy indeed is to be found in the 'Picture of Paris,' for Mercier with his frank realism described the squalor, the poverty, and the pain which cankered the painted city. He declares that his faithful pencil found within the walls of the capital more of hideous misery than of honest ease, more of grief and disquiet than of the joy and gaiety popularly attributed to the Paris people. But his noting of these causes led Mercier no more to any deduction of possible events therefrom than the powerful picture in 'Faublas' impressed Louvet to any purpose. On the contrary, we shall find in the 'Picture of Paris' a prophecy so laughably, so ludicrously unlucky that it is almost enough to cover poor Mercier's name with unquenchable ridicule. Any kind of disturbance in Paris he declares which might degenerate into serious sedition has become morally impossible. The watchfulness of the police, the regiments of Swiss guards—there is a curious unconscious tragedy in this touch—and of French guards embarracked and ready to march at a moment's notice, not to speak of the vast number of men devoted to the interests of the Court, all seem well adapted to repress at any time any appearance of a serious revolt, and to maintain that calm which becomes the more assured the longer it endures. Thus complacently Mercier, prophet of the Revolution, assured the world of the impossibility of Revolution. But, as if to make assurance doubly sure, Mercier went on to consider what might be done in the absurdly unlikely case of the Parisian ever asserting himself unpleasantly. If the Parisian, he said, who has his instants of effervescence, should really rise in mutiny, he would promptly be shut up in the vast cage he inhabits, his grain would be cut off from him, and when he had nothing more to eat in the larder, he would very soon have to knuckle down and plead for pity. Alas and alas for the prophet of the Revolution! The instant of effervescence became a geyser spring; the scarcity of bread was bad for the baker; and insurgent Paris did no knuckling down at all, but enforced that process upon its oppressors. Never was a prophet more woefully out. That touch about the Swiss guards is the one thing not wholly laughable in the whole absurd prediction. There came a time indeed long later when Paris, girt with steel and forced by famine, was compelled to yield after a heroic defence, but there was no dream of such a possibility in Mercier's mind then; nor in any man's mind for nearly three generations to come.

Let anyone who wants to understand his French Revolution get if he can a map of Paris of a date as near as may be to its outbreak. Such a map is before me now as I write: 'Plan de la Ville et Faubourgs de Paris, avec tous ses Accroissemens et la Nouvelle Enceinte des Barrières de cette Capitale. A Paris: chez Mondhare et Jean, rue Sainct Jean de Beauvais, près celle de Noyers, 1789.' This solemn setting forth is surrounded, as was the good old graceful fashion of antique map-makers, with an elaborate allegorical device in which a nude nymph, no doubt intended to represent the deity of the Seine, pours water from a jar at the left, while three baby Hermes at the right count over money on a corded box, and represent no doubt industry, commerce, and the like.

A river with a comically stiff bridge, a triumph of the engineering art, is in the background, and over all at the top are emblazoned the arms of the good city of Paris in the congenial company of overflowing horns of plenty and a pair of globes. It is impossible to look at this faded fantastical old map without emotion. Here on that square of dirty yellowed paper lies old Paris, the Paris that Mercier saw, that Burke, and Johnson, and Charles James Fox visited, that Marie Antoinette queened it over, that Beaumarchais set laughing, that Voltaire beheld with dying eyes, that Mirabeau loved. Little men thought of what the Revolution was to do when that old map was printed with its gardens of the 'Thuilleries,' and its Place Louis XV., and above all with its duly recorded Bastille.

With such a map for basis of operations, the curious student of history can now if he pleases reconstruct for himself the city of Paris as it appeared to the eyes of its visitors one hundred years ago. M. Albert Babeau, who has done so much and such excellent work in bringing the France of the Old Order home to the readers of French history, whose studies of the town, the village, the rural and the military life during the Ancien Régime are already classics, has added greatly to the debt the world owes him by his elaborate and exhaustive study of Paris in 1789. What M. Auguste Maquet did for the Paris of the Sun-King in his delightful and magnificent 'Paris sous Louis XIV.,' M. Babeau has done for the Paris of well-nigh a century later. With these two works, with the labours of the Bibliophile Jacob, with the magnum opus of M. Hippolyte Gautier, 'L'An 1789,' the student can almost remould that lost Paris of the year of Revolution, can with a little pains conjure it up for himself, and see it almost as vividly as it seemed to the eyes of those deputies from all the corners of France who came toiling across the country roads to be present at the opening of the States-General. With 'Paris à travers les Âges,' with Mercier's inestimable volumes, 'written with his legs,' with A. de Champeaux' 'Les Monuments de Paris,' with Pierre Bujon's 'Petite Histoire de Paris,' his apparatus is fairly complete. He is indeed additionally fortunate if he possess or can gain access to the magnificent, monumental, and rare 'Tableaux de la Révolution Française,' a sumptuous folio in three volumes which the Restoration suppressed in 1816, and of which we are lucky enough to own one of the few remaining copies. He will do well, too, in getting hold of the quaint little work in two volumes, 'Nouvelle Description des Curiosités de Paris,' published in the year 1791, which gives in alphabetical order a vast amount of information about the city of Mercier's days. But though a knowledge of these chief works on Paris is precious, M. Babeau is such a master of condensation and skilful presentation, that with his work alone the student may get a very satisfactory picture of what Paris was like on the eve of the Revolution.

It is difficult now to find any hints of old Paris in the Paris of to-day. Mercier, indeed, after the Revolution found, as he shows in his 'Nouveau Tableau,' much of the city that he had described before the Revolution as completely a thing of the past as Babylon or Troy Town. But still, in the days when Charles Lamb visited Paris, when Thackeray first visited Paris, when Carlyle first visited Paris, some half a century ago, it was far more possible for the traveller to conjure up some image of the city of Desmoulins and Danton, of Besenval and Lauzun, than it now is after the Haussmannizing of the Second Empire and the energy of the Third Republic. When one thinks that the custom of giving names to the streets was only sixty years old, having been begun for the first time in 1728, when one thinks that any system of numeration for houses only began at the same time, and was carried out in the clumsiest way, the existing system not coming into use until seventeen years after the Revolution began, in 1806, one begins to understand how far off one is from the city into which Faublas rode with his father on the memorable occasion.

Happily for us, however, we are in something of the position of Lesage's hero when the limping devil so agreeably unroofed Madrid for him. We may almost say that we too have our Asmodeus, that we can at least conjure up a familiar spirit who will enable us to see the Paris of a hundred years ago almost as clearly as if we had been present and beheld it in the flesh. For we can call up a witness who saw Paris with keen intelligent English eyes, and who could put down his impressions very vividly in his keen English way; we can call up Arthur Young again, and ask him to reveal old Paris to us. The very fact that Arthur Young saw Paris as a stranger, and saw it as an Englishman, makes his account the more real and the more intelligent to us. We can put ourselves in his place all the more readily, and with a little effort can almost succeed in seeing what he saw.

It is curious to find that he, like that Faublas of whom we have spoken, was first impressed disagreeably by his arrival in Paris. The cause of the disagreeable impression was not quite the same, but the fact remains—a curious alliance of the evidence of Louvet's fictitious rascal and of the high-minded living Englishman. Being in a post-chaise, he tells us, he travelled to Paris, as other travellers in post-chaises do, knowing little or nothing. For the last ten miles he was eagerly on the watch for that throng of carriages which near London impede the traveller. But he watched in vain; for the road, quite to the gates, was, in comparison, a perfect desert. So many great roads joined here, that the stranger supposed this must be accidental. The entrance seemed to him to have nothing magnificent; to be only ill-built and dirty. To get to the Rue de

Varenne, Faubourg St. Germain, he had the whole city to cross, and he crossed it by narrow, ugly, and crowded streets.

Some time later, when he entered Paris again, he was confirmed in his idea that the roads immediately leading to that capital seemed deserted when compared with those of London. By what means, he asked in amazement, can the connection be carried on with the country? He decided that either the French must be the most stationary people upon earth, or the English must be the most restless; and find more pleasure in moving from one place to another than in resting to enjoy life in either. He shrewdly said that the roads could not be more solitary if the French nobility went to their country seats only when exiled there by the Court.

In the beginning Paris struck him as being more or less like any other city. He went about at first 'upon the full silly gape' to find out things that he had not found before, as if a street in Paris could be composed of anything but houses, or houses formed of anything but brick or stone—or that the people in them, not being English, would be walking on their heads. After a while, however, he began to change his note, to find many points of difference, for and against. From the tower of the cathedral, he got a complete view of Paris. It seemed a vast city, even to his eyes that had seen London from St. Paul's; its being circular gave an advantage to Paris; but its greatest advantage was its atmosphere.

It was then so clear that he could have supposed it the height of summer. The clouds of coal-smoke that enveloped London always prevented a distinct view of that capital, but Arthur Young took it to be one-third at least larger than Paris. The buildings of the parliament-house were disfigured for him by a gilt and tawdry gate, and a French roof. The Hôtel de la Monnaie he thought a fine building; and the façade of the Louvre one of the most elegant in the world. These pleased him because they had, to the eye, no roofs. In proportion, he says, as the roof is seen a building suffers, and he adds that he does not recollect one edifice of distinguished beauty, unless with domes, in which the roof was not so flat as to be hidden, or nearly so. What eyes, he asked, must the French architects have had, to have loaded so many buildings with coverings of a height destructive of all beauty? 'Put such a roof as we see on the parliament-house or on the Thuilleries upon the façade of the Louvre, and where would its beauty be?' At night he went to the Opera, which he thought a good theatre, till he was told it was built in six weeks; and then it became good for nothing in his eyes, for he immediately supposed it would be tumbling down in six years. 'Durability is one of the essentials of building; what pleasure would a beautiful front of painted paste-board give?' The Alceste of Gluck was performed by Mademoiselle St. Huberti, whom he considered an excellent actress. As to scenes, dresses, decorations, dancing, and the like, he admitted that this theatre beat the Haymarket to nothing.

Another time he went to L'Ambigu Comique, which he called a pretty little theatre, with plenty of rubbish on it. He noted the coffee-houses on the Boulevards, the music, the noise, the women of the town without end ; everything but scavengers and lamps. The mud was a foot deep ; and there were parts of the Boulevards without a single light.

Indeed, Arthur Young was not much captivated by Paris. It is curious to note what best pleased his sturdy British sense of the practical. He liked the Boulevards, and the Place Louis XV., which he held was not properly to be called a square, but a very noble entrance to a great city. The union of the Place Louis XV. with the Champs Elysées, the gardens of the Thuilleries and the Seine he found open, airy, elegant, and superb, and called the most agreeable and best built part of Paris. There, he said, one could be clean and breathe freely. But by far the finest thing he saw at Paris was the Corn Market. That vast rotunda, with its roof entirely of wood, upon a new principle of carpentry, to describe which would, he declared, demand plates and long explanations ; that gallery, one hundred and fifty yards round, and as light as if suspended by the fairies ; that ground area, where wheat, pease, beans, lentils, were stored and sold ; those staircases doubly winding within each other to spacious apartments for rye, barley, and oats, won his agricultural heart. The whole, he said, was so well planned, and so admirably executed, that he knew of no public building that exceeded it in either France or England.

What an eminently sensible way of looking at things!—very English, very un-French. How it would have astonished Restif de la Bretonne, who wrote a little earlier his rhapsody about the charm of those serried ranks of beautiful women who lined the noble avenue of the Tuileries on summer evenings, and during the fine days of spring and autumn. Restif loved to think lingeringly of the attraction of the varied groups of people, all awakening a continuous series of ideas which charmed the mind, as the beauty of those who gave rise to them delighted the eyes. Much the fantastic novelist would have cared for the best possible of all corn-markets compared with that brilliant butterfly scene in the Tuileries Gardens which his pen can re-create for us. What a different Paris the two men saw, and yet, between them, they help us to see it as it was.

The streets were mostly very narrow and very dirty, with gutters that rushed torrents in time of rain and compelled dandies and neatly shod damsels to cross them on the backs of obliging men for a few sous. The chief open places were the gardens of the Tuileries and the Luxembourg, of the Temple and the Arsenal, and the vacant spaces by the Cathedral of Notre Dame, in front of which a kind of perennial fair was carried on, and behind which people amused themselves by playing games on holidays. But three years earlier, in 1786, the principal bridges of Paris had been covered with houses, like old London Bridge and like the Ponte Vecchio at Florence. Not very long before, the famous Court of Miracles, which was slowly crumbling into ruins, after a long and fantastic career, had been swept away and a market was established on its site. There were an astonishing number of churches, enough to have amazed Sir Roger de Coverley, destined many of them to fall before the fury of the Revolution. In their shadows nestled, to the injury of the public health, a dangerous number of cemeteries, disused or in use. Nothing probably would have more impressed the stranger in Paris in 1789 than the astonishing amount of building that was going on. A kind of mania of reconstruction seemed to have seized upon authority, and in all directions new streets were stretching out, bridges being projected, and stately buildings rising to heaven amid their scaffoldings. Paris might have been the securest city in the world, the Old Order the most durable of human institutions, to judge by the way in which the administrators of a system that was falling to pieces occupied themselves with the rehabilitation of Paris.

The sidewalk took a long time to establish itself in Paris. London in the last century was an uncomfortable place enough, but it was a kind of

Earthly Paradise compared to Paris as far as street comfort and convenience went. In most of the Paris streets the pedestrians picked their way as best they might along the highway in common with all the wheeled traffic. Only in a few favoured streets were strips of the pavement at each side of the street marked off with posts to form a species of side-walk. This amazed and irritated Arthur Young. It appeared almost incredible to him as a person used to London, how dirty the streets of Paris were, and how horribly inconvenient and dangerous walking was without a foot-pavement. The dirt seems to have surprised everyone, even in that astonishing last century, which set so little store by cleanliness. Paris was famous or infamous for its mud. On days when it rained, and it rained a good deal in Paris, the streets were given over to a horrible, glutinous, evil-smelling compound of earth and refuse and filth of all kinds, which poisoned the air with its stench and destroyed the garments to which it clung. Through these streets poured the interminable procession of Paris life, the great lumbering gilded carriages of the aristocracy, painted with a whole heathen mythology and drawn by four or six horses, the many public conveyances, the cumbrous hackney coaches with their bright yellow bodies, the mud-carts and water-carts. The fiacres, as the hackney coaches came to be called from their first establishment bearing the sign of Saint Fiacre, were dear, dirty, detestable, some two thousand in number. Once, we are told, the wild Duke of Orleans and his wild companions actually hunted a stag through some of the Paris streets. Amidst all the wheeled traffic, generally going as fast as it could be driven in defiance of regulations of police and the well-being of the foot-walkers, the Paris population made its way as well as it could and certainly as rapidly as it could.

Long before 1789 Montesquieu had hit off the Parisian passion for rapid motion. In his Persian Letters he made his imaginary Oriental describe a residence of a month, during which he had not seen a single person walking at a foot-pace. There was no one in the world like a Frenchman to get over the ground; he ran and flew. The mimic Persian, accustomed to walk leisurely, sometimes lost all patience, for, to say nothing of being splashed with dirt from head to foot, he could not put up with being elbowed at every turn. Some man coming up behind him compelled him to turn right out of his path, and then somebody else, coming in another direction, drove him back to the place from which the former had pushed him; until before he had walked a hundred yards he was as tired as if he had been ten leagues. This astonishing activity is gravely explained by Mercier. The Parisian learned when quite young to keep his footing on the pavement, to get out of the way of horses and carriages, to diminish his bulk like a true Gascon, to jump over the gutters, to run up seven storeys without losing breath, and to come down like a flash of lightning. It must indeed have been a curious sight to look down from an upper window upon the mass of carriages of different kinds which were going to and fro; to watch the foot-passengers who, like birds when they see someone coming with a gun, flutter off in all directions, one putting his foot in the gutter and splashing himself from head to foot, and another getting the dust driven in his eyes.

A very bewildering, perplexing, variegated crowd it was too that jostled and pushed and hurried its wild danse macabre along the unsavoury Paris streets. And what a danse macabre it was! Its beggars alone would have delighted Callot. Blind beggars were numerous; pickpockets were plentiful; rogues of all kinds were ready to take advantage of the throng. The din was tremendous; the street cries alone were enough to make the town a very Babel. The sellers of fish, the sellers of cakes, the sellers of gingerbread, of oysters, of oranges, of old clothes, all made it a point of honour to advertise their wares at the shrillest top of their shrill voices. The women, according to Mercier, cried like men and the men like women. There was one perpetual yelling, which made it impossible to describe the sound and accent of all these multitudinous voices uplifted in chorus. Auvergnat porters pushed along; Savoyards carried Sedan chairs, which were still used; hawkers of all kinds filled the air with their strange cries in commendation of their wares; beggars, burgesses, soldiers, nobles, strangers, servants, shop-girls, ladies, work-women, all blended together in the incessant panorama of the Paris streets. Dangerous in the daytime, they were no less dangerous at night, for the lighting was of the poorest lantern kind, almost as bad as London in the days of Anne, and in some parts of the town even the wretched lanterns were not lit when there was a moon. We can well understand how a stranger would dislike the Paris streets. Arthur Young lost his honest English temper with those same streets. Paris, he declared, was in some respects the most ineligible and inconvenient city for the residence of a person of small fortune of any that he had seen; and was vastly inferior to London. It is curious to compare with this Montesquieu's declaration in the Persian Letters that Paris was perhaps the most sensual city in the world, and the one in which pleasure was carried to the highest pitch; but that at the same time it was the city in which men lead the hardest life. Arthur Young was provoked out of all patience by the narrow streets, the crowd, the dirt, the want of foot-pavements. Walking, which in London was so pleasant and so clean, that ladies might do it every day, was here a toil and a fatigue to a man, and an impossibility to a well-dressed woman. What especially irritated Arthur Young were the infinity of one-horse cabriolets, which were driven by young men of fashion and their imitators, alike fools, with such rapidity as to be real nuisances, and render the streets exceedingly dangerous, without an incessant caution. He saw a poor child run over and probably killed, and was himself many times blackened with the mud of the kennels. This beggarly practice, of driving a one-horse booby-hutch about the streets of a great capital, flowed either from poverty or despicable economy, and could not be spoken of with too much severity, since it rendered Paris an ineligible residence for persons, particularly families that could not afford to keep a coach; a convenience which was as dear as at London. If young noblemen at London, he proudly reflected, were to drive their chaises in streets without foot-ways, as their brethen do at Paris, they would speedily and justly get very well thrashed, or rolled in the kennel. The hackney-coaches he found much worse than in London; and chairs were rare, as they ran the risk of being driven down in the streets. To this circumstance also it was owing, that all persons of small or moderate fortune were forced to dress in black, with black stockings. It was not so much the dusky hue of this in company that annoyed Arthur Young as the too great distinction which it marked in company between a man that had a good fortune and another that had not.

These same black stockings that annoyed Arthur Young so much were something more, however, than a mark of social inequality. They were the outward and visible proof of the change that was coming over the country, of the increased simplicity in dress which was owing partly to Rousseau, partly to Marie Antoinette, partly to the Anglomania of the Duke d'Orleans and his set, and partly to the spread of democratic or semi-democratic opinion. The colour of dress was nowhere very brilliant, not so brilliant as in former days. Dark blues and browns, homely greys and blacks, were the chief wear; the simplicity which came in with the new ideas had had its effects upon daily dress, and the shining foppery of the Old Order had already begun to fade. The trouser, that useful but singularly ugly garment, had already begun to assert itself, and was worn by many instead of the old knee-breeches. Paris was still in 1789 the mistress of modes, but the mode just then was swayed by the Anglomania which had already exercised its sway on science, on sport, and on political opinion. With the sober colours and cut of English cloth came other English customs. Gentlemen in 1789 did not so generally carry swords as of old; a cane was sufficient unless the wearer was, as it were, in full dress. While men still wore powder, women began to leave it off, and the amazing head-dresses of the earlier days had given place to a more natural arrangement of the hair. Women's hats and bonnets were enormous and much beribboned and beflowered. A keen observer might have almost predicted from the change in Parisian dress that other and more momentous changes were in the air.

There are three things which everyone instinctively associates with the last century and the Old

Order—patches, powder, and periwigs—but the use of all these was already on the decline in 1789. M. Alfred Franklin, in his interesting and admirable studies, 'La Vie privée d'Autrefois,' claims to have discovered the origin of the use of the patch. In a rare French book, the 'Diverses Leçons' of Louis Guyon, published in 1625, it is stated that at the end of the previous century physicians sought to cure the toothache by applying to the temples tiny plasters stretched upon velvet or taffety. It was easy for a beauty to perceive that these black patches greatly heightened the whiteness of a fair skin, and lent a certain lustre even to a waning complexion. The patches were useless against the toothache, but they soon became essential to the toilette. They were worn all through the seventeenth century, but they retained their greatest influence in the eighteenth century. Fantastic poets attributed their origin to Cupid placing a fly upon the breast of Venus and the 'mouches,' as the patches were called, had different names according to the different parts of the face to which they were applied. Thus one near the eye was 'passionate,' one near the mouth the 'kisser,' one on the lips the 'coquette,' one on the nose the 'impertinent,' on the forehead the 'majestic,' on the cheek the 'gallant,' on the lower lip the 'discreet,' on a spot the 'thief,' on the fold of a smiling cheek the 'playful,' and so on. During the reign of Louis XV. every lady carried her box of patches, and, as they were sometimes cut in quaint devices of ships, and stars, and animals, a lady's face was often a very gallery of shadows.

One of the great features in Paris life were the cafés, which had become so numerous since the success of the Café Procope, and which continued to increase. To these establishments, as to their London kindred, the St. James's coffee-houses of the Georgian age, people resorted to take a cup of coffee, to talk and hear the news. A writer of the time calmly asserts that the urbanity and mildness discernible upon most faces in Paris was due to the establishment of so many cafés. Before they existed, nearly everybody passed his time at the wine-shops, where even business matters were discussed. Since their establishment, however, people assembled under their roofs to hear what was going on, drinking and playing only in moderation, with the consequence that they were more civil and polite, at least in appearance. The cafés grew rapidly in number. There were six hundred in the reign of Louis XV. They were the daily meeting-ground of the idlers, the talkers, the domino, chess, and draught-players, and the newspaper-readers. Billiard-rooms were not added, says Bibliophile Jacob, until the Revolution, and no one would ever have ventured to smoke there. The fondness for tobacco led to the creation of estaminets and tap-rooms, which ranked much below the cafés. In the cafés there was little or no drunkenness, coffee and other simple drinks being almost the only things supplied. Though they were, for the most part, plain and little decorated, each had its peculiar physiognomy. Some of them quiet even to silence, while others were noisy even as Babel. The Café de la Régence and the Café du Quai de l'Ecole had inherited the renown of the Café Procope. Lovers of gossip, rakers up of rumours, men of letters, retired officers, and strangers formed their chief customers.

For wilder spirits, caring for fiercer joys than coffee, chess, news, and scandal, there were the taverns, the wine-shops, and above all the guinguettes. The guinguette was much smaller than the tavern, and the frequenters, taking their refreshments at tables, were regaled with dancing and singing. We are told that these establishments were especially numerous in the faubourgs and at the approaches to the barriers, as at these places the wine and spirituous liquors did not pay octroi-duty. The guinguette, as we learn, merely consisted, in most cases, of a large tent, around the inside of which were long rows of rough deal tables, a place being left vacant in the centre of the tent for the dancers, whose orchestra was made up of a squeaky violin and a discordant flute. The guinguettes outside Paris were more frequented, on account of their rustic aspect. They were veritable arbours, hidden in greenery, standing in a garden or shrubbery, whence they were called Courtilles, which means plots of ground planted with trees.

There was the Grande Courtille at the end of the Faubourg du Temple, on the road to Belleville, and the Petite Courtille, near the Porcherons, on the road to Clichy.

The beautiful Marie Antoinette herself was taken to one of these places by the Count d'Artois, and is said to have declared that she never enjoyed anything so much in her life as the wild humours and the wild dances of the place. We are told that her incognita was respected by those present, who affected not to recognise her. Still she was recognised, and the harmless freak went its way to swell up the long list of the offences against queenly dignity which were to tell so heavily against her.

There was an immense deal that was very bright about that old world Paris, though its crowd was not so brilliant as of old, and though there was such a preponderance of black stockings. It was not always raining, it was not all walking in crowded streets. We must remember Restif de la Bretonne's enthusiasm about the Tuileries. We must remember Dulaure's rhapsodies in his description of Paris curiosities written in 1786, when he avowed that the old Boulevard combined all the attractions longed for by loungers; varied sights, splendid houses, and delightful gardens, down even to the cafés and wine-shops, which, with their flowers and shrubs, had quite a fairy appearance. On the afternoons of Sundays and Thursdays the Boulevard was patronized by the prettiest women in Paris, and the long strings of carriages were an ever-varying source of curiosity. But in spite of Dulaure, in spite of Restif de la Bretonne, it is not in the many tinted Tuileries with its coveys of plumaged dames, it is not in the old Boulevard with all its emphasized splendours, that we are to look for what was most characteristic of the Paris of 1789.

There is really only one part of the Paris of to-day where the student may for a moment forget himself and fancy that he is back again in the days when the States-General were coming together and the Bastille still lifted its head over turbulent Saint Antoine. That is of course the Palais Royal, where if, like the Marchioness, we make believe very hard, we can almost conjure up the scene where the people used to throng to discuss the things that were being done over at Versailles and to duck in the fountains individuals who were supposed to be hostile to the popular cause. It did not dream indeed of gas or electric light, but it made a brave show with lamps and candles at night, and was crowded then, as it is crowded now, with the curious of all nations. That part indeed which was devoted to ladies of the lightest character has happily vanished. It existed long enough: Balzac's Lucien de Rubempré saw it when he came to Paris to make his fortune, and it impressed him a good deal. But altogether the Palais Royal of 1789 would not so greatly differ from the Pálais Royal of 1889, if it did not lack its Café de Foy.

Ah, that Palais Royal! Taine, in his 'Ancien Régime,' sighs for eight days of the stately splendid old Versailles life. We should rather, we think, if we were to choose, get a glimpse of the life of the Palais Royal. If we were but possessed of those goloshes of fortune which we spoke of a little while ago, we would gladly wander in that Palais Royal of the year 1789. We would mix with its marvellous crowd. We would study the shops which made it a kind of world's fair for all the luxuries of body and mind. We would test the merits of the restaurants, the best and dearest in Europe, the 'Barrier,' and the 'English Tavern,' the humbler 'Flemish Grotto,' the cafés like that Café Militaire with its device 'Hic virtus bellica gaudet,' and the Café de l'Ecole, kept by Charpentier, whose pretty and wealthy daughter was wooed by an obscure young advocate whose name was Danton, and who was not always to be obscure. We would visit the waxworks of Curtius, uncle of Mdlle. Gresholtz, who served Madame Elisabeth, and who should be famous as Madame Tussaud. We should perhaps meet his friends Marat and Robespierre. We would study the marionette shows and the Chinese shadows and make our way into the lively theatre of Varieties. The Palais Royal is the capital of Paris, said Mercier. It is the heart, the brain, the soul of Paris, said Karamsine the Russian.

Arthur Young naturally gravitated, as all strangers did gravitate, to the Palais Royal, and was much annoyed by the National Circus there, a building in the gardens of the palace, which seemed to him the most whimsical and expensive folly that could easily be imagined. It was a large ball-room, sunk half its height under ground; and, as if this circumstance were not sufficiently adapted to make it damp enough, a garden was planted on the roof, and a river was made to flow around it, which, with the addition of some spirting fountains, undoubtedly made it a delicious place for a winter's entertainment. Arthur Young angrily reflected that the expense of this gew-gaw building, the project, as he supposed, of some of the Duke of Orleans's friends, would have established an English farm, with all its principles, buildings, live stock, tools, and crops, on a scale that would have done honour to the first sovereign of Europe; for it would have converted more than five thousand acres of desert into a garden. As to the result of the mode that had been pursued, of investing such a capital, he knew no epithet equal to its merits. It was meant to be a concert, ball, coffee, and billiard room, with shops, something in the style of the London Pantheon. There were music and singing on the night when Arthur Young visited it, but the room being almost empty, he found it equally cold and sombre.

All round Paris in the last century were the seats of princes, of nobles, of opulent financiers. The city was cinctured with stately parks and ancient woods. At the north the groves of Enghien and Montmorency led to the glades of Compiègne. At the south lay the fair forest of Fontainebleau and at the south-west the rabbit-haunted wilds of Rambouillet and the brakes of Meudon. West lay Saint Germain. Eastward lay Bondy and Vincennes. The Boulogne wood was still sylvan in fact as in name. But of all the woods, the wood of Senart was Louis XV.'s favourite hunting ground, and of all his country seats Louis best loved Choisy—Choisy-le-Roi as it had come to be called from his predilection for it. In the gardens of Choisy, famous for jasmine and roses, and thronged with the gods and satyrs of Greek mythology, Louis loved to linger after the hunting at Senart. The gods have vanished long ago; the roses and jasmine have disappeared like the roses that the Persian poet weeps; not a trace remains of the château which Mansard built for the great Mademoiselle after the Fronde wars.

But the two places near to Paris of special interest to the stranger were Versailles and Trianon. Arthur Young went to both, and recorded his opinions in his usual matter of fact way. He had a letter to Richard, which procured admittance to Trianon, to view the Queen's English Garden. It contained about one hundred acres, disposed in the taste he had read of in books of Chinese gardening, whence it was supposed that the English style was taken. He found more of Sir William Chambers there than of Mr. Brown—more effort than nature—and more expense than taste. He observed that it was not easy to conceive anything that art could introduce in a garden that was not there; woods, rocks, lawns, lakes, rivers, islands, cascades, grottos, walks, temples, and even villages. He admitted that parts of the design were pretty, and well executed. The chief fault was too much crowding; which led to another, that of cutting the lawn by too many gravel walks, an error to be seen in almost every garden Arthur Young met with in France. But the glories of La Petite Trianon in his eyes were the exotic trees and shrubs. The world had been successfully rifled to decorate it with curious and beautiful plants to please the eye of ignorance, and to exercise the memory of science. Of the buildings, the Temple of Love seemed to him truly elegant.

The palace of Versailles, however, one of the objects of which report had given him the greatest expectation, made no impression on him; he viewed it without emotion. Nothing could compensate him for its want of unity. From whatever point he viewed it, it appeared to him an assemblage of buildings; a splendid quarter of a town, but not a fine edifice; an objection from which even the beautiful garden front was not free. The great gallery was the finest room he saw; the other apartments were nothing; but the pictures and statues he hailed as a capital collection. The whole palace, except the chapel, seemed, to his surprise, to be open to all the world; for he tells us that he pushed through an amazing crowd of all sorts of people, many of them not very well dressed. But the officers at the door of the apartment in which the King dined made a distinction, and would not permit all to enter promiscuously.

At another time he again visited Versailles, and was again surprised. While viewing the King's apartment, which he had not left a quarter of an hour, Arthur Young was amused to see the blackguard figures that were walking uncontrolled about the palace, and even in his bed-chamber. The rags of these men betrayed them to be in the last stage of poverty, and the English stranger was the only person who stared and wondered how the devil they got there. It was impossible for the English stranger not to like this careless indifference and freedom from suspicion. He declared that he loved the master of the house, who would not be hurt or offended at seeing his apartment thus occupied, if he returned suddenly.

The curious mixture of magnificence and dirt which characterized Paris was not uncharacteristic of its people. It must be confessed that in some respects the refinement of the last century was disagreeably artificial, the thin veneer that cloaked a great deal of coarseness. Washing of the person was, unhappily, an infrequent process. A modern gentleman, accustomed to cleanliness from his youth upwards, would be beyond measure disgusted if he could step back for half an hour into the Paris of the polite last century at the very filth with which luxurious living was environed. Sanitary arrangements were of the most primitive, most detestable kind. It is unpleasant to think that the stately palace of Versailles was chiefly characterized to its familiars by its abominable smells. Bathing of the body as a daily institution, even for the nobility, was practically unknown. A palace did not always think it necessary to include a bath-room among its appointments. There were indeed public bath-houses upon the river, but they were few in number, and the semi-private bath-houses had a certain shadiness of character. People of the middle classes who wished to take a bath could hire one from an ironmonger for a few pence. These baths were shaped something like the shoe of the old lady who had so many children that she didn't know what to do. Such baths, although no doubt highly uncomfortable, had the advantage in economic eyes of requiring less water than those of more oblong shape. In the houses of great nobles, baths were of a more luxurious nature, and were fashioned in many forms all seeking after the comfort of the human body. It is a curious example of the manners of the day that great ladies did not hesitate to receive their friends, male as well as female, while in their baths. Decency was, however, respected. A pint or two of milk, or a quantity of prepared essence, rendered the water white and opaque. Some baths, again, were covered with a perforated lid, which left the bulk of the body quite concealed while still permitting evaporation. In many cases, too, ladies took their baths enveloped in a bathing-gown from head to foot. Madame Campan declares that Marie Antoinette was so particular in this respect, that she always bathed clad in a long flannel robe, buttoned up to the neck, and when she left the bath she always insisted on having a cloth held up before her to conceal her from the eyes of her women. This statement is curiously and decisively in contradiction with that of Soulavie, in his memoirs of the reign of Louis XVI., in which he records the incredible story of a visit paid to the Queen by an aged and eminently virtuous ecclesiastic. On entering the room he found the Queen, entirely naked, in her bath. He was about to retire, but the Queen called him to her side, and held him for some time in unwilling converse, compelled to admire 'the fairest form that nature ever moulded.' The story would seem on the face of it to be apocryphal, but it is certain that some great ladies made no scruple of being seen completely unclothed, at their toilette or in their bath, by the male lackeys, and this from no indecency but from their contemptuous unconsciousness that a lackey could be regarded as anything but an automaton.

Gouverneur Morris gives some very remarkable pictures of the freedom of social life in Paris in this regard. On May 27, 1789, he called on Madame de la Suze. 'She is just going to dress, but that is nothing.' 'M. Morris me permettra de faire ma toilette?' 'Certainly.' So we have the whole performance of undressing and dressing except the shift. On July 26 in the same year he notes: 'At five go by appointment to Madame de Flahaut's. She is at her toilette. Monsieur comes in. She dresses before us with perfect decency, even to her shift.' That same year, November 13, Madame de Flahaut, says Mr. Morris, 'being ill, goes into the bath, and when placed there sends for me. It is a strange place to receive a visit, but there is milk mixed with the water, making it opaque. She tells me that it is usual to receive in the bath, and I suppose it is, for otherwise I should have been the last person to whom it would have been permitted.'

Madame de Flahaut, who was so frank in this respect, was a very charming woman, who impressed every one she met from Montesquieu and Talleyrand to the clever, whimsical, conceited Gouverneur Morris, who was destined to be a good friend to her in later days. She was very beautiful, very witty; she wrote romances and talked philosophies; she was unhappily married to a man much older than herself, the dissipated, indifferent Count de Flahaut—for whom the guillotine waits. Talleyrand, then Abbé de Périgord, was her friend, her lover, and the father of her child Charles, named after him. Possibly this may have influenced Morris when he wrote of the abbé. 'He appears to be a sly, cunning, ambitious, and malicious man. I know not why conclusions so disadvantageous to him are formed in my mind, but so it is; I cannot help it.'

Gouverneur Morris is of immense value to us in enabling us to appreciate the social life of Paris on the eve of the Revolution. Born in 1752, he had been exceptionally well educated; his father had desired that he should have 'the best education that is to be had in England or America.' In his young manhood he devoted himself to the law; when the Revolution broke out he played a prominent part in asserting the need for American independence, and was gallantly prepared 'to fall on the last bleak mountain in America rather than yield.' He was with Washington during the long winter at Valley Forge, and earned the lifelong friendship of the American leader. In 1780, in consequence of an accident in Philadelphia, Morris had to have his left leg amputated below the knee, and for the remainder of his life we learn that he wore a wooden leg of primitive simplicity, 'not much more than a rough oak stick with a wooden knob at the end of it.' Such was the man who, in the February of 1789, found himself in Paris on some business of his own and his brother's concerning the shipment of tobacco to France. His excellent introductions brought him into the best Parisian society, and his keen quick appreciations of all he saw render his diary and letters second only in importance to Arthur Young's writings in dealing with the time. With a good deal of conceit and a good deal of humour, he stumped his way through the bright Parisian society, often amazed at its morality, often amused at its behaviour, always intelligent, appreciative, and reliable. If he seems to have believed that he could easily set things right in France if he had the chance, he only shared a delusion common to many persons less intelligent than himself. A little later in this year of 1789 he and his enchanting Madame de Flahaut began to scheme out the ideal policy for the hour. Her suggestions that Mirabeau should be sent to Constantinople and Lauzun to London do not say much for her diplomacy. Morris's great idea was that Madame de Flahaut should command the Queen, whom he described as ' weak, proud, but not ill-tempered, and, though lustful, yet not much attached to her lovers," so that a superior mind— Madame de Flahaut's superior mind—' would take that ascendency which the feeble always submit to, though not always without reluctance.' Madame de Flahaut seemed to be pleased with Morris's plan, and declared that she would take care to keep the Queen supplied with an alternating succession of gallants and masses. It was impossible, Morris thought, not to approve of such a régime, and felt confident that ' with a due proportion of the former medicine' Madame de Flahaut ' must supplant the present physician.' After all, outsiders do not always see most of the game.

CHAPTER XXIII

THE PEOPLE OF PARIS

Such was Paris in that memorable year 1789, a huge hive of humanity, more animated, more excited than it had ever been before in all the course of its turbulent history. The decision of the King and his ministers to summon the States-General had aroused the keenest excitement in every part of the city. Every section of the social scale shared in and swelled the general stir. In the salons, in the clubs, in the wine-shops, in the coffee-houses, in the streets, above all in the Palais Royal, Paris buzzed, and fluttered, and discussed, and doubted, and wrangled, and was perturbed or hopeful according to its mood. Let us study some of these centres of excitement and see what they are doing.

Parisian society still thronged its various salons, still glittered in satins and embroideries, silks and laces; the courtly clink of swords was still heard and the rustle of hoops. The salons still made up a world of powder and of patches, but they were not the salons of old time, for which some eighteenth-century Villon might weep, the salons of the Regency or the Fifteenth Louis, the salons of light wit, the salons of fashionable science and patronized Encyclopædiaism. Politics have turned all heads, and the salons have mostly become political centres. Madame de Sabran swayed the most aristocratic of the salons that professed reaction and clung to the Court principles. To her rooms came the fine flower of the nobility, the wits and politicians, who thought that the Old Order could still somehow be bolstered up. Madame de Sabran was no longer in the enjoyment of that first youth which made her so famous some twelve years earlier. Madame Vigée-Lebrun, to whom we owe so living a knowledge of so many of the lords and ladies of that old time, has left a ravishing picture of Madame de Sabran. It shows her dark eyes smiling divinely under their beautiful brown lashes, the beautiful face beneath its cloud of fair hair, the exquisitely fine skin, the daintily delicate body, which conquered the heart of the audacious and brilliant Chevalier de Boufflers. Madame de Sabran was a woman of wit, a woman of taste and scholarship; her wit, her taste, her scholarship, and her beauty captivated de Boufflers in 1777, when she was twenty-seven and he was thirty-nine. Madame de Sabran returned the passion of de Boufflers, and for the rest of her life was devoted to him. He was now in 1789 the chief ornament of her salon, and one of the most remarkable, one of the most typical figures of that antique world.

The brilliant figure of the Chevalier de Boufflers shines eccentrically radiant through the whole revolutionary period. He is indeed a wandering star : the Old Order is to be seen at its best in him. His portraits confirm what the praises of his contemporaries assert, that he was singularly attractive. The gracious oval of his face is instinct with a witty intelligence ; his bright eyes seem to question mockingly ; his nose is large and sensual ; so are the large firm lips, but their sensuality is tempered by a sense of cynic humour. The son of that Madame de Boufflers who was so dear to the old King Stanislas of Poland, Louis XV.'s father-in-law, young de Boufflers was originally destined for the Church, not indeed from any spirit of belief, but solely from ambition and a desire that the red hat might some time shade his high and handsome forehead. In an age of strange Churchmen there never was a stranger servant of the Church than the young Abbé de Boufflers. The traditional Parisian abbé of a world of tales and comedies finds its finest realization in this dainty disciple of the lighthearted Abbé Porquet, this love-making, verse-making scapegrace, who delighted, like Faust, to reel from desire to desire and to rhyme his way none too decently through life. It is of de Boufflers that Métra tells a tale—Métra the journalist, who tells so many and so strange tales. De Boufflers offended some great lady by an epigram : the great lady wrote to him making an appointment and proposing conciliation. De Boufflers came to the appointment with a pair of pistols in his pocket. He had hardly spoken to the lady before four tall lackeys came in, who, in obedience to the lady's command, seized de Boufflers and administered a severe castigation. De Boufflers bore it composedly, then producing his pistols made the affrighted lackeys, on pain of death, administer the same castigation to his treacherous hostess, and afterwards to each other in turn. This amazing child of the Church, whom Rousseau despised and in whom Voltaire delighted, suddenly set the literary and polite worlds on fire one day by the little tale, 'Aline,' which enraptured Grimm, captivated Madame de Pompadour, and overtaxed the patience of his ecclesiastical superiors. De Boufflers was made aware that he must really choose between letters and the Litany. De Boufflers did not take long to choose. With a light heart he laid down the cassock and caught up the sword and fought his way gallantly through the Hanover campaign. Yet still there was something of the Churchman in him. He was no longer an abbé, but he was a Knight of the Order of Malta, so that we have that strange picture of him given by M. Octave Uzanne in which, being at the same time a prior and a captain of Hussars, he assists at Divine Office in the costume of a soldier-abbé, a long white surplice on his shoulders and a long sword beating against his heels. The contradiction which is here implied is really typical of De Boufflers' entire nature. He was a creature of contradictions. His friend and emulator, the Prince de Ligne, in one of those exquisite portraits from his gallery of contemporaries, has left a very living and charming picture of the man who was in turn abbé, soldier, author, administrator, deputy and philosopher, and who, in all these various states, was only out of place in the first. Laclos has left a grimmer portrait of him under the name of Fulber, as of one born eighty years too late, a fanfaron of another time who being serious seeks to be gay, frivolous seeks to be grave, good would fain be caustic, and idle plays at being industrious. Perhaps de Boufflers did come a little belated into the world. His bright butterfly figure seems out of place in the stormy hours of 1789. Rivarol, in his brisk way, summed him merrily up as a libertine abbé, philosophical soldier, rhyming diplomatist, patriotic emigrant, and courtier republican. From the moment of meeting Madame de Sabran he took life and love a little more seriously. It became his ambition to win a position which would allow him to marry the beautiful widow. When, in 1785, he was sent as Governor to Senegambia, he showed very considerable ability as an administrator, and was heartily regretted by both blacks and whites, it is said, when he returned to France in the end of 1787, and to his adored Madame de Sabran. He was now the shining light of Madame de Sabran's salon, and perhaps we may as well part company with him here. He got elected to the States-General as a noble deputy; he played no considerable part in the Assembly; in 1790, he with Malouet, La Rochefoucauld-Liancourt and others, founded the 'Impartials' club; he married Madame de Sabran, emigrated, came back to France under Bonaparte with all his light wit worn out of him, settled down as a kind of gentleman-farmer, and died in the January of the year of Waterloo. He wrote himself an epitaph, which may be thus rendered:—

> Here lies a lord who without ceasing sped;
> Born on the highway, there he lived, and dead
> He lies there still to justify the Sage,
> Who says that life is but a pilgrimage.

No less characteristic of their age were the two brothers Louis Philippe de Ségur and Joseph Alexandre de Ségur, the Castor and Pollux of the Royalist salons. The elder brother, Louis, born in 1753, was noted for a kind of grave sweetness, a gallantry and address which had in them a reserve, almost an air of melancholy, which gave them an additional charm. An impassioned Voltairean in his youth, he was destined in his time to play the part of a kind of glorified Vicar of Bray and to serve a variety of autocratic masters with a whimsical indifference to the liberalism of his early years. Madame de Sabran did not esteem him too highly when she described him in a biting little epigram as an empty-headed philosopher and a pedantic and timid rake. We may think a little better of him if we please. He was a dexterous and delicate political epigrammatist; he wooed a frolic muse like most young men of his station, and with an average success. No one has painted better than he the kind of brilliant life

which the young nobility lived in the reign of Louis
XVI., when 'we saw the brief years of our spring-
time wheel by in a circle of such illusion, and such
happiness, as I think through all time was reserved
for us alone. Liberty, royalty, aristocracy, democracy, prejudices, reason, novelty, philosophy, all
united to make our days more delightful, and never
surely was so terrible an awakening preceded by so
sweet a sleep or more enchanting dreams.' There
is a picture in little of the Old Order, as it seemed
to the eyes of golden youth in those exciting, intoxi-
cating days, when the new ideas were blending with
the old like the junction of two rivers.

His brother, the Viscount Alexandre, who was
three years younger than Louis, was a fribble of
a lighter type. In later years he classified himself and his elder brother. 'He is Ségur the cere-
monious; I am Ségur without ceremony.' In these
days of the Sabran salon he was chiefly distinguished
as a man of taste and wit, gliding gracefully through
life with the support of a rose-crowned and rose-
coloured philosophy all his own. He wrote clever
little poems; he wrote clever little plays; he uttered
clever little epigrams. The character of the man
may be best estimated from this, that he found fault
with those who caused the Revolution chiefly because
they 'spoiled his Paris,' and 'turned the capital of
pleasures into a centre of disputes and dulness.' He
got into grave royal disfavour once in 1786 for
saying with an affected gravity at a social gathering,

when pressed for the latest news, that the King had abdicated. As he persisted in this piece of laboured witticism with all possible solemnity, it naturally got bruited abroad and came to the King's ears, who forbade Ségur the Court and Paris for a season. Ségur had little idea how true a prophet he was, but when his prophecy did come true it scarcely seemed so good a jest. Perhaps he deserves to be best remembered, after all, for having happily and certainly ingeniously defined taste as only the art of putting everything in its place, and for saying that taste is to the mind what grace is to beauty. It must be confessed that these seem strange popinjays to defend a threatened throne; they were as witty, as brilliant, as lightly profligate as the Cavaliers of Charles II., but they did not make quite so good a stand for the institution which allowed them to live and adorn the Sabran salon. Madame de Sabran's little son was typical of that institution. When he was eight years old, he was brought before the King and Queen to play a part in Voltaire's 'Oreste.' A beautiful Court lady began to talk to him about the classic authors, whereupon the tiny courtier, with a grave bow, said, ' Madame, Anacreon is the only poet I can think of here.'

Madame de Chambonas held another and less select salon in defence of reactionary principles. Of this salon Rivarol was the prevailing spirit—Rivarol the witty, the audacious, the violently royalist. The name of Rivarol has come to the front considerably of late years. Always remembered for the brilliant services he rendered to the royalist cause, he has recently, however, been made more of, more written about, more thought of; instead of being bracketed with Champcenetz or with Chamfort, he stands alone, and is studied individually. There is a kind of sect formed under the shadow of his name, a sect of Rivarolists whose mission it is to keep his memory green and stimulate themselves with his writings. The name of Rivarol does not appear to have been his name by any other right than the right of choice. He first flickered upon Paris, comely, needy, esurient of success, in 1777, that same year in which de Boufflers first met Madame de Sabran. He introduced himself to d'Alembert under the name of the Abbé de Parcieux, de Parcieux being the name of a distinguished physician and geometrician lately dead, with whom the warm imagination of the chestnut-haired youth constructed a kinship. D'Alembert introduced him to Voltaire, who welcomed him well. He soon began to make his way in Paris, and to make enemies. His bitter tongue, his mordant epigrams, made him feared and hated. No longer bearing the name of Longchamps or of de Parcieux, he was now the Rivarol who was to be famous. The son of a worthy man who in his time had tried many trades, from silk-weaving to school-teaching, and from school-teaching to inn-keeping, Rivarol boldly declared himself a descendant of a stately Italian family, and with a light heart elected himself first chevalier and then count. Why, it has been asked, while he was about it did he not make himself a marquis or a duke?

The son of the innkeeper of the Three Pigeons was well content with himself and his name and his rank, but they afforded excellent opportunities for his enemies to fasten upon. He attacked the 'Jardins' poem of the Abbé Delille with a critical acridity which entertained Grimm, but which raised a cloud of enemies against the critic. Cerutti, Chamfort, La Harpe, and many another waged epigrammatic war with him. It was not an over-nice age, and the champions of the Abbé Virgile, as Rivarol called Delille, found much sport in the fact of Rivarol's marriage to sour-tempered, pretty, pedantic, devoted, Scotch Miss Flint, from whose ill-temper Rivarol soon shook himself free, to the poor lady's despair. Rivarol's enemies revelled in his domestic troubles; it was a merciless age; men fought like Indian braves, neither giving nor taking quarter; all was fair in those hideous literary feuds. But Rivarol held his own. He bit his way like an acid into society; now, on the eve of the Revolution, he was one of the props of the reactionary party, for whom he was to do battle so long and so courageously.

Champcenetz was perhaps a wilder spirit than Rivarol. He was born in 1759, the son of one of the governors of the Louvre, and he rattled through his earlier youth in the liveliest manner—a haunter of taverns, of fencing schools, of houses of ill-fame, like a better-class François Villon. Desperately dissipated, a sparkling talker, a skilful stringer of satirical rhymes, he made sufficient mark upon his time by his super-scandalous reputation to earn for himself the honour of more than one incarceration in the Bastille. Wild as a Cavalier of the House of Stuart, he was no less Royalist, and cherished no hatred to the Bastille which had imprisoned him, nor the institutions which it represented. He walked his wild way with his light songs and his biting epigrams; his ideal world was a world of full flagons and pretty women, and the new revolutionary spirit was not in the least to his liking, nor to the liking of such as he. Against the bitter epigrammatist bitter epigram was employed to some purpose. There is a description of Champcenetz extant written by Rulhière, which is as severe and stinging as Champcenetz could himself have written. 'To be hated but not to be feared, to be punished but not to be pitied, is a most imbecile calculation. Champcenetz has failed. In seeking to be hated he is only despised. He takes lettres de cachet for titles of glory; he thinks that to be notorious is to be renowned. He who does not know how to please is unwise to slander; it is of little avail to be spiteful if one does not know how to write, and if one goes to prison one should go at least for good verses.' Champcenetz was lieutenant in the Gardes Françaises, but was not to hold his lieutenancy much longer. He was brave enough, and his ready sword was time and again at the service of Rivarol, whose stinging satires he was more willing to defend than their author was.

Another journalist of the race was Jean Gabriel Peltier, of Nantes, who was born in 1758. He came early to Paris. According to his own account, he received his education in the College of Louis le Grand, and had the misfortune of having some shirts stolen from him by a fellow-student named Maximilien Robespierre, a statement which it surely required a rabid Royalist to believe. In Paris, Peltier found a place after his own heart and friends after his own heart, among whom he promptly dissipated a very pretty patrimony. His tastes and inclinations jumped with those of Rivarol and Champcenetz; he liked the nobles, liked to rub shoulders with them, to wear their modes and ape their manners; he became in time more royalist than the Royalists themselves. He was a brilliant, audacious, unscrupulous adventurer of letters, a good swashbuckling henchman; not perhaps quite the best man to help to save a losing cause; still a faithful free-companion enough.

A much better man than Peltier was not at this time shining upon the salon where Rivarol and Champcenetz and their like glittered. The man who was to be their ally in their desperate fight for the Old Order against the New Order was now wandering in America and dreaming of settling down there for the remainder of his days. It would have been much better for unhappy Suleau if he had done so instead of coming home to fight a lost fight and perish by a woman's hand for an unworthy epigram. Louis François Suleau was young like the others. He was born in 1757; he too was educated at the College of Louis le Grand, where he had a great friend in a fellow-student named Camille Desmoulins: he had served in the army and got tired of it; he had served the law and known a lawyer named Danton, and got tired of the law in its turn and had set off in 1787 for America. He will return in the late July of this year 1789 to a changed world and to his fate.

A somewhat darker and more dangerous spirit is the Count Alexandre de Tilly, the beau Tilly, whose memoirs, as sparkling and as venomous as a poisoned wine, have left behind so curious a representation of the age in which he lived. Tilly was an Osric doubled with Iago; a dandy and a rake, he was also something of the assassin; his beauty, his wit, and his malignant malice gave him a little of the character of a fallen angel. All his comprehensive love for women, all the passionate adoration that women paid to him, all the loves he inspired and the hates he felt, all the witty things he said—and some of them are incomparably witty—all the unconquerable envy, hatred, malice, and all uncharitableness of his nature, all the impertinence and the treachery and the cruelty were to end very dismally and very shamefully in desperate self-slaughter in the years to come. For the moment he was one of the brightest of the courtly satellites, one of the strongest too; if there had been more men like Tilly and another king, the royalty might have had a different fate. For a time he was a friend of Rivarol's, and with him and his allies was to fight a stout fight for the monarchy with rapier-like pen. But the 'Acts of the Apostles' are not yet.

High constitutionalism, high finance, high philosophy, high diplomacy, found their home in the salon of Madame Necker. Since the old days when Madame Necker's salon first became a centre to be shone upon by Grimm's rouged ambitious face, to be longed for by Galiani in his distant desert of fifty thousand Neapolitans, to echo to the sighs of d'Alembert for Mdlle. de l'Espinasse and to catch the waning rays of Buffon's glory, Madame Necker had found a new ally in making her salon attractive. That new ally was her brilliant ugly daughter, who had married a Swedish ambassador when she might have married Pitt, and who was watching the world with her keen eyes and meditating literary immortality in her quick brain. To the Necker salon came all the distinguished people who put their faith in Necker and whose devotion to the Court meant devotion to the King and hostility to the Queen, or, at least, to the Polignac section, which was supposed to sway the Queen. It was a ministerialist salon, a salon that looked with suspicion alike upon the rising democratic spirit and upon the extreme feudalism of the Old Order as it was represented by the Queen's party. The most brilliant and conspicuous of the new men who were now thronging to Paris did not swell the crowd at Madame Necker's receptions. The men whom Burke would have called men of light and leading went elsewhere; a Sieyès, whom we shall meet with presently, a Clermont-Tonnerre, whom we shall also meet with, were the most remarkable lions of the salon where Marmontel had glittered and Galiani played Harlequin Machiavelli, and St. Lambert slightly chilled the company with his icy exquisite politeness.

A very different salon from any of these, and yet a very important salon in its way, was that of a very beautiful lady of the lightest of light reputations who came from Liège and set up her staff in Paris. Théroigne de Méricourt was the daughter of a rich farmer; she had been betrayed and abandoned, such was her story, by a noble: she gravitated to London and to Paris, where she was ambitious of playing the part, not of a vulgar courtesan, but of a revolutionary Aspasia, a hetaira of the type that was to find its Pericles among the enthusiasts of the New Order. She was very beautiful, she was very clever; her house came to be the centre for all the men of the most advanced ideas. Here came men who were yet to be famous—Pétion, Romme, Sieyès, Target, Maximilien Robespierre, Populus, as Popule was called, Populus who was regarded by many as the real Pericles of Théroigne's Aspasia. At this moment the star of her vexed and unhappy destiny was shining very brightly. The betrayed farmer's daughter Anne Josèphe Terwagne was the idol of advanced Paris, a revolutionary goddess before the days of revolutionary goddesses.

Among the smaller salons were that of Madame Helvétius—she with whom Turgot had played at battledore and shuttlecock—frequented by the leading philosophers and men of science; the revolutionary salons of Madame Dauberval, the dancer's wife, and of Madame d'Angiviller, where a ridiculous, bedizened old woman played at youth; the salon of the Countess de Tessé, who is to be enthusiastic about Bailly, and many another of less note and scant importance where the new ideas were assiduously discussed, fiercely championed, or bitterly arraigned. Gouverneur Morris describes Madame de Tessé as a Republican of the first feather, 'a very sensible woman,' who has 'formed her ideas of government in a manner not suited, I think, either to the situation, the circumstances, or the disposition of France, and there are many such.'

Very unlike the salon of the wild Théroigne was that in which Madame de Genlis received the more respectable of the queer crowd which composed the Duke d'Orleans' party. As the lady of honour to the Duchesse de Chartres, Equality Orleans' daughter-in-law, she acted in some measure as hostess in the Palais Royal. Her daughter Pamela was there to add the charm of her rare beauty, that beauty which a few years later was to captivate a young Irish gentleman, the 'gallant and seditious Geraldine' Lord Edward Fitzgerald, who loved her, so the legend goes, less for herself than for the fact that her beauty reminded him of one whom he had adored too wildly, the beautiful wife of Richard Brinsley Sheridan. But in these days the beautiful Pamela was a slender stripling of a girl, and the young Irish gentleman was far away. To Madame de Genlis's salon came Choderlos de Laclos. Most able among profligate penmen, he had come into the world at Amiens in 1741, chiefly, as it would seem, to be of service to a Duke d'Orleans who needed such service badly and to write an obscene book. The book is still dimly remembered by the lovers of that class of literature; Laclos himself is dimly remembered, the shadow of a name. Here, too, came Saint-Huruge, bull-necked and boisterous, loving his cups and the sound of his loud voice, an immense believer in himself, a brazen creature, hollow and noisy as brass is hollow and noisy. In these later years Madame de Genlis had grown sourly prim. She was virtuous now, and heartily desired that there should be no more cakes and ale. Probably of all women in the world she liked Madame Buffon least. So she sits now in that 'blue-room with its golden beading and its magnificence of mirror,' sour, austere, compelling even Saint-Huruge to lower his voice and even Laclos to moderate his sallies.

Hers was decidedly the dismalest of all the salons, but very important.

There was another blue-room of a brighter kind, where Madame de Beauharnais held her little court. Madame de Beauharnais was no longer young; she had never been very witty, but she possessed the happy art of wearing years gracefully, and of seeming witty, which is almost as good as being witty. And then she gave such excellent dinners. It might almost have been said of her by the uncharitable that she intended to found a salon and only succeeded in starting a restaurant, for certainly her dinners were the things most immediately associated with her name. There was a queer atmosphere of dead days forgotten about that little room in blue and silver. The ghosts of a former generation of wits, and philosophers, and statesmen, seemed to flit like bats through its dim air. Rousseau was here in his time, and many another famous man now quietly inurned, the Dorats, the Crébillons, the Colardeaus—ghost, ghosts, ghosts. The memory of Dorat was disagreeably perpetuated by Dorat-Cubières—most unadmirable of mean men, a weary rhymer of foolishness, 'the delirious mite who wishes to play the ant,' as Rivarol kindly said of him. He played the host in this salon and the fool, and was yet to play the knave when his time came. Here came distinguished strangers; an exiled Prince de Gonzague Castiglione, whom we shall scarcely meet again, and an atheistic Prussian baron whom we shall certainly meet again, and come to know more closely. For the present he was known as Jean Baptiste Clootz. Here, too, came Vicq-d'Azir and Rabaut Saint-Etienne, the excellent, high-minded Protestant enthusiast, seeing no shadow of the axe upon his path. Here came Mercier, noting with his keen eyes the Paris that he loved, and little dreaming what a service he had rendered to mankind by his book. Here, too, came one of the most remarkable figures of a fading past, Restif de la Bretonne.

Restif de la Bretonne was one of the strangest figures that literary France of the eighteenth century produced. That curious sloping forehead and long nose, those thick lips, that retreating chin, that large sleepy eye with its vague air of speculation, suggest more the tenth transmitter of a foolish face than the brilliant and amazingly voluminous novelist whose works are so vivid a picture of the France of the Old Order. Compared to a writer whose works occupy some two hundred volumes, the poor half-century of volumes of Balzac's fiction sinks into insignificance. But while Balzac lives, Restif de la Bretonne is forgotten; a few bibliophiles rave about him, because his books are hard to obtain—it is said that no one possesses a complete set. A kind of Restifomania, as it has been called, has seized upon a few individuals who offer up to the memory of their eccentric genius an almost Buddhistic devotion. He has been hailed as the French Defoe, but his popularity has not endured like Defoe's. He has been styled the Rousseau of the Halles, and the Rousseau des ruisseaus; but while the influence of Rousseau is as enormous almost as ever, the influence of Restif is exercised over a little handful of queer bookworms. Nicholas Edme Restif was born in Burgundy in the October of 1734, the eldest son of the second marriage of a farmer who had been a clerk. He was brought up to the life of a peasant, and the knowledge of the Bible. Before he was fifteen he was educated for a while in Paris among the Jansenists of Bicêtre. In 1751 he was apprenticed to a printer in Auxerre. In 1755 he came to Paris, which was to be his home for the rest of his life. In 1767 he first essayed literature, and for the rest of his life he literally showered books upon a world that was equally willing to welcome them when they came, and afterwards most heartily to forget them. He had always enjoyed astonishing health, which was no doubt the great secret of his alliance of long life with such indomitable work. He ate little, drank less; his weakness was a devotion for women, which made his life one long procession of amours, of passions, of intrigues of all kinds. An unhappy marriage darkened his life for a season, but he shook himself free from the tie and walked his amorous way after his own heart. His greatest enthusiasm was for the dainty shoes, the dainty stockings, the dainty feet and shapely legs of women; about these he raved assiduously through all the interminable length of his many books. But if he was a gallant he was not a dandy. We can almost see him in his habit as he lived, in the costume which he persisted in wearing for twenty years—the old blue coat, the heavy black mantle, the huge felt hat. He was always indifferent to linen and the cares of the person. He had a way when he was working hard at a book of not shaving till it was finished, which did not add to his attractions, but which sufficiently displayed his absolute and serene indifference to the mere minutenesses of existence. In these days of revolution in the air his spirit is all Republican; he is one of the strangest figures to whom it was given to live through the more thrilling part of the great drama that was now upon the eve of beginning.

To the salon of Madame de Broglie, wife of the young Prince de Broglie, came certain brilliant thoughtful young men who had a distinguished part to play. One of them was named Barnave; we shall meet with him again. Here came the two noble sons of an ancient Picardy house, Charles Malo de Lameth, born in 1757, and his brother Alexandre Malo de Lameth, who was three years younger. They had both shared with Lafayette, and Lauzun, and Boniface Barrel Mirabeau in the honours of the American campaign; they had both been chosen by an affectionate province to share in the honours of the States-General; they represented the desperate, honourable attempt to unite loyalty to the monarchy with advanced constitutional ideas. Here too came Armand de Vignerot, Duke d'Aguillon, son of the d'Aguillon of the du Barry days, and himself a gallant soldier. Here came the Vicomte de Noailles and the young Duke Mathieu de Montmorency, who entered the National Assembly as a youth of twenty-two—he was born in 1767—who was only a child when he followed Lafayette to America, and who was one of the most advanced of the advanced nobility. In consequence he will soon share with the Lameths and their like the merciless hatred of the Royalists quand même, such as Tilly and the Rivarol gang.

The salon of Julie Talma, the great actor's wife, was no less political than dramatic. Joseph Marie Chénier was as interested in the events of the day as in his plays. Ducis' honest if queer admiration for Shakespeare, whom he never read in the original, was allied with a no less honest interest in the events of the hour. Ducis was a Republican of a high ideal kind like Chénier, like another frequenter of the Talma home whom we shall have much to do with hereafter, and whose name was Vergniaud.

One of the queerest of all the queer centres of Parisian life was dominated by an English nobleman. The Duke of Bedford, fifth duke of the name, was an ardent sympathiser with the earlier revolutionists, held open house for them and for the light ladies who sympathised with them, Grace Dalrymple Elliott, the Duke of Orleans' mistress, who wisely left memoirs, and Madame de Saint Amaranthe, and the rest. He was a man of new ideas; he disliked the Duke of Dorset, who reigned at the Embassy; these two motives were enough to tar him on to toy with revolution. But the strongest motive was the first, which led him a few years later to become the leader of the crops or shavers, as the Radical peers and gentlemen were called who showed their affection for advanced ideas by wearing their hair short, and irritated the Tories by thus avoiding the tax on hair-powder. The Marquis de Villette of infamous reputation was always a conspicuous figure at the Bedford entertainments.

A much more sober salon was that of Madame Panckoucke, the wife of Panckoucke the publisher, the Panckoucke who shall yet apply for the privilege of reporting the debates of the National Assembly. Panckoucke himself was an enterprising, ambitious man, sprung from an old printing stock at Lille. He was born in 1736; when he was eighteen years old he came to Paris to make his name, and he succeeded. He had a lucky instinct; he married a clever woman more ambitious than himself, whose sister was married to the Academician Suard; he bought the 'Mercure,' the oldest paper in France, and afterwards bought the 'Gazette de France.' Such a man naturally gathered a number of authors about him, and when the Revolution was dawning, and Madame Panckoucke saw her way to playing a part in politics, she was not likely to want for visitors of distinction. Here came La Harpe, acrid, pedantic, energetic classicist, writer of poor tragedies, compiler of a portentous 'Course of Literature,' which was not without merit, a man who in his fifty years of life—he was born in 1739—had earned perhaps more hatred than usually falls to the lot of critics. Here, too, came the older and less ill-tempered critic Marmontel, sixty-six years of age, with a memory going back over the brilliant days of the Pompadour, and the great Titanomachia of the 'Encyclopædia,' 'quorum pars parva fuit.' Both he and La Harpe, belonging as they did to the old school, were yet to outlast the fever heat of the Revolution after seeing the world in which they lived turned completely topsy-turvy after a fashion intolerably perplexing to compilers of 'Eléments de Littérature,' and 'Cours de Littérature.' Here came Condorcet, whom we shall make closer acquaintance with at the Paris elections. Here came Barère, dreaming not of terror as order of the day, or guillotine Anacreontics, and heedless of a certain Zachary Macaulay, of whom Brissot could have told him somewhat, and who was yet in eleven years to bear a son who should lend Barère's name a cruel immortality. But Madame Panckoucke's most important guest was the grave, high-minded, honourable Genevese Mallet-du-Pan. An austere man of forty, born in 1749, he had seen many things with those grave, judicious, earnest eyes, but nothing yet to prepare him for what he was still to see. His childhood was passed in the beautiful little village of Celigny, on the right bank of the Lake of Geneva, where his father was pastor. He studied and earned high honours at the College of Geneva which Calvin founded; for a while he studied the law. He was fifteen when he entered the Geneva Academy; when he left the Academy at twenty years of age he plunged at once with a strangely matured mind in the political and journalistic life of the little Republic. He early earned the warm friendship of Voltaire, and no one saw more of the aged philosopher in his shelter at Ferney than the young Mallet-du-Pan. The persecutions inflicted upon Linguet aroused the indignation of Mallet-du-Pan; when Linguet appeared at Ferney, as most people in trouble did, he greatly attracted the young man, though he greatly irritated Voltaire, and in 1777, under Linguet's influence, Mallet-du-Pan went, first to London, and then to Brussels, where Linguet decided to publish his 'Annales politiques, civiles, et littéraires du Dix-huitième Siècle.' During Linguet's imprisonment in the Bastille, Mallet-du-Pan kept up a sequel to the 'Annales.' When Linguet came out of the Bastille he quarrelled with Mallet-du-Pan, and denounced him as an imitator. Mallet indignantly and justly repudiated the charge, and carried on his own paper under the title of 'Mémoires historiques, politiques, et littéraires, sur l'État présent de l'Europe,' with the motto, 'Nec temere, nec timide.' In 1782, when Geneva was torn by Revolution, and three armies thundered at her gates, Mallet played his part in a mission to General la Marmora, and in counselling prudence to his fellow-citizens. In

1784 Mallet-du-Pan came to Paris. Panckoucke had been longing for him since 1778; now at last he induced him to edit the political part of the 'Mercure,' and in Paris for the five years till 1789 he lived in great quiet and seclusion with his family—he had married young—devoting himself heart and soul to his journalistic life. Of a strictly simple nature, brought up in the austerity of Swiss life, he was little attracted by the glitter of Paris life. Paris began, he said, by astonishing, it afterwards amused, then it fatigued. No higher-minded man ever gave his services to journalism; no purer spirit devoted itself to the Royalist cause; if that cause could have counted on more supporters like him it would have been happier.

A very different type of journalist had just come to Paris in the early part of this year 1789. This was Elysée Loustalot, who was born in 1761 at Saint-Jean d'Angely. His family occupied an honourable place at the Bar; it was in accordance with the fitness of things that the young Loustalot should go to the Bar too. Accordingly he studied law at the college of Saintes, studied law at Bordeaux, and became a lawyer there. He got into trouble on account of a vehement attack he made upon the administration of his native town, he was suspended for six months from the practice of his profession; irritated, he shook off the dust of provincial life, and came to Paris in the beginning of 1789 to follow the Paris Bar. While pursuing his profession he was keenly attracted by the new political life and activity that was teeming around him, and he was ready enough when the time came—and the time was now near at hand—to plunge into journalism, and to fight vigorously for the principles of the Revolution. His extraordinary energy, his unwearying capacity for work, his clear and caustic style, were to make him an invaluable supporter of the new men and the new ideas that were coming into play.

The time was not far off when the active life of literary and political Paris would be in her clubs, but the time was not yet. The Breton Club, germ of the Jacobins, was not yet formed; the Cordeliers was yet to be famous. Still Paris, under the influence of its Anglomania, had its clubs—the 'Société des Amis des Noirs,' which Brissot had founded, Brissot who was always being fired by hissing hot pseudo-enthusiasms; the Lycée, which was much associated with Condorcet; the Club de Valois, of which that energetic American gentleman Gouverneur Morris was delighted to become a member. There were other smaller clubs too, but the fierce club-fever had not yet set in. But none of these were as yet serious political centres. The real political centre of Paris was the Palais Royal.

CHAPTER XXIV

THE ELECTIONS

To this excited and exciting Paris in the spring of 1789 men were tending from all parts of France. From north and south, from east and west, the high roads saw a steady stream of men rolling like the single drops of water to be amalgamated into the shining sea of Versailles. For the elections, the great elections to the States-General, had taken place. After an infinity of speculation and discussion, of publication of pamphlets, of study of precedents, of consideration of time-honoured formulas and propositions of radically new notions, the States-General had somehow or other got elected. It had soon become clear that the old rules were obsolete, exploded, useless. On January 24, 1789, the regulation was issued which decided the way in which the elections should be managed in that part of France known as pays d'élection. The old administrative divisions known as royal bailiwicks in the northern part of France, and as royal seneschalries in the south, were used as electoral units, and a little later the part of France known as pays d'état, and which comprised such semi-independent provinces as Burgundy, Brittany, and Languedoc, were also divided into electoral units. In each of these electoral units all the nobles, all the clergy, and all the electors of the Third Estate who had been previously elected in primary assemblies in town or village were to meet together to choose their representatives for the States-General.

Now all this lay behind those wandering deputies; a portion and parcel of the dreadful past. The primary assemblies in the towns and villages had got through their difficult and complex method of choosing the electors, who were in their turn to elect their deputies at the large assemblies. The large assemblies in their turn had met and chosen their deputies, and those deputies were now speeding as swiftly as might be along all the roads of France to Versailles. They had not come to pass, however, without an immense deal of friction, and sometimes more than friction. All manner of jealousies and rivalries agitated the bailiwicks; all kinds of mistakes were made, leading to the issue of supplementary regulations; all kinds of quarrels, disputes, bickerings rent the civic and the country air. The old nobility did not always get on very well with the new nobility, proud of their fire-new brand of honour. The upper and the lower clergy were not in cordial union, naturally enough. Again and again the orders fought among themselves and fell asunder. In some cases the nobility took no part in the elections, in others they protested against their results. In Brittany they refused to elect any deputies at all. The Third Estate all over the country were fortunate in having the good example and the good advice of Dauphiné. The wise men of Grenoble, with Mounier at their head, guided, advised, directed, encouraged the electorate of the Third Estate with marvellous prudence and tact. It is impossible to over-estimate the services Mounier and his friends rendered to their cause at this difficult and perplexing crisis.

The legend of the imprisoned Titan who only waits the magic watchword to shake aside the chains that bind him, the mountains that are piled upon his breast, found for the first time its parallel in history. The French people played the part of the prisoned Titan; the magic words States-General were the new open sesame that set the Titan free. It is unhappily the vice of Titans to play sad pranks with their newly-found liberty, pranks that a respectable Swiss Protestant banker could not dream of, much less dread. Enfranchise the people as much as you please; Necker can always control, Necker can always guide; such were the confident convictions of Necker the Man, such were the confident assurances of Necker the Minister. So the work went on, and no one felt afraid. All over France there was a great throbbing of new life, the quickening experience of new vital forces. The new privileges were immense. Everybody might vote, everybody who had a plaint to make might freely make it heard. Town and country, city and hamlet, all alike were equal as regards the new assembly. Never was so desperate an experiment attempted before. The bulk of a nation that had lain for long generations insulted and ignored, the patient victim of well-nigh intolerable abuses, was suddenly entrusted with the rights and privileges of free men. The question was what these free men would do with these rights and privileges, and that was just the question which nobody could presume to answer, though everybody made bold to hope after his own fashion.

It is said that five millions of men took part in the elections. Five millions of men, of whom the greater part could not write, were summoned to play their parts as citizens and choose their representatives. The nobles fondly imagined that the flock would follow its old shepherds of the Church and of the State and prove a sufficiently submissive instrument in the elections of delegates agreeable to the Old Order. The Old Order was decisively disappointed. The untrained masses showed an astonishing alacrity to avail themselves of the unexpected opportunity offered to them. They did not know their strength, but they were dimly, vaguely, conscious of it, and they bowed to their old lords no longer. In every part of France men flocked to the elections. In every part of France men put pens to paper, for the drawing up of 'cahiers,' in which the national wrongs were for the first time recorded, and recorded with striking uniformity. France was wakening up with a vengeance; even the privileged orders were not free from the new democratic spirit. There were children of the Church, two hundred and more of the smaller clergy, who were in some degree inspired with the new ideas, who were hostile to their spiritual heads very much as the peasantry were hostile to their temporal heads, and the elections brought some of this democratic leaven into the lump of the Second Estate.

But of all the elections that sent deputies to the States-General, by far the most important were the Paris elections. The sixteen quarters of the city were divided into sixty electoral districts. To Paris had been allotted no less than forty deputies—ten from the nobility, ten from the clergy, and twenty deputies of the Third Estate, in accordance with the principle that had been decided upon that the Third Estate was to be represented by as many representatives as the two other orders put together. The Paris elections began much later than any of the others, and most of the deputies from the other parts of France had actually arrived in Paris or Versailles and were witnesses of the great election which was in some sense the key-stone of the whole business. The nobility on the whole were strongly liberal. Their ten deputies included the Count de Clermont-Tonnerre, the Duke de La Rochefoucauld, Count de Lally-Tollendal, Adrien Duport, and the Marquis of Montesquieu. Clermont-Tonnerre was a gallant cavalry colonel, forty-two years old, and exceedingly popular with the Constitutionalists on account of his liberal ideas. His face was singularly striking, even handsome in an imposing, severe kind of way. The sharp straight slope of the forehead continued along the nose, the long upper lip and slightly protruding lower lip, the advanced and rounded chin, the high arched eyebrows and deeply set eyes with a certain menacing sternness in their regard, seem the appropriate facial symbols of the calm and lofty eloquence he had so readily at command.

Lally-Tollendal was a gallant captain of Cuirassiers, the devoted son of an unhappy father, whose unjust sentence he had succeeded in reversing in spite of the opposition of another Paris deputy, d'Éprémesnil, nephew of Dupleix and inheritor of his hate. Adrien Duport was the Duke d'Orleans' right-hand man, aspiring to success through the success of his chief, a councillor in the Paris Parliament, with a vast ambition and a genius for intrigue. He was now about thirty years of age. Duport's influence was very great in the country. He had correspondents in every part of the kingdom, who kept him in close touch with the progress of opinion, and who were the means of extending his influence. His house in Paris was a kind of Cave of Adullam, to which all who were discontented and all who were in distress and all who were in debt were quite welcome to repair so long as they permitted Adrien Duport to make himself a captain over them. Here came all the young ambitious lawyers of advanced opinions; here came the liberal nobility; here came the subtle friend of Madame de Flahaut, Talleyrand Périgord, bishop of Autun; here sometimes came a greater man than any or all of these whose name was Mirabeau. Duport played his game well. He was ambitious; he saw in himself an excellent prime minister, to some puppet king, some roi fainéant such as the Duke of Orleans might easily be made under his skilful manipulation. That rounded face, with its queerly compressed lips, its large sleepy looking eyes with lowered lids, its spacious forehead and prominently marked eyebrows, has on it an air of quizzically smiling at the follies of mankind and dutifully suppressing the smile. Certainly a man who aspired to greatness by the aid of Equality Orleans had every reason to smile at mankind.

It was considered somewhat surprising that two members of the primary assembly of the nobility, who helped to draw up its cahier, were not chosen either as deputies or as the supplemental deputies, who were in all cases chosen to be in readiness in case any accident should prevent any of the elected deputies from fulfilling their functions. The two men thus omitted were Choderlos de Laclos and Condorcet. No one except the members of the Orleans faction could regret the absence of Laclos from the Assembly. All parties might well have considered the presence of Condorcet an advantage. Still a comparatively young man—he was only in his forty-sixth year—he was already one of the most distinguished scientific men in France, and his name was the link between the thinkers of the Encyclopædic age and the radical thinkers of the New Order. The admirer of Voltaire, the intimate friend of d'Alembert, the disciple, the friend and the biographer of Turgot, the victor over Bailly at the Academy of 1782, Marie Jean Antoine Nicolas de Caritat, Marquis of Condorcet, would certainly have added a lustre to the brilliant Assembly of men into whose hands the task of regenerating France was given.

Condorcet was a liberal of the truest type, the advocate of all the oppressed. There was no more zealous advocate of the Cause of the Blacks. The young Lally-Tollendal, striving to redeem a father's name, found no firmer friend and helper than he. Injustice everywhere found in Condorcet a staunch opponent. That wide inquiring eye, that high and curiously domed forehead, the large nose of Roman curve, the prominent lips and firm, forward chin, went to compose a face in which an air of extreme gentleness and good-nature masked an ardent, impulsive nature. His tall, slightly stooped form, his huge head, his massive shoulders made him always a conspicuous figure, and contrasted somewhat oddly with his usual shyness, even timidity of manner, a shyness and timidity that only quitted him within the narrow circle of a few intimate and dear friends. D'Alembert called him a volcano covered with snow. Mdlle. de

Lespinasse said that most people looking at him would think him rather a worthy man than a wise man. He had none of the belligerent fierceness which characterized so many of the Philosophers, and no man was ever more ready to admit himself in the wrong when he believed himself to be in the wrong. No sweeter spirit adorned the last century. One critic described him as a mad sheep. Madame Roland illustrated the relation of Condorcet's mind to his body by saying that it was a subtle essence soaked in cotton. His early education was curious enough. His father was a cavalry officer who died when his son was three years old. Most of the child's relatives would have liked to see him become in his turn a stout man-at-arms, as his father had been before him, and were sufficiently disappointed at his becoming a mere economist and philosopher. But his mother's treatment was hardly of a kind to train him either as a good soldier or philosopher. She dedicated him to the Holy Virgin, and for eight years made him wear the dress of a little girl, as a sort of shield against the evils of the world. Achilles in Scyros seems hardly stranger to us than the little Condorcet going about in girl's clothes. Who shall say how profound an influence this extraordinary experience may have had upon the child to whom a little later the Jesuits were to impart so profound a mathematical knowledge! The boy in girl's clothes, the pupil of the Jesuits, grew up an impassioned mathematician, but also an ardent politician, eager in a hot-headed, uncompromising way for the bettering of the world. His resolves were more impetuous than strong. He was little fitted for that golden mean in life upon which Aristotle insists. The more we read his writings, the more we study his life, the more we understand, even while we refuse to agree with, that 'mad sheep' criticism. For what he believed to be right he contended with a passion which was the sign rather of strong emotions than of the strong capacity to lead. With all the most honourable ambitions of a statesman he lacked the essential capacity of a successful statesmanship, the capacity for seeing how much of a desirable work can be accomplished at a certain time, and of appreciating with a fine infallibility the exact time in which the desired work can best be done. He played his part in forming the Revolution; he was one of the many gallantly ambitious Frankensteins who found their creation too much for them.

The Parisian clergy displayed none of the liberalism of the nobility. Their ten deputies were all strongly conservative; their leader, Antoine Leclerc de Juigné, archbishop of Paris, especially. The archbishop was an excellent good man, charitable, well-esteemed; utterly out of sympathy, however, with the advanced political opinions of the hour. It will take the stones of an infuriated populace to temper his hot conservatism by-and-by, and to make his pride bend to the demands of public opinion.

The real interest of the elections, however, centred in the Third Estate.

There was trouble in Paris. The weak King, oscillating between Necker and the Court, between the rising democracy and an imperious consort prompted by an ambitious Polignac, was making some desperate efforts to shackle his liberated Titan. By delay of elections, by postponement of the opening of the States-General, by such clumsy devices the poor King strove to shuffle aside the inevitable, and to pack cards with fortune. In Paris especially, Paris, where the popular feeling was most alert and most intelligent, the Court resorted to its rashest measures. The Paris elections were not fixed until the very eve of the opening of the States-General. By this juggle the Court hoped to keep the Paris deputies out of the way until the essential preliminaries might be arranged which were to assure to the privileged orders the majority of the Third Estate. Moreover, the conditions of election were by a special decree made more severe in Paris than in any other part of the kingdom. Only those who paid six livres of impost, instead of those who paid hardly any impost at all, were allowed to vote. To overawe the electors thus minimized, the streets were filled with troops, the place of election surrounded by soldiers; all that the display of force could do was done to bring the electors of Paris to appreciate their position and to submit. The electors did appreciate their position rightly, and they did not submit. They started off by declining to accept the presidents proposed for them in the royal name. Sixty presidents had been thus proposed for the sixty districts of Paris, and out of these sixty only three were accepted, and then only on the express understanding that they must consider themselves as duly elected by the will of the people and not as the nominees of the Court. On April 21 the various districts chose their representatives for the general assembly of the Third Estate of Paris. On April 26 the general assembly of the Third Estate met separately, after the nobles and the clergy had refused to join with them, elected Target for their president, Camus for second president, Sylvain Bailly for secretary, and Dr. Guillotin as assistant-secretary. Gui Jean Baptiste Target was born in Paris in 1733. He was a member of the Academy; he was the foremost leader of the Paris bar. He had always before his eyes as an ideal the British Constitution, a monarchy tempered by parliamentary government. An air of humorous surprise throned upon his large and heavy face, a magisterial face, to which a slight obliquity of the eyes appeared to give an oddness of expression. He was, according to the testimony of his colleague Bailly, whom we shall meet with and estimate later, a man of flawless probity, of infinite political learning, of rare memory, eloquent and logical, of profound and critical judgment. Armand Gaston Camus, his colleague, was, like him, a Parisian; he was born in Paris in 1740, and up to this time he was chiefly remarkable for his translation of Aristotle's 'History of Animals,' which had earned him a place in the Academy of Inscriptions. He was a jovial-looking man, with an air of roguish sensuality.

Assistant-secretary Guillotin we shall meet with again and again. At present he was simply a successful doctor, fifty-one years of age, with a somewhat skull-like face, large mouth and smiling eyes. Questions of hygiene, questions of humanity occupied his mind even more than questions of politics. But he was a keen politician too, no doubt acquainted with the rising of the English people against their King, Charles I., and pained probably by the blundering method of decapitation employed. Could there not be some better way, he thought, with no idea of what that better way was. We have seen that the fate of Charles I. appears to have made a profound impression upon the French mind. We have seen what Turgot wrote to Louis XVI. Arthur Young speaks of the opinion some Frenchman of his acquaintance passed upon that act. This Frenchman, speaking for himself and his countrymen, said that the French had too profound a respect for their monarchy to allow such a crime ever to become possible in France. Yet the example was always there, ominous and disquieting. We read that Madame du Barry was at great pains to obtain a portrait of Charles I., and that she was wont to stimulate the flagging zeal of Louis the Well-beloved against his parliaments by pointing to this portrait, and warning him of what he might expect if he did not keep turbulent forces well in check. So, too, in much the same manner the Count d'Artois about this time of the States-General presented Louis XVI. with a picture of Charles I., as a warning to him of what happened to kings who conceded too much to their subjects. How portentous the warning was, stupid d'Artois and blundering Louis had no idea. Guillotin was the man to drive the warning home.

CHAPTER XXV

THE SPRING OF '89

PARIS had seldom known a harder, a crueller winter than that of 1788–89. When the year began, the thermometer registered eighteen degrees below freezing-point. It had been freezing for thirty-six days, ever since November 24, and the suffering was intense. The Seine had begun to freeze on November 26, and the cold showed no signs of diminishing. It was not so bad for the wealthy, who, cloaked in furs, skimmed along the frozen boulevards in fantastic sleighs, capriciously delighted with the new toys that Nature allowed them to sport with. But to the needy and the really poor, the winter was one long agony. People died of cold in the streets; the hospitals overflowed with luckless wretches, men, women, and children, struck down by the merciless intensity of cold.

Lalande, who had startled Paris before by a threatened comet, predicted that the cold would endure, and his prophecy proved correct this time. Until January 13 there was no thaw, and then, though there was a slight frost on the 16th, the bitterness of the cold began to break, and was succeeded by pitiless, endless torrents of rain. The horrors of that wild winter are difficult to appreciate. The suffering was appalling, the mortality great. Charitable people like Langrier de Beaurecueil, curé of Sainte-Marguerite, like Monseigneur de Juigné, organized dispensations of food and fire in the form of soup and charcoal, but there was not enough soup to feed all the starving mouths, nor charcoal to warm the pinched bodies. In some cases the poor wretches to whom the burning charcoal was given were found in their miserable slums dead, asphyxiated by the subtle fumes over which they had cowered in their aching passion for warmth. The Hospice de la Garde de Paris opened its doors to the poor who passed by, that they might come in and warm themselves at its fires on their way.

From the dawn of the year Paris was as warm with political excitement as it was cold with climate. Day by day thrilling news came pouring in from the provinces. Now it was the Dauphiné elections begun before the solemn sanction of the State had been given in its published regulation. Now it was riots in Nantes. Now it was the imbecile action of the Breton nobles. Now it was the controversies in Franche Comté between the liberal and antiliberal nobility. Now it was the dissensions and disturbances in Rennes. Now it was the protest of the nobility of Toulouse against the States of Languedoc. Now it was the meeting of the three orders in

Lorraine, and de Custine's declaration that the order of the Third Estate constituted the nation. Now it was the Roussillon nobility renouncing their pecuniary privileges. Now it was the discord in Provence, and the name of Mirabeau blown about on Provençal winds. Now it was the orders of Châteauroux and of Languedoc renouncing their pecuniary privileges. Never had a more momentous January passed over Parisian heads. Every day brought fresh news from the provinces, and with the news always the wildest of rumours, which turned out in the end to be no news at all, but idlest inventions of popular fancy or popular fear. Poverty drove unhappy women to expose their new-born children almost naked in the street to touch the pity of the passers-by. 'It is baptized,' one of these women is reported to have said; 'what does it matter whether it dies of cold or of hunger?' Paris had its own excitements too. Duval d'Éprémesnil was denouncing Necker in the Parliament. The Parliament was issuing profitless orders against gambling. The worshippers of the Reformed Churches began to agitate for the opening of their places of worship, shut since the days of Louis XIV. The town and the Châtelet, headed by their two provosts, the Provost of the Merchants and the Provost of Paris, were wrangling fiercely over the right to convoke the Paris electors. Neither of these provosts was over-popular. The Provost of the Merchants, Lepeletier de Mortefontaine, a babbling man of pseudo-gallantries with a taste for rouge, was reproached with having dabbled in monopoly of woods and charcoals. The Provost of Paris, who led the Châtelet faction, Bernard de Boulainvilliers, was popularly accused of a comprehensive system of smuggling. It was said in those early January days that the Cardinal de Rohan had actually been permitted to pass through Paris incognito, the cardinal whose name was to figure in so many of the cahiers of the nobility protesting against his treatment. Cerutti was filling all literary Paris with his fury against Mirabeau for publishing the correspondence between them ; energetic Jesuit Giuseppe Antonio Gioachimo Cerutti from Turin, whose fifty years of life had made him liberal in his opinions, but had not taught him how to write good verses. The frosty air was so full of wild ideas that the wildest cease to excite surprise. A proposal, with which Dr. Guillotin and new-made notorious Marquis de Villette were associated, was set on foot to erect a statue to Louis XVI. on the Place du Carrousel. Then some one else proposed that the Bastille should be pulled down, and a statue of the King erected there, with an appropriate inscription to the King as the destroyer of state prisons. This proposal was to seem curiously ominous and prophetic presently.

In the midst of all this excitement, a couple of distinguished men passed from the scene for ever. On January 21, Baron d'Holbach died, d'Holbach the learned chemist, the aggressive atheist, the patron of Diderot, the friend of Grimm. On the

27th, d'Ormesson died, Louis François de Paule le Fevre d'Ormesson, first President of the Paris Parliament. He was the son of that incompetent controller-general who muddled the finances in 1783, and who survived his son some sixteen years.

Slowly the winter slipped into spring; slowly the cold abated. But two things did not abate—the flood of exciting news that came daily pouring into Paris, and the flood of political pamphlets and publications of all kinds that poured daily from the Parisian presses. The air was thick with these 'Black Butterflies' as they were playfully called. Seldom has the world witnessed such a flight of political papers since Gutenberg first plied his dangerous craft. In the midst of all this seething mass of printed tirades, attacks, propositions, and programmes, there appeared, by way of the strangest contrast, a book which had nothing to do with politics, and which might have made its appearance in a happier age. This was the 'Voyage du Jeune Anacharsis' of the Abbé Barthélemy. For thirty years the good abbé had been at work upon this, the magnum opus of his life. For the time its scholarship was profound, and the scholarship was agreeably gilded with the thin gold of a narrative form. It is not perhaps the most agreeable kind of fiction, the kind which seeks insidiously to distil learning under the guise of romance. The 'Gallus' and the 'Charicles' of Becker are not exactly exhilarating books; they suggest Mr. Barlow and his methods too much. But the young Anacharsis had success enough to delight the heart of the old Barthélemy. That long, kindly, smiling, wrinkled face, over which seventy-three winters had passed, had every reason now to beam with pleasure. Some friend had advised him, when the book was printed, to hold back its publication until the approaching States-General had come to an end. Luckily for the Abbé Barthélemy, he did not take this advice. Suppose he had, poor old man; would anybody have ever heard of the young Anacharsis at all? As it was, the book had a great success. Everyone who had time to read anything save pamphlets read it. The literary world, the polite world, were delighted with it. Greece, to anticipate a phrase that soon became disagreeably familiar, was the order of the day. People thought Greece, talked Greece, played at being Greek at Madame Vigée le Brun's, where that pretty paintress gathered her friends about her. The enthusiastic Hellenists got up Greek tableaux and Dorat-Cubières played with a lyre, and Le Brun Pindare shook the powder from his hair and sported a wreath of laurel. Nothing could be more queerly in contrast with all that was happening, with all that was going to happen, than this affected aping of Hellenism, this assumption of mere literary ease and enjoyment in a world that was about to fall to pieces. It was dancing on a volcano, indeed, with a vengeance. Yet this sudden Hellenism was to have its influence, too, in days a little later, when the mania for being Greek or Roman shall assume grimmer proportions.

Steadily the winter went its course, steadily the elections went on all over France, steadily the news of them came pouring into Paris, steadily soon the deputies themselves began to pour into Paris and to settle themselves in Versailles. The Versailles municipality had arranged a regular tariff of charges for their lodgment to prevent them from being victimized by the cupidity of the eager flock of people who had rooms to let. At last, as we have seen, when the elections in the country were practically all over, the Parisians got their chance of electing their deputies.

CHAPTER XXVI

THE ROW AT RÉVEILLON'S

AT this moment the first jet of pent revolutionary flame pierced the crust and leaped into the air, at once portentous and perplexing. Among the Paris electors was a certain wealthy manufacturer of wallpaper, a self-made man who had been but a working man, Réveillon. De Besenval says of him in his kindly soldierly way that he was an honest man, charitable, well-approved, who little merited the fate he underwent. Réveillon's paper works were in the Faubourg Saint-Antoine, within the very shadow of the Bastille. In that troublous, truculent ant-hill of Saint-Antoine, where men felt the pinch of poverty very keenly, and where rumours flew abroad as swiftly as they fly through Eastern bazaars, some one had set going an accusation against Réveillon. The opulent paper-maker was accused of saying scornfully that fifteen sous a day was ample pay for the workpeople. This seemed to angry Saint-Antoine to sound badly from the lips of one who had sprung from the ranks of the people, who had known their sufferings, their privations, who knew better than most the little way a scant wage went. Saint-Antoine was angry for another reason too. It was bruited abroad that Réveillon was to receive the order of the Saint Michael. Saint-Antoine grumbled ominously in its wine-shops, its garrets, its cellars. Who was this man, who cheapened the pittance of the poor, who accepted the decorations of the rich? Saint-Antoine did more than merely grumble. It marched in considerable numbers to the door of Réveillon's factory, and there placed an effigy of the obnoxious paper-maker sus. per coll., with the decoration on the puppet's breast. After a while they took the image down, carried it in triumph to the Place de la Grève, and there burnt it to ashes under the very windows of the Town Hall, with many denunciations of Réveillon and threats that they would return again to wreak sterner justice.

A marvellous affair, this affair Réveillon. A matter of small moment it would almost seem, and yet a matter of great moment as the first flare-up of revolutionary fires. It is difficult to make head or tail of the whole business, so desperately has it been confused, by the different stories told of it. Réveillon was the first to thrive in France upon the making of wall-papers in the English manner. He was wealthy after the labours of some eight and forty years. His factory was more like a palace. He had magnificent gardens from which a few years before the Mongolfier balloon mounted to heaven.

He employed about eight hundred workmen. He was one of the electors of the Paris delegates for the Third Estate. Saint-Antoine, suspicious, populous with small artizans, seems to have looked with no loving eye upon him. Who started the damning story about the fifteen sous? Réveillon said, then and after, that it was started by a certain Abbé Roy, a needy ecclesiastic, patronized by the Count d'Artois. Roy came near to being hanged for it later, innocent or guilty; he was not hanged; he was forgotten. But according to Réveillon he was his enemy, and went abroad spreading tales against him, including that worst tale of all about the fifteen sous. There were plenty to believe the story, as Réveillon found to his cost.

That worthy soldier and amiable story-teller, M. de Besenval, was much perturbed by these proceedings. For eight years de Besenval had been entrusted with the command of the provinces of the interior—the Soissonnais, the Bourbonnais, the Orléannais, Berry, Touraine, Maine and the Isle of France, the City of Paris excepted. The command, sufficiently engrossing at all times, became very arduous in the April of 1789, in consequence of the disette and the scarcity of grain. The markets became the scenes of stormy riots. Attacks were made upon Government convoys. De Besenval, at his wits' end to protect all parts, was obliged to divide his troops in order to watch over all the markets in his command, and to keep in check the 'brigands,' grown audacious by the excitement of the time. Still, de Besenval proudly records that he accomplished his task, that he kept order with the greatest success, that everything went well until, alas, until the unexpected came to pass. De Besenval had nothing to do with the maintenance of order in Paris. But when the good city began to 'ferment,' authority in Paris had to call for the aid of the two regiments of the French Guards and the Swiss to help them in maintaining order. The command of these two regiments devolved upon the Duc du Châtelet and the Count d'Affry. As luck would have it, the Count d'Affry had an accident which brought him to death's door, and de Besenval, who was his second in command of the Swiss, had to take his place, and add the care of Paris to all his other cares. Poor de Besenval! some sleepless hours were in store for him. No more writing of graceful tales, no more dreamings of a fair royal face. The cares of Paris, the correspondence of his command, the duty of seeing Paris properly supplied with corn; these duties, which keep him busy day and night, were among the last services he will be called upon to render to royalty.

In the opening days of April, de Besenval was duly informed of the arrival in Paris of large bodies of most ill-looking strangers, vile fellows in scarecrow tatters, brandishing huge batoons, and babbling all the thieves' lingoes under heaven. These uncanny crews, it seemed, always set in their staff in the

Faubourg Saint-Antoine, and mischief might confidently be expected from them. On April 27 news was brought to de Besenval and to du Châtelet of the disturbance in Saint-Antoine and the menaces levelled at paper-maker Réveillon. Du Châtelet despatched a sergeant and thirty men of the French Guard to the spot, and hoped all would be well.

All was by no means well. The men who had menaced Réveillon kept their word. They came back again, vast battalions of rascaldom, and made ferociously merry at the expense of du Châtelet's poor thirty men. They sacked the house of Réveillon's neighbour, Henriot; Henriot had to fly for his life. The little handful of soldiers dared do nothing, could do nothing, against the furious mob. They had to stand quietly by, thankful that nobody troubled about them. Nobody did trouble about them; all that the wild crowd wanted was to get hold of Réveillon, and, failing that, to do as much damage as might be to Réveillon's property. Réveillon himself they did not get. He had prudently slipped across to the Bastille. Behind its massive walls he deemed himself secure. From its towers he could behold the ruin of his splendid house, fair with the paintings of Le Brun.

The electors of Paris were seated tranquilly at the Archbishopric, proceeding to fuse together the cahiers of the different districts into a common cahier. Bailly had noted, indifferently, the absence of Réveillon from the council. Suddenly the proceedings were interrupted by a clattering at the door, and the irruption of an armed and angry crowd raving for the absent Réveillon's head. About the same time or earlier de Besenval's morning hours were broken in upon by du Châtelet, alarmed, and excited with the news of the wildest disturbances in the Faubourg Saint-Antoine. Every moment fresh tidings came in to the two perplexed officers. News came of riot, of pillage, of a large crowd growing momentarily larger, of the helpless handful of soldiers who had not dared to fire a shot. Du Châtelet saw that something must be done more decisive than the despatch of thirty men. He sent off some companies of grenadiers, with orders to fire if need be.

There is a picturesque episode in the Réveillon riot which is not generally noted. When the mob, bandits, blackguards, bravoes, whatever they were, had swept du Châtelet's luckless thirty men to one side, and were beating in the doors of the factory, an old woman suddenly appeared upon the threshold, and boldly called upon the assailants to pause. She was old, it seems, in the Réveillon service; she called loudly for pity, for justice; she declared that the people were deceived. Poor, impassioned, eloquent old lady, the brigands put her aside in no time, but not unkindly, and the work of ravage began.

In the midst of all the clamours and the crashing

timbers, gilded coaches came upon the scene, stately coaches with delicately painted panels, bearing delicately painted ladies and delicate attendant lords to Vincennes. Saint-Antoine, pausing in its work of destruction or witnessing destruction by others, raged at the gilt carriages and their occupants in an ominous, uncomely manner, and the pretty pageant dispersed, rolling its wheels rapidly. Only the Duke of Orleans, recognised by the crowd, and raising his plumed hat, passed on his way in curious triumph. It was said that he came on purpose to encourage the rioters.

When du Châtelet's men arrived on the scene of action they found the street so choked with people that it was difficult to force a way to the paper factory, in which the assailants had now lodged themselves, and in which they were making wild carnival, breaking everything they could break, and drinking everything they could drink, to the cost of some of them who took some patent acid employed in the preparation of Réveillon's painted papers for some choice cordial and drained a terrible death. Those who found wine drank deep and desperately, as sailors will do in a sinking ship, and, fiery with false courage, they faced the disciplined soldiers that now marched down against them. The rioters had only sticks to oppose to the bayonets of the soldiers; they could only exchange a rain of tiles from the roof against the rain of lead from the levelled muskets; but they held their own, fighting desperately.

Defeated, dispersed in the street, they rallied within the walls of Réveillon's gutted building, and held it, fighting with tigerish tenacity all through that livelong day. The police spies kept coming and going between the scene of fight and the quarters where de Besenval and du Châtelet waited and wondered. Very difficult these spies found it either to penetrate into the crowd around Réveillon's door or to get out of it again when they had so penetrated. To make up for delay, they brought back the most astonishing stories, spoke of people they had seen inciting the rioters to further tumult, and even distributing money.

The fight still raged on, desperate as that last wild fight in the halls of Atli which we read of in the great Icelandic epic. At last de Besenval determined that this should end one way or the other. He sent companies of his Swiss off as fast as they could go to Saint-Antoine, taking with them two pieces of cannon, and the concise instructions, if they were resisted, to kill until not one of the rioters was left. The sight of the cannon produced a calming effect upon the bulk of the mob, which speedily evaporated. But the desperate men inside Réveillon's still held good, still fought and defied. The Swiss fired upon them again and again, carried the factory by storming, forced room after room of the place, bayoneting and shooting the rioters. A great many were killed, a great many were wounded and died later. It was a bloody piece of work from first to last, but to de Besenval belongs such credit as there was for stamping it out. It was indeed only like stamping out a small piece of lighted paper while the forest is taking fire behind you; but still it was something, and poor de Besenval got small thanks for it. The Court looked coldly upon him, as he thought. Paris was not profoundly grateful to him. The stamping-out process came too late. It saved Réveillon, it could not save the monarchy. The carnage left its bitter memories. The number of the slain has been much exaggerated. Bailly has even left it on record that he did not think anyone was killed. But a great many were killed, and their deaths were not found deterrent.

So ended the Réveillon episode, which may be looked upon as the lever de rideau, the curtain-raiser of the Revolution. To this hour it is uncertain who the men were who instigated the attack, who led it, and who defended themselves with such desperate courage. Réveillon's workmen were not with them or of them. For it would appear, in despite of that rumour about the fifteen sous, that he was a kind master, in good favour with those in his employment. Nor was it either a rising of the Faubourg Saint-Antoine. Children of Saint-Antoine may have mingled in the mass, may have taken part in the fray for sheer desperate love of fighting, and a kind of devilish Celtic delight in the fun of the thing. But the faubourg at large, the faubourg as a faubourg, if we may be permitted the phrase, looked on with folded arms, and, if it said much, did little or nothing. All sorts of fantastic theories flutter, carrion-like, round the graves and the gibbets of Réveillon's mysterious assailants. De Besenval, disliking to distrust even so scapegrace a kinsman of the royal house as the Duke of Orleans, decided in a convenient, indefinite way that it must have been the English. Others, less particular, insisted that it was done by Orleans and his faction. Later students have actually thought that it was a put-up job on the part of the Court, in the hope that by the wholesale complicity of Saint-Antoine they would be provided with a sufficient excuse for flooding Paris with soldiery and suppressing the inconveniently disaffected. Whoever set the thing going, there were certainly in Paris enough desperate characters, ready to bear a hand in any desperate enterprise which might be rewarded with a pocketful of coin or even a skinful of liquor. News of any kind of disturbance or possible disturbance in the capital naturally attracted to Paris all the seedy rogues, all the vagrom men, all the queer kinsmen and dependents of the chivalry of the road. On every highway and byway in France thievish tramps turned their thoughts and their steps towards Paris. If anyone wanted to foment a disturbance, there was plenty of material ready to hand to be had for the buying. The result, in any case, told for the Revolution. The fierce bloodshed enraged Saint-Antoine, the desperate strife showed Saint-Antoine how such things might be done, and how hard it was to cope with the doers. Réveillon, shivering and sighing behind the Bastille walls, might have felt still less at ease if he could have seen but a poor six weeks ahead into futurity, and learned that the fortress of a king was no more stable than the factory of a maker of painted papers. But he was no seer. He was compensated by the King for his losses, and straightway vanishes from history and leaves not a rack behind. He earned the distinction of being the first plaything of the Paris mob; he had better fortune than their next playthings, as we shall presently see. What became of him afterwards, where he drifted, and how he ended, we have not been able to find out.

It will probably never be known how the Réveillon business did actually originate. The fact, if fact it be, as would seem on Réveillon's own showing, that nothing was stolen, puts the affair out of the category of a mere vulgar raid for plunder upon a building exposed to assault by its owner's unpopularity. The desperate resistance, again, which the rioters offered to the royal troops implies a degree of courage and determination not usually to be found in merely needy or merely mischievous rioters. The stories of men in rich attire, of men in women's garb, who were seen egging the mob on are a trifle cloudy and incoherent; so too are the tales of sums of gold in the pinched pockets of meagre rascaldom. That the killed and wounded came to be talked of by their kind as 'defenders of the country' counts for something in the argument that the movement, such as it was, was largely popular and spontaneous. After all, there is nothing very surprising, in the then electric condition of Paris, in the fact that a mob, irritated by what they believed to be a rich man's scorn of the poor man's need, should incontinently proceed to break the rich man's windows and express a large desire to break the rich man's head. The rash words of another man cost the speaker far dearer not very many days or weeks later. It would not be surprising either if unscrupulous persons were to be found, of any party, ready to take advantage of an inflamed popular feeling to manipulate riot for their own ulterior purposes and advantage. Whatever we may think, with Réveillon, of the participation of Abbé Roy, with de Besenval of the machinations of England, with others about the dodges of Orleans, and with yet others about the militant purposes of the Court, one thing remains clear and incontrovertible, that Réveillon became suddenly unpopular on account of words attributed to him, that a mob ravaged his premises, and that the riot was bloodily suppressed. The democratic eye, heedless of minute possibilities, saw in the whole affair a movement of not unjustifiable popular passion savagely suppressed by the soldiery of a not too popular King.

CHAPTER XXVII

STATES-GENERAL AT LAST

Two days after the battle round Réveillon's shop, or rather palace, the not too popular King was reviewing his deputies at Versailles, and not increasing his popularity in the process. The deputies of the Third Estate, to begin with, were by no means pleased at the choice of Versailles for the session of the States-General. Paris seemed the most obvious place for the purpose; Paris would have been a much cheaper place for deputies not too well off. The choice of Versailles made the States-General resemble too much a plenary court to please the Third Estate. Then, too, the manner of presentation to the King irritated the susceptible. The deputies were presented, thanks to Master of Ceremonies de Brézé, by order and not by their bailiwicks, which would have seemed the simpler, more natural course. These were small things, but they rankled. It was plain from the first that concord was not the order of the hour.

On May 4, amidst vast crowds, the States-General paraded through Versailles from the parish church of Our Lady, where they heard the Veni Creator, to the church of St. Louis, where a Mass of the Holy Ghost was celebrated. It is the most famous pageant in history; it has been described a thousand times; the thought of it always stirs the blood and thrills the pulses. Versailles was resplendent for the occasion. The streets were hung with tapestries; the French and Swiss Guards kept the line between the two churches; all the balconies along the way were hung with precious stuffs. By one of those chances which sometimes make Nature seem in exquisite harmony with the actions of men, the day was divinely fair, an ideal May day. The air was steeped in sunlight, the streets were brave with banners, the air rang with martial music, and the swell of sacred bells, the beat of drum and blare of trumpet, blended with the chanting of the priests. The world glowed with colour. When did the skies seem deeper blue, the trees and grasses more richly green? The clear sunlight lent a rarer value to the delicate dyes of silken garment, to the jewels on women's bosoms and the gold on courtly swords. The Court shone in its brightest splendour for that brilliant hour. It thought to participate in a triumph; it shared unawares in a sacrifice. It gleamed and dazzled then for the last time, and walked all unconsciously in its own funeral. For in front of all that world of plumes and jewels, of fair powdered heads and fair painted faces, of chivalrous long-lineaged nobility, walked, arrayed in solemn black, their judges, their executioners, their fate, the deputies of the Third Estate.

All France, says a historian, was at Paris, all Paris was at Versailles. Every inch of available standing room was thronged. At every window, on every balcony, bright eyes watched the marvellous sight, and fair lips praised or blamed as the speaker leaned to the Court or to the new ideas. First of all, at the head of the procession, came a sombre mass of black relieved by touches of white; this was the Third Estate, lugubriously attired, raven-like, ominous. More than five hundred deputies, in the gloomy garb that ceremony forced upon them, moved slowly along, a compact body, while the warm air trembled to the enthusiastic cheers of the spectators. The cheers lulled suddenly into a grim silence as the black band of the Third Estate was succeeded by the rainbow brightness of the many-hued nobility. There were friends of the people in those butterfly ranks, but one alone was noted out for salutation, the dark, adventurous Orleans, who ostentatiously stood ahead of his own order to mingle with the later ranks of the Third Estate. 'Long live Orleans!' the people cried, and for a moment the weary vicious face glowed with exultation, as it had glowed but four days earlier when the Réveillon rioters had acclaimed him. 'Long live Orleans!' Perhaps he thought as he smiled of a lengthy life, of a royal crown.

The same silence that had greeted the nobility

greeted also the clergy, the clergy in whose own ranks a division into two orders was distinctly visible. Some thirty princes of the Church came first in purple and fine linen, a resplendent hierarchy. Then came a company of musicians, and at their heels trod the clerical Third Estate, the two hundred parish priests in their black gowns. Thus, in funereal melancholy sable, the procession of the deputies of the States-General began and ended. That, too, was ominous to the perception, to the prophetic eye. Those black-garbed priests were to be the first to join with their black-clad brethren of the Third Estate. Both alike represented the people.

At the end of the procession came the King and the Court. Some cheers were accorded to the monarch, partly the cheers of not ungenerous victors, partly cheers of gratitude for the convocation of the States-General. The Queen was greeted only by a grave and menacing silence, which she affected to brave with a proud indifference. But some women in the crowd cried out in mocking hostility to Marie Antoinette the war-cry, 'Long live Orleans!' The Queen heard the sounds, she saw a gleam of joy, of triumph, in the eyes of the Duchess of Orleans; for a second her courage failed her; she reeled, almost fainted, had to be sustained by the fond arms of Madame de Lamballe. In another moment she was herself again, and went with head held high to the end.

Among all the spectators of that splendid scene,

one of the most interested, one of the most interesting was Necker's daughter, Madame de Staël. Madame de Staël was in the wildest spirits. She saw in all that was happening only a tribute to the genius of the father she adored. It was all the creation of his majestic mind, to Madame de Staël, and she exulted accordingly. With her, watching from the same window, was Madame de Montmorin, wife of the Minister of Foreign Affairs. She strove to check Madame de Staël's exuberant gaiety. 'You are wrong to rejoice,' she said gravely. 'Great troubles will come from all this for France and for us.' Pathetic, prophetic speech, dimly foreshadowing her own death on the scaffold, her son's death on the scaffold, her husband's death in the September massacres, her daughter's death in a prison hospital. She was not, Madame de Staël thought, a very wise woman; but she was wise enough to see more in the pageant of that day than Necker's daughter saw in it, and to gather vaguely some dim tragic perception of the awful forces that lay latent behind its noise and pomp and glitter. It is characteristic of the fateful time, this queer gleam of second sight vouchsafed to the commonplace wife of a commonplace minister of state. Wiser eyes did not see so far: wiser tongues were less truly prophetic.

Inside the church of Saint Louis the three orders took their places in the nave. The King and Queen sat under a canopy of purple velvet starred with the golden lily flowers of their line. Round them were ranged the princes of the royal blood and the flower of the Court. A sweet-voiced choir raised the hymn O Salutaris hostia as the host was placed upon the altar. Then M. de la Farre, archbishop of Nancy, passed into the pulpit and preached. His sermon was inspired by the feeling of the hour, it became a kind of political pronouncement. Royalist writers reproached him promptly for declamations on the luxury and despotism of courts, the duties of sovereigns, and the rights of the people, but he certainly succeeded in arousing at least the temporary enthusiasm of his audience. When, after a glowing picture of the evils of the fiscal system and the sufferings of the country, he asked if such barbarous exactions should be done in the name of a good, just, and wise King, the enthusiasm of his hearers took fire and vented itself in loud and prolonged applause, oblivious alike of the sacred character of the edifice and of the presence of the King, before whom it was not etiquette to applaud, even at the play. With the echo of that applause in their ears, noting markedly how the old traditions were losing hold, the States-General came out of the church of Saint Louis at four o'clock of the May afternoon, to wait patiently or impatiently according to their temperaments for the morrow.

CHAPTER XXVIII

THE PLAY BEGINS

VERSAILLES woke up on the morning of May 5, 1789, with the memory of all the brave doings of yesterday still buzzing in its brain, to take part in, or to take an interest in a no less imposing and a yet more important ceremony. The proceedings of May 4 were like the overture before the curtain rises. With this May 5 the play was really to begin. The three estates of the realm were to meet their monarch for the first time for two centuries, and nobody could be confident, except perhaps the ever-confident Necker, as to what might come of the meeting. The Assembly was to open in the Salle des Menus in the Avenue de Paris. The Salle des Menus exists no more. If a new Villon, weary of regrets for the lords and ladies of old time, were to tune his verse to a ballade for the lost buildings of the world which men might most regret, he should include the Salle des Menus, with the temple of the Ephesian Diana and the palace of Kubla Khan, in the burden of his despair. For, never since man first reared houses out of reeds or quarried holes in the sides of the eternal hills has any edifice been the theatre of a more momentous event or more deserving to be preserved for the sake of its deathless associations. But the Salle des Menus has passed away in fact; in fancy, however, we can reconstruct it. The painter's and the graver's art have preserved for us its seeming, and it needs no great effort of the imagination to call up that stately hall, large enough to hold more than five thousand persons, and rich on this May day with all the splendour of a courtly ceremony. We can see the spacious floors, its carpets glittering with the golden fleurs de lis of the Bourbon House, the majestic curve of the painted ceiling where a picturesque mythology gambolled, the range of massive pillars on either side of the hall which separated the eager beholders from the centre field for the performers in the pageant of the day. We can note the lofty daïs, with its terraced lines of steps, at the summit of which the throne was placed, and over which the velvet canopy extended. We can watch the royal pages in their bright apparel as they moved hither and thither on their courtly duties. We can catch the gleam of steel and the blending of blue and gold and scarlet where here and there a soldier stood on guard. The Salle des Menus is gone, its bricks and mortar, its marble pillars, its painted walls and lily-laden carpets have had their day and ceased to be. The wind has carried them all away. But fancy lingers for an instant fondly over the fair theatre it has re-fashioned for the great Mystery

Play of the Deluge. Here it was at last, this deluge Louis XV. had lightly prophesied, its first waves rising round the throne with the beginning of that May day's proceedings.

The proceedings opened, if not stormily, certainly irritably. Foolish Court etiquette barred the entrance of the Salle des Menus to the deputies. None was suffered to pass in save after a regular summons from the heralds-at-arms, which done, the master of the ceremonies marshalled each man to his place according to his degree and the degree of his bailiwick, in accordance with the fusty precedent of 1614. This fusty precedent had for first result to keep a large number of deputies wedged together in a dark and narrow lobby or corridor, and for second result to arouse considerable spleen against the pedantic, slow formality. Deputies pushed, clamoured, refused to answer to their call or take their places; it took hard upon three hours to get them into their places. In the midst of the hubbub, Equality Orleans, avid of popularity, won some thunderous applause by insisting on the humble priest who shared with him the representation of Crépy en Valois, passing into the great hall before him.

The deputies, seated at last, and comparatively tranquil, had nearly an hour before them in which to survey the stately Salle des Menus, to gaze at and be gazed at by the glittering mob that thronged the side galleries, and to study each other with that half-timid speculation peculiar to all large bodies of strangers brought suddenly into close association. Nigh on to one o'clock the King made his appearance, a royal sun with a train of shining satellites, and the enthusiastic deputies—for Robespierre still was loyal and Orleans still shammed loyalty—sprang to their feet and hailed him, so official record assures us, 'with cries of joy.' The King and Queen took their places, the royal princes and the rest of the courtly following settled down too, the ministers sat at the table allotted to them, the 'cries of joy' died down and faded out, Master of Ceremonies de Brézé lifted his hand for silence, announced that the King would speak. The King got up, and the great play began.

So, from all the ends of France, the States-General had come together, and faced each other, in the Salle des Menus—a kind of unnatural Trinity, a three that were by no means one. 'August and touching ceremony,' said the Marquis de Ferrières, when he re-wrote for his memoirs the description he had penned for his own pleasure immediately after the event. August it certainly was, touching too, though not perhaps quite in the sense in which De Ferrières intended it. It was the tragic preface to the most tragic epoch in history. Mirabeau, with his fine perception, caught and immortalized the true meaning of the situation, as he looked upon that splendid scene. He saw the King with all his Court about him; the princes of the blood royal, a glittering bodyguard behind him; Necker and his ministers in front at the foot of the daïs; to right the ranked hierarchy of the Church; to left the representatives of the nobility of France; in front the sombre masses of the Third Estate. Comprehending all this with one swift glance, Mirabeau turned to certain of his friends, and, embracing the scene with a gesture, slightly pointed to the King upon his daïs and said—very audibly it would seem—'Behold the victim!' That was indeed the situation, though no one but Mirabeau guessed it, and even Mirabeau can scarcely have guessed how prophetic he was. Louis the King, in opening his States-General, was in fact performing Hara-Kiri with all conceivable pomp and all conceivable unconsciousness.

Let us glance for a moment while Necker is pronouncing his somewhat tedious, terribly long-winded discourse, upon the sober-coated gentlemen of the Third Estate who sat there facing their King. They were some six hundred men, all attired alike, in accordance with due etiquette, all very unlike, when once we forget the coat, waistcoat, and breeches of black cloth, the black stockings, the short mantle of silk or stuff, such as the legal were wont to wear at Court, the muslin cravat, the hat cocked at three sides with neither band nor button, which royal rescript had endued them with. We shall find them all in the triple columns of the 'Moniteur,' from Afforty, cultivator at Villepinte, of the provostship and viscounty of Paris, to Wartel, advocate of Lille, in the bailiwick of Lille.

These two, the Alpha and the Omega of the Third Estate, we shall not hear of again. Agriculturist and advocate, they have come here from the extremes of the alphabet and the extremes of France, to do a certain work, and, having done it, to be speedily and fortunately forgotten with the majority of their six hundred fellows. But there was a minority not likely to be forgotten so long as men care to remember anything. Here and there in those sombre masses of the Third Estate, staring with their eager curiosity at the victim King, were men with names then unknown or little known who were by-and-by to be famous, most famous or infamous according to their several destinies and degrees.

Out of all that six hundred present or not present, Time the winnower gleans only a little handful of names. After the two most famous names, we must remember Barnave, and Bailly, learned among men, little dreaming that a colleague from one of the divisions of Paris was occupying his busy brain with an instrument of justice and of injustice that should shear close. We see Buzot and Pétion, sitting together now, who shall lie closer yet in the cold fields by-and-by. We recall Camus and Lanjuinais and Rabaut-Saint-Etienne, and Mounier and Malouet, and Rewbell, and the ingenious, nimble-witted Abbé Sieyès. We may note, too, sturdy Père Gérard and M. Martin of Auch, whom we shall meet again. One man we have mentioned already, the Parisian delegate whose busy brain was forging a surer sword for justice, Dr. Guillotin. Of all the men on that 'august and touching' occasion, he—not indeed, we believe, bodily present owing to some electoral delay—was the one most to be dreaded by his fellows if they could have got one sure glance into the wizard's glass of the future. How many heads, from the King to the Arras lawyer, from pocked Equality Orleans to Bailly, pedantic Mayor of Paris, were doomed to fall beneath the grim machine with which the name of Dr. Guillotin has been so indissolubly associated! It matters little whether Guillotin did or did not actually invent the particular form of death-dealing machine which has borne his name so long. He advocated expeditious decapitation; the instrument which expeditiously decapitated bears his name. Dr. Louis may have planned the construction of the engine, but the engine was called, is called, will be called the guillotine. That is enough. Inexorable humour of history! From the crowned king of the stately Capet line, proud representative of divine right, to brilliant young Barnave, no one heeded Guillotin much, present or absent, and yet Guillotin was their fate and the fate of thousands more. Carlyle has written his undying epitaph, 'his name like to outlast Cæsar's.'

CHAPTER XXIX

THE WILD GABRIEL HONORÉ

MOST Englishmen, when they think about Mirabeau, think of him and of his stock and kin as they stand on Carlyle's picturesque, impressive canvas. In his presentation of Mirabeau in the famous procession, and in his separate essay devoted to Mirabeau and the Mirabeaus, the world is afforded a strongly marked, highly coloured, eminently attractive portrait and series of portraits. But if the Carlylean Mirabeau is eminently picturesque, if the Carlylean House of Mirabeau takes an historical dignity akin to that of the House of Pelops, they do not altogether stand the test of modern criticism. Of the real Mirabeau it was almost impossible for Carlyle at the time when he wrote, except by a kind of magnificent guess-work, to know much. Of the 'great House of Mirabeau' he seems to have accepted implicitly the astonishing statements of the family and their yet more astonishing pretensions. Not a man of the line, Riquet or Riquety or Riquetti, for the name is spelt all these ways and even other ways besides, very perplexingly, who does not seem to have been bustling, ambitious, esurient of dignity, proud of the grandeur of his race, with a kind of blustering pride that almost invites scepticism by its challenging air of swagger. In the greatest study of the Mirabeaus that has yet been made, that of Louis de Loménie, the Riquettis show to less theatrical advantage. It threatened to be one of the gravest losses in modern literature that De Loménie's book, like the unfinished window in Aladdin's Tower, 'unfinished must remain.' Happily within the last few months the materials left by Louis de Loménie for the conclusion of the book have been admirably put together and brought out by his son Charles de Loménie.

The Mirabeaus stemmed from a house of noble Ghibellines who during an epoch of Guelf supremacy were banished from Florence in the middle of the thirteenth century. Such at least is the notion Mirabeau himself strove to make current, and succeeded in making current posthumously in the famous 'Vie de Jean-Antoine de Riquetti, Marquis de Mirabeau, et Notice sur sa Maison. Redigées par l'aîné de ses Petits Fils d'après les Notes de son Fils.' M. Lucas de Montigny, who gave this document to the world at the beginning of his 'Mémoires de Mirabeau,' was under the natural impression that it was founded by Mirabeau upon mere notes jotted down by his fiery old father. As a matter of fact, however, Mirabeau was deceiving the world. The life of Jean Antoine de Riquetti was entirely by his father, as the discovery of the original manuscript has since made certain. Mirabeau merely copied it, amplifying it here and there to the greater glory of the House of Mirabeau, and altering and softening the archaic vigour and richness of the paternal prose. That the elder Mirabeau suspected some trickery on his son's part is made plain by M. de Loménie, who quotes a letter from the Marquis to his brother the Bailli, in which he expresses a fear that Mirabeau has copied a manuscript lent him for his instruction, and adds that if any copy comes before the world it must be through the son.

In the original manuscript the Marquis de Mirabeau makes much of the splendour and dignity of his race, but their grandeur grows and swells under the copying hand of Mirabeau. The son intensifies terms of grandeur, interpolates adjectives of greater stateliness, and in every way endeavours to heighten the picture of the ancestral dignity. Illustrious Ghibelline nobles banished from Florence, the great house transferred itself to Provence, and took rank at once among the loftiest Provençal nobility. Such is the Mirabeau contention; but the contention, unfortunately, does not stand the test of cold historic inquiry. To begin with, the Riquettis of Provence do not appear to have made up their mind as to whether the Arrighettis of Florence were Ghibelline or Guelf, a matter of some small importance in the history of a stately house. There is next no existing proof of any kind of the marriage of Pierre, the first of the French Riquettis, with Sibylle de Fos, 'of the house of the Counts of

Provence, of whom the Troubadours have sung the talents and beauty.' A fragment of genealogy in the National Library in Paris gives the wife of the first French Riquetti as Catherine de Fossis, a name which has no connection whatever with the house of the Counts of Provence. It is, indeed, as M. de Loménie shows, truly remarkable that if the first French Riquetti was of sufficient standing to wed the daughter of a princely house, no mention whatever of his descendants should be made for two and a half centuries, until the middle of the sixteenth century, in any historical record, not merely of France but of Provence. Nor is it less remarkable that the first conspicuous bearer of the Riquetti name seems to have had some difficulty in escaping, by alleging nobility, the payment of a tax levied only on the lowest classes. A strange drop in the world indeed for illustrious Ghibellines—or Guelfs—wedded to ladies of the princely lines of Provence.

This John Riquetti of the tax was the son of an Honoré Riquetti of Digne, who settled in Marseilles at the beginning of the sixteenth century. He seems to have engaged in commerce of some kind. His son Jehan appears to have worked with success in the coral trade, and to have founded besides a manufactory of scarlet stuffs. He married in 1564 a lady of the old Provençal family of Glandèves, bought the house and lands of Mirabeau, and took its name. Hitherto the castle and estate of Mirabeau had belonged to the Barras family, 'li

Barras viei coumo li roucas'—old as the rocks they were called in Provence. The castle and lands passed by marriage into the Glandèves family, and from Gaspard de Glandèves Jehan Riquetti, successful coral merchant and manufacturer of scarlet stuffs, bought it when he wedded a lady of the line. It must be admitted that in these acts we see more the ambitious, pushing, prosperous coral merchant than the descendant of illustrious Florentines and of the highest nobility of Provence. Twenty one thousand crowns of forty-eight sols each was a pretty good sum to pay for a tumbledown castle, so knocked about and dilapidated that it was wholly uninhabitable. He seems to have been as eager to bear the name of Mirabeau as Glossin was in 'Guy Mannering' to be called Ellangowan. His ambition brought him into trouble. Lawsuits rained on him for dues, the castle and lands were even for a season sequestrated, but Jehan Riquetti was hardy, and fought pertinaciously, and won his case at last. In the documents of these various processes he is alluded to as a merchant of Marseilles, and in the final act is called Lord of Mirabeau, with no title of nobility whatever. The second lawsuit was for payment of that right of Francs Fiefs, which was only taxable upon roturiers who had acquired noble property. Jehan stood out for his nobility, and an inquiry into his claims was set on foot. The inquiry was held first at Seyne, the oldest abiding place of the family, then at Digne. Various persons testified in a vague sort of way to the nobility of the family. The absolute absence of documentary proof was accounted for by the destruction of precious papers in the turbulent year 1574. Dim memories of a destroyed shield with a blazon, of a vanished portrait, of a shattered tomb, were offered in evidence. Worthy persons remembered hearsay statements as to the nobility of the Riquettis. All this was not much for a family belonging to the highest Provençal nobility, but it was something in the eyes of the commissioners. They accepted the kind of general impression of nobility, acquitted Jehan of the Francs Fiefs, and Jehan styled himself écuyer thenceforward.

Thomas de Riquetti, grandson of Jehan, squire and lord of Mirabeau, gave his family another lift in the world by his marriage with a daughter of the house of Pontèves. The difference between the social status of the Riquettis and the lady of Pontèves is curiously marked in the marriage contract, in which the simple squireship of Thomas of Riquetti contrasts with the pompous and swelling epithets of the people of Pontèves. When this same Thomas, nineteen years later, in 1639, wished to set a younger son's name upon the roll of the Knights of Malta, he had to obtain what was called the secret proof of nobility in the solemn declaration of four gentlemen of old stock that the Riquettis were a family of the first water. It is really curious and pathetic to note the struggles the Riquettis had to keep up their dignity and assert their nobility. Inclusion in the

Order of Malta was a much-desired dignity, we may imagine, for the Riquetti Mirabeaus. There had been Mirabeaus before in the Order, but they were Barras-Mirabeaus, a very different matter. The Riquettis were making their way, however, patiently and perseveringly, step by step. Thomas's next move was to secure himself a dignified blazon. He had recourse accordingly, not to the official genealogist, Charles d'Hozier, who saw through his pretensions, but to a kind of swindling herald, Jean Baptiste L'Hermite de Soliers, who turned him out a genealogy and any number of brilliant armorial bearings, just in the same way that a heraldic stationer of to-day will supply, for a consideration, arms and old descent to any ambitious pork-butcher. This amazing rogue of a herald coolly falsified citations from Italian historians, and converted genuine Arrigucci of Zazzera's book into Ariqueti. On the basis of this audacious swindle the great Mirabeau coolly declared that the only mésalliance in his family was with the Medicis. In all probability Mirabeau accepted L'Hermite's work in all sincerity, but the fact remains that it was no Ariqueti or Arrighetti who wedded into the Medici line, but one of the Arrigucci, a most ancient house of Fiesole. There did indeed turn up a certain Count Giulio d'Arrighetti in the service of the Grand Duke of Tuscany, who, travelling in Marseilles, was hailed with joy by Thomas de Riquetti as a relation, and who seems to have been good enough to recognise the relationship. But as his arms were wholly different from the Riquettis of Provence, and different again from those of the genuine Arrighettis, who are to be found in Florence at a much later period, however, than that of their alleged banishment, this testimony only adds a fresh complication to the ingenious little family swindle. It was not, however, owing to the audacity of L'Hermite, or the complaisance of Giulio Arrighetti, that Thomas was able to hold his nobility in 1688, when Louis XIV. ordered the verification of titles of nobility. Two documents did this for him —one dated 1398, which calls Antoine Riquetti 'vir nobilis juris peritus de Regio,' that is, of Riez; and another of 1410, which calls Antoine Riquetti 'judex curiæ regiæ civitats Dignæ,' that is, of Digne. In 1685, Thomas, who had been a loyal King's man all through the Fronde, received letters patent permitting him to take the title of Marquis from the estate of Mirabeau, and so for the first time a Riquetti entered the ranks of the high nobility.

In 1693, a new prop for the great house of Riquetti made its appearance in a ' Nobiliaire de Provence,' by the Abbé Robert of Briançon. This book, dedicated to Jean Antoine, second Marquis of Mirabeau, our Mirabeau's grandfather, repeats most, if not all, of L'Hermite's lies, invents the mysterious Sibylle de Fos, and fills in the foggy period of the Riquetti record with a crowd of remarkable and purely imaginary figures and events. Against this prodigious performance a zealous antiquarian, the

Abbé Barcilon of Mauvans, immediately ran a-tilt, especially assailing the imaginary grandeur of the Riquettis, and, rushing impetuously to the other extreme, he brings forward a throng of Riquettis in humble walks of life, labourers, artizans, and the like, who may, however, belong to those Riquettis with whom our Riquettis always sought to disassociate themselves. It is certain, however, that Barcilon quotes the act of marriage of Honoré Riquetti in 1515, which, if genuine, proves that instead of the nuptials between a lord of Sieyès and the daughter of a lord De la Garde of the 'Nobilier de Provence,' a simple schoolmaster of Digne married the daughter of a tailor of Marseilles.

But the final support of the glory of the Riquetti line is in Louis d'Hozier's 'Armorial de France,' in the volume of 1764. Here we have an Azzuccius Arrighetti, banished from Florence in 1267 or 1268 as a Ghibelline, and assumed to be the father of Pierre Riquetti, who died in Seyne in Provence in the middle of the fourteenth century. Here all the older assertions of the Riquettis are completely upset. The Pietro Ariqueti, who was a Guelf banished from Florence, becomes Azzuccius Arrighetti banished as a Ghibelline. Moreover, there is not the slightest proof that Azzuccius Arrighetti was the father of Pierre Riquetti beyond the assumption, unsupported by any documentary evidence, of an Abbé Octavien de Buon-accorsi and a Father Soldani, whom Louis d'Hozier cites. Truly the whole business is an amazing muddle, a veritable genealogistic Slough of Despond, in which we flounder despairingly. The tissue of lies which the Riquettis and their friends built up, generation after generation, not only do not stand separate tests, but do not hold together at all. The account of one friend differs from the account of another friend. The Biblical genealogies are less perplexing, are easier to reconcile than the astonishing assumptions, assertions, and fabrications of the ambitious Riquettis. M. de Loménie took a world of pains to get at the truth. He sought and sought in vain for the decree of banishment. It seems as certain as anything well can be that in 1267 the triumphant Guelfs issued no decree of banishment against the Ghibellines. The name of Arrighetti does not occur in the lists of important families of the two parties drawn up by Machiavelli or Villani, nor in the 'Nobiliaire Florentin' of Scipione Ammirato, nor in Zazzera's 'Nobiliaire Italien,' nor in Paolo Mini, nor in Litta. There is indeed a document, a 'Priorista,' in the National Library, in which eleven Arrighetti figure as having been successively Priors in the Corporation of Woodcutters. This fact would not interfere with their nobility, but merely would imply that they were at the head of one of the twelve trade bodies. But these Arrighetti belong to 1367, a century later than the alleged banishment of the whole family. Their arms, too, are different from those described in the Seyne inquiry as belonging to Pierre Riquetti, and from those of the complaisant Giulio of the seventeenth century.

Perhaps the most curious part of all this amazing story is that the time came when these very dubiously noble Riquettis were called upon to give their aid in bolstering up a family of the Riquets. In 1666 a Riquet, family of Languedoc who had been in obscurity, and who now became distinguished by the enterprise of the canal of the two seas, made rapid progress in wealth and honours and gained first the countship and later the marquisate of Caraman. By a curious chance it came about that in the eighteenth century the Marquis of Caraman found that it would be advantageous for him to seek relations with the Riquettis of Provence, the Mirabeaus. They had succeeded in inscribing their name in the Order of the Knights of Malta. The Count of Caraman wished to get his younger sons on the roll, and in order to do this he sought to give a more ancient lustre to the firebrand newness of his nobility by attaching himself to the Riquetti Mirabeaus, and so pleading precedence for one of the Riquetti kin in the Order. The then Marquis of Mirabeau accepted the relationship graciously, much as Giulio the Complaisant had accepted his ancestor; but in spite of the amiable fraud they never forgot or allowed others to forget that the Riquetti Mirabeaus were a very different order of beings from the Riquets of Caraman. Was there ever in the history of man a more curious example of one family of sham grandeur backing up its pretensions by the aid of another family whose sham grandeur was furbished forth a little earlier? There seems to have been something in the very name of Riquet or Riquetti which awoke in its wearers a mean and eager hunger for a splendour and an ancestry not their own, a craving after titles, honours, and the glitter of sham genealogies. In all probability Riquets and Riquettis alike were French of origin and of no great beginnings. The wild tempestuousness of the race which is supposed to point to an Italian origin is not more characteristic of Italy than of Provence.

As for that magnificent example of the earlier and stormier Riquettis, the mad knight who chained the two mountains together in some such fit of fiery humour as led the hysterically feminine Xerxes to scourge the raging waves of the sea, he must, it is to be feared, be dismissed bodily from the great Riquetti mythos. Mr. Carlyle, as was natural, loved this wild Titanic ancestral Riquetti and made much of him, and deduced characteristics of the race from his fierce spleens. But it seems certain, as far as anything is certain in the Riquetti muddle, that the famous chain, with its star of five rays in the centre, has naught to do with Mirabeaus or Riquetti. The chain, if it ever existed at all—and its existence seems scarcely more certain than of the chain which bound Andromeda and some links whereof were still visible, says Herodotus, in his time—belongs not to any Mirabeau but to a Blacas. Old Marquis Mirabeau, in telling this tale, admitted its highly mythical and problematic character, but Mirabeau, the Mirabeau, judiciously editing his father's simpler honesty, omits the qualification and converts a Riquetti as legendary as Amadis or Gawain into an undoubted fourteenth-century ancestor of tempestuous passions becoming to one of a great race. Vanity was the strongest passion in the Riquetti race, and that seems to be the quality of all others which our Mirabeau derived most largely from his predecessors.

One of the Mirabeaus, and one alone, succeeded in attaining the slightest notoriety outside the limits of Provence before the eighteenth century. This was Bruno de Riquetti, a captain in the French Guards, who appears to have been a hot-blooded, tempestuous kind of person, with little or nothing of the courtier in his composition, and a great deal of the reckless dare-devil. We hear of his batooning some offensive usher in the very cabinet of the King, coolly ignoring the royal order for his arrest, and swaggering with broad audacity into the monarch's presence. Louis XIV. had always a liking for a soldierly quality and he forgave the mad Mirabeau. The mad Mirabeau is more celebrated still for another example of canteen insolence. A stately ceremonial had been organized by the Duke de la Feuillade in honour of the equestrian statue of the King in the Place of Victories, and in this ceremony mad Mirabeau bore his part, chafingly no doubt, at the head of his company of Guards. Riding away afterwards with his Guards, he passed the statue of Henri IV. on the Pont Neuf, whereupon, turning to his soldiers, he roared in the big Bruno voice, ' Friends, let us salute this fellow ; he is as good as another,' and so rode clattering on, leaving his audacity to be the scandal and delight of courtly chroniclers. He was altogether the sort of man whom we may imagine M. d'Artagnan, of his Majesty's Musketeers, would have found by no means bad company.

Bluff Bruno apart, John Anthony is the first of the Mirabeaus who occupies any serious place in history. His son, the old Marquis and Friend of Man, wrote a life of him, which, as we have seen, the grandson, the great Gabriel Honoré, got hold of, and copied out with alterations and amplifications, intending to pass it off, and succeeding, posthumously, in passing off as his own. Thanks to M. de Loménie, we know what old Marquis Mirabeau wrote, denuded of the interpolations and additions of the tribune. John Anthony was a remarkable man, and it is curious that he has left so little impression upon his time. A distinguished soldier, his name figures in few of the ' Mémoires,' few of the military chronicles of the age in which he lived and battled. Saint-Simon, the only one who mentions him at all, mentions him passingly and inaccurately, in connection, be it noted, with that very Cassano fight in which, according to his son and biographer, he played the most conspicuous and brilliant part. The probability is that John Anthony was a good and gallant soldier in an age of good and gallant soldiers; that his deeds, not sufficiently remarkable in such a warlike epoch to earn him any exceptional fame, loomed out enormous in the eyes of Mirabeau, always eager in family glorification, and that this is the explanation of the fact that the living Mars of the Marquis's memoir only obtains the honour of a misspelt reference in the record of Saint-Simon.

This casual and inaccurate mention is made all the more remarkable when it is contrasted with the glowing account which the old Marquis gives of the part his sire played on that memorable day. The Mirabeau muse of history, always ready on the least possible prompting to sing the deeds of her heroes in the bombastically epic vein, here surpasses herself. According to the story of the Marquis, John Anthony was the hero of Cassano fight, where he played a part akin to that of some Titan of old time, some Roland at Roncesvalles, some Grettir at Drangey. He alone offered his colossal form to the pikes, the bullets, and the sabres of an overwhelming force. He was struck down with a hundred wounds, the least a death to nature—indeed, the old Marquis, with a calm indifference to scientific possibilities unworthy of such a hero, declares that his jugular was severed by a shot—and the greater part of an

army charged full tilt over his ruined body. A
faithful henchman, pausing from the charge, flung an
iron pot over his master's head—it was all he could
do—and galloped on, leaving John Anthony to his
fate. The iron pot saved him. The hoofs and the
heels of Prince Eugene's horse and foot rattled over
it in vain. When the fight was done, the body was
still found to have some signs of life. Vendôme
wailed for John Anthony, as Priam wailed for
Hector. 'Ah, Mirabeau is dead!' he exclaimed—
in the narrative of Mirabeau the tribune—as if
Cassano fight had no other result than that. But
Mirabeau was not dead. Prince Eugene, eminently
the 'edle Ritter,' had the body picked up, and finding it animate, like a more courteous Achilles, sent
it back to Vendôme's camp, to Vendôme's delight,
unrecorded by other history than that of the Mirabeaus. John Anthony recovered, had himself patched
together, bound up his marred and mangled neck in
a stock of silver, and coolly faced the world again.
There is a certain hero of French fiction, a Captain
Castagnette, a mythical hero of the Napoleonic
wars, who gets knocked to pieces and has gradually
to replace every portion of his shattered body with
some foreign substance, who would almost seem to
be an exaggerated reminiscence of John Anthony
'Col d'Argent.' We may well pardon John Anthony
the harmless pleasure he took in alluding to Cassano
fight as 'the little affair in which I was killed.' For
surely no man in history or fiction came to such

close quarters with destiny before and got off on the whole so well. If he was a stout soldier, he was a poor courtier, as poor as mad Bruno himself. When Vendôme presented him to the King, all John Anthony could find appropriate to say was, 'Sire, if I had left my flag to come to Court and bribe some strumpet, I should have had more advancement and fewer wounds.' Louis discreetly pretended not to hear, and Vendôme hurried his unruly favourite away, saying, 'Henceforward I will present you to the enemy only, and never to the King,' which, on the whole, was perhaps the most prudent course for all concerned.

In his youth John Anthony must have been singularly handsome, and the description of the portrait of him which still exists in the Castle of Mirabeau somehow suggests the Aramis of Dumas' immortal Quadrilateral. He had, we learn, a charming face, which, though exceedingly animated, did not suggest the stern vigour which showed itself in the brave squares of war, and which his children so well remembered. The great blue eyes are full of sweetness, and the young musketeer's beauty is qualified as almost feminine. Our dear Aramis was just such a musketeer, and it is hard to think that Dumas had not John Anthony in his mind when he gave some touches to more than one of his heroes. Though this delicate beauty must have been considerably impaired by the bustle and scuffle of Cassano fight, it did not make John Anthony less attractive to woman. While taking rest at the waters of Digne with his forty-two years, his broken arm, his silver neck and his body honeycombed with wounds, he met a certain Mademoiselle de Castellane-Norante, beautiful, wealthy, high-born, wooed her and won her, and wedded her, and she bore him seven children. The eccentricity of the battered musketeer comes out strongly in this marriage. Not in choosing a young and beautiful girl—for though he is said to have been jealous, his strong left arm was as terrible as ever his right had been —but because of the extraordinary preliminaries and conditions of the marriage. First, he wanted the young lady to marry secretly, and when she refused this, he tabled a series of conditions for her family to obey. She was to come to her husband in garments which he had prepared for her, taking nothing, not even her linen, from her home; and he further stipulated, and 'that peremptorie,' as Dugald Dalgetty would say, that her mother should never put her foot inside her daughter's new home. This was certainly anticipating the advances of a mother-in-law with a vengeance. It seems, however, certain that John Anthony did after all consent to wed his wife encumbered with her worldly gear to a very considerable amount of property, and that he showed himself a more business-like and less disinterested person than his son and grandson would have had the world believe. However all that may be, the marriage seems to have been a happy one, as it was a fruitful one. It lasted some twenty-nine years. The shattered old warrior died, thanking heaven that it spared him from a sudden death, and allowed him to meet his end in tranquillity and composure. Of his six children, five sons and a girl, only three sons survived him.

John Anthony left three sons, as we have seen; the eldest, whom we know as the Marquis of Mirabeau; the second, Jean Anthony Joseph Charles Elzear de Riquetti, whom we know as the Bailli; and the third, Louis Alexander, of whom history takes little heed. The last may be set aside in a few words. He was not his mother's favourite. He was neither the handsomest nor the wisest of his family. Yet he was good-looking enough, and M. de Loménie hits him off happily as the type of a gentleman of the eighteenth-century comedy. He was in the Order of Malta like his brothers; he was a soldier, and did his devoir gallantly, but his head and heart were not of the strongest. He got entangled at Brussels in the lures of an adventuress, half actress, half harlot, a Mademoiselle Navarre, who was one of the many mistresses of Marshal Saxe. She was the mistress of Marmontel also, and that meanly voluptuous moralist was just screwing his resolution to the point of asking the adventuress to marry him when young Mirabeau stepped in and carried off the poor prize. The Mirabeau family were furious, strove to move heaven and earth against the marriage before and after it was accomplished; their efforts were suddenly ended by the death of the new Countess of Mirabeau at Avignon in 1749. Louis Alexander, renounced by his family, and at his wit's end and his purse's end, was suddenly taken up by the Margrave of Bayreuth and his wife. He went with them to Italy. He accompanied them to Bayreuth. He rose in honour and dignity at the little German Court, played a part in Franco-German diplomacy, and married a Julia Dorothea Sylvia of Kunsberg, a young German girl of rank. He became reconciled to his brothers, and at last to his mother. Then in the high tide of prosperity and felicity he was struck down by disease, and died at Bayreuth in the autumn of 1761. His widow, who had won all the Mirabeau hearts, came at their urgent request to take her home with them, and the Marquis seems never to tire of singing her praises.

The Bailli Mirabeau may be summed up as a good sailor, a bad courtier, a gallant gentleman, an illustrious ornament of the waning order of Malta, and an ideal brother. His affection for his brother the Marquis knew no bounds, and their sympathetic intimacy is one of the most pleasing episodes in the history of their house, and indeed in the history of the century. They never quarrelled, they seldom disagreed; even when Gabriel Honoré set his wits to work, he could not set them at odds. As a sailor he fought the English time and again; now defeated, wounded, and a prisoner in England; now defeating, as in the affair at Saint Vaast. As he battled with the English, so he battled with the bureaucracy at the Admiralty, striving in a shower of pamphlets after all manner of reforms. As a governor of Guadeloupe, he distinguished himself by his sympathies with the native, as opposed to the planter classes, a policy which had its usual effect of making him highly unpopular with the privileged order. He took the final vows at Malta, and rose to high distinction in the fading Order, regretting gravely that there were no Turks to fight. For his brother's sake he left Malta and came home to live with him.

Few historical characters have been more harshly entreated than old Marquis Mirabeau, the 'Friend of Man.' Sneering critics have alluded to him as the Friend of Man who was the enemy of his son. He has been held up as an example of crabbed dogmatism. He has been reviled because he did not appreciate the deterioration and decay of the stately manners of the French nobility. His attitude towards his tempestuous son can be best understood by comparing it with his relations to his own father. His horror at the disregard of etiquette which made him growl at Marie Antoinette running about in the short skirts of a stage peasant was natural in a man whose sire represented the formality of the age of Louis XIV. For the rest, if he was dogged, obstinate, stubborn, it is hard to imagine how he could very well have been anything else, sprung from such a sire and such a dame. Victor de Riquetti was born on October 4, 1715. It was a stormy year and a stormy season. Bolingbroke had just arrived in Paris, an attainted peer, flying for his life. James Stuart was about to set forth on that expedition which came for a moment near to placing the crown of England on the head of a Stuart prince. The life that had just begun was destined to have a good deal of experience of ruined royal houses.

The young Victor was received in his childhood into the knighthood of Malta. It must be admitted that his education was of the Spartan kind. To the curious in the effects of education upon character it is interesting to contrast the method of John Anthony de Riquetti with the method of Pierre Eyquem and to note the result of each method in Victor of Mirabeau and Michael of Montaigne, in the author of 'L'Ami des Hommes' and the author of the 'Essais.' Two wholly distinct schools of education are represented in the story of these two sires and their sons. Pierre Eyquem may be said in some degree to have anticipated the method of 'Levana,' and to have adopted beforehand the views of Jean Paul Richter on the education of children. The result was the formation of one of the most lovable of natures. That education left in the mind of Michael of Montaigne the tenderest affection for the father who reared him. The educational system of John Anthony was wide as the poles asunder from the method of Eyquem. He held it as his cardinal belief that all display of sentiment or of familiarity between parents and children should be rigidly abolished. The business of John Anthony and his wife was always to keep up what we may well call a masquerade of superiority to all the weakness of humanity in the eyes of their offspring. It would be hard to expect a son who had seen his parents after the loss of a child go about with an air of 'full and entire serenity' to extend any great degree of sentimental emotion towards his own children. The chief emotion which John Anthony aroused in his children was fear. He seems to have interpreted the duty of a parent towards his family much as a lion-tamer interprets his duty towards the wild beasts under his control. So long as they are kept in subjugation by fear, all is well. Even at a great distance from his austere sire, the terror of his influence held the young Victor in check, and he himself records the fact that as his mother was accustomed to write his father's letters, and as he was always afraid of his father's letters, he could never all through his life open a note from his mother without a beating heart. Yet he had no such Spartan dread of his mother. For her from the earliest days he seems to have cherished the liveliest affection. When Victor was five years old a strange and terrible plague swept across Provence. The great seaport of Marseilles was panic-stricken and deserted. Fugitives from Marseilles came swarming into Mirabeau's village. Françoise de Mirabeau insisted upon leaving the plague-threatened place with her husband and children. So one of Victor Mirabeau's earliest recollections was of the family flight across the mountains to the town of Gap, which they found in wild disorder. At first, entry was refused to the fugitives from Mirabeau, but John Anthony of the Silver Neck was not a man to be trifled with. He practically took the town by storm, forced his way in, assumed command at once, and in twenty-four hours had completely restored it to order and tranquillity.

Victor and his brother the Bailli were educated chiefly in a Jesuit college either at Aix or Marseilles. Their schooling was of necessity brief. The younger entered the navy at twelve and a half. The elder Victor was attached at thirteen to the regiment of Duras which his father had so long commanded. The father sent him off to the army with a characteristic affectation of Roman austerity. When the son waited upon the sire to say farewell, John Anthony, finding that the carriage had not yet come, and unwilling to waste any time in sentimentalisms, made Victor take up a book that was being read to him, and continue the reading until the carriage came. Then it was simply 'Good-bye, my son; be wise if you wish to be happy.' And so, with no other or tenderer words ringing in his ears, the son turned upon his heel and went to face the world.

The educational theory of John Anthony was rich in maxims. Two of his favourite counsels to his son were never to loot an enemy, and never to expose himself from mere foolhardiness. On matters of etiquette he was a precisian and a martinet. Once the young soldier appeared before him at Aix in his uniform. 'Sir,' said the indignant John Anthony, 'when we come before people whom we respect we take off our corporal's coat. A corporal appears nowhere save at the head of his men. Go and take it off.' The Friend of Man, recording this, wonders what his father would have thought of an age in which generals and even marshals of France wore uniforms.

The youth of Victor Mirabeau was sufficiently stormy. In 1731 he was withdrawn for a time from his regiment to enter a military academy in Paris, and the life of the young academician was sufficiently turbulent. By quietly suppressing a letter from his father he exempted himself from submission to the authority his father wished him to obey, and gave himself up to a riotous enjoyment of the capital. There is something of Tom and Jerry, something of the mad escapades of Lever's heroes, in the record of the young soldier's Paris life. Play, debauch, quarrels, laid their usual tax upon light-hearted youth. But what Victor seems to have liked best of all was to frequent the playhouse with his wild companions, and interrupt the progress of the piece by all manner of mad buffooneries. We have an amusing picture of the reckless lads shouting songs in their soft Provençal and Languedocian dialects in order to silence the orchestra, and clamouring loudly for some other play than the one which happened to be the piece of the evening. Soldiers were called in to repress the tumult and were promptly driven out again by the rioters. The actors were shouted and howled into silence. The audience laughed and fumed alternately. At last peace was restored at the direct request of a princess of the blood royal, the Duchess de Bourbon, who sent to demand an interview with the leaders of the riot. She saw Victor Mirabeau and a musketeer named Ducrest, and persuaded them to extend a gracious forgiveness to the unlucky mummers.

All this playhouse-haunting had its inevitable result upon Victor. The bright eyes of a pretty actress set fire to his boy's heart. Perhaps at no time has the stage been more successful in its attractions than in the eighteenth century. The fair playing-women were worshipped with a kind of desperate gallantry in which mere passion was blended with a semi-chivalrous poetry which makes the stage loves of the Old Order eminently picturesque. Of all the pretty women whose names are preserved for us in the amorous chronicles of the day, few were prettier than the little Dangeville, and her charm, in the Shakespearean phrase, overlooked the young Mirabeau. The young fellow seems to have been very seriously in love, for though he had not a penny in his pocket he won La Dangeville's heart with words, and was for a sweet season wildly, madly happy. But the happiness was of brief duration. John Anthony of the Silver Neck seems to have heard of it. There came to the young Mirabeau a captaincy in his regiment of Duras, and orders to join it immediately. Young Mirabeau set off with a breaking heart. The farewell between him and his flame was almost tragic, and the vows of mutual fidelity were deeply sworn. However, the young soldier soon heard that La Dangeville had allied herself with a wealthy nobleman whom she soon ruined, and so he says that his heartache was completely cured, and that he forgot all about her, which we may be permitted to doubt.

Victor's stage love was happier in its beginning and its ending than his more regular alliance with Mademoiselle de Vassan. In 1743, being in Paris on certain military business, the idea seems to have occurred to him that it would be a good thing to marry. He was eight and twenty then, but for so young a man he seems to have acted with the chill composure of a more than eccentric Stoic. He seems to have pitched upon Mademoiselle de Vassan as his future wife in a most casual manner, chiefly in consequence of the good opinion, founded upon hearsay, of the business-like capacities of her mother. Marie Geneviève de Vassan was a young lady in a very peculiar position. There was a law feud between the two branches of her mother's family concerning the land of Saulvebœuf, and it was decided to extinguish this suit by a marriage between M. de Vassan's eldest daughter and her cousin, the young Saulvebœuf. Death carried off the eldest daughter, so the transaction was transferred to the next, Marie Geneviève, then only twelve years old, who was duly married to her cousin. Owing to her youth the marriage was not consummated, and the young Saulvebœuf died the next year, so that in 1743 the young lady was wife, widow, and maid. Victor de Mirabeau had not, it would appear, seen her at the time when he entered into the negotiations for the marriage. The marriage took place and proved most unhappy. Mirabeau himself describes the twenty years he passed with his wife as twenty years of nephretic colic.

It would be difficult to find a more melancholy or a more touching story than that of John Anthony's wife, the grandmother of our tribune. That old saying of Solon's about counting no man happy till his death has been quoted and quoted till we are sick of it; but it never received a more remarkable application than in the case of Françoise de Castellane. As a young woman she appears to have been singularly charming. She bore with very rare modesty the beauty which attracted John Anthony; she even in her youth thought herself ugly, because she saw no other faces that resembled hers. In her young maidenhood she was characterized by an unusual soberness and wisdom. She said of herself that she always found herself too young or too old for the world. Her married life was a pattern of wifely and motherly devotion. Her long widowhood was firm, austere, and blameless. Her association with that grim ruin of a John Anthony had imparted a certain sternness to her nature. She had moulded herself, as it were, into a stony, uncompromising inflexibility, which lent a kind of Roman hardness to her relations with her children and the world. She did not love her youngest son, and she did not love the youngest son of her own eldest and well-beloved son. Much of the misfortunes of our Mirabeau's life may be traced to the severity of his grandmother. But that very severity of discipline and rule, that austerity of morality, only serve to throw into more terrible relief the last act of that rigid life. After eighty-one years of virtue and of piety, the widow of John Anthony was afflicted with the most cruel visitation. Her reason left her, and left her under peculiarly poignant conditions. Although the story of her strange affliction has been much exaggerated, it is certain that her madness led her mind in a direction very different from that of its lifelong course. The tortured spirit seems to have railed in unwitting blasphemies against heaven; the pure tongue to have uttered language of a gross impurity. It is inexpressibly tragic to think of this lofty nature reduced in extreme old age to abject insanity, accepting only the attentions of an old serving-man for whom she is said to have conceived a servile affection, and at moments, in brief lucid flashes, sending instructions to the religious to pray for her soul as for one already dead. Perhaps one of the strangest features of this amazing case is that with the delirium of the mind the favour of the body altered. Something approaching to the freshness and the forms of youth returned to the aged body and gave an unnatural and ghastly air of rejuvenescence to the unhappy woman. For three years the victim lingered in this case, devotedly guarded and tended by her son the Marquis. The letters exchanged between the Marquis and his brother the Bailli are touching examples of filial affection and filial grief. At last, in 1769, she died; her long and noble life of one and eighty years, her long and ignoble agony of three years, were sealed by the sepulchre of Saint Sulpice.

The Vicomte Mirabeau thought a good deal of himself; his brother the Bailli estimated himself more modestly. They were both remarkable men; they were destined not to be the most remarkable of their race. Never since the world began was a stranger child born into it than Gabriel Honoré Mirabeau. He was born on March 9, 1749, at Bignon, near Nemours. He was not born into a happy world; he was not born into a happy family. The Marquis Mirabeau, the wild old Friend of Man, was a friend of woman too, but not, as we have seen, of the particular woman who happened to be his wife. Indeed, he had come in time to hate her with a very decided detestation, which she returned in kind. The young Gabriel Honoré, pushing up through his sturdy stubborn childhood, throve under curious and trying conditions. There was an eternal family Iliad always raging about his ears. The mother and the father fought like wild cats. There was, too, the fitful influence of a certain lady, a De Pailly from Switzerland, whom the old Marquis, in his capacity of friend of woman, found very beautiful, altogether delightful, but whose presence did not tend towards domestic peace. It was a mad, unlucky household for such a child to be born into.

The very birth was remarkable, Rabelaisian, almost Gargantuesque. The huge head of the child put the mother's life in imminent peril. That huge head was already adorned with teeth when its lips parted for its first lusty cry. Never, so the gossips said, was a bigger child brought forth. The Marquis seemed to take a kind of pleasure in its great proportions. 'I have nothing to tell you about my enormous son,' he writes to his brother the Bailli, 'save that he beats his nurse, who beats him back again: they pitch into each other lustily; they make a pretty pair of heads.' Some three years later, the smallpox, that terror and scourge of the last century, attacked the child. The frightened mother applied some ill-advised salve to the child's features, with the result of scoring his face with ineffaceable marks. From that time forth the heir of the Mirabeaus was, to use a familiar phrase, as ugly as sin. Alas for the pride of race of the old Marquis! It was part of the good old family tradition, that tradition fostered and kept alive by so much scheming, so much self-deception, so much deception of others, that the Mirabeaus were always comely to look upon. Comely indeed they almost always were; but now, here, by perverse chance, was the latest Mirabeau destined to go through the world the reverse of comely. The Marquis was furious, inconsolable. It may be that the child's misfortune, instead of stirring the pity, only awoke the aversion of the Marquis; it may be that the extraordinary harshness with which the Friend of Man pursued his son had its origin in an illogical, savage dislike to see a Mirabeau bearing a scarred and disfigured visage through the world. In a being so unreasonable, so inconsistent, as Marquis Mirabeau, even this aberration is scarcely surprising.

Never probably had any infant in this world a more astonishing education. Montaigne's education was curious enough in fact, that of Martinus Scriblerus was curious enough in fiction, but Mirabeau's overtops the fact and the fiction. His father tried his hand; his mother tried her hand; the grandmother tried her hand. The boy did a good deal in a strange independent way towards his own education. When he was only seven years old he solemnly drew up of his own accord a little Rule of Life in which, addressing himself as 'Monsieur Moi,' he tells himself his duty. He is to give heed to his handwriting. He is not to blot his copies.

He is to obey his father, his master, and his mother. The order in which obedience is due is characteristic of a child brought up in the household of the Friend of Man. He is not to contradict, not to prevaricate. He is to be always and above all things honourable. He is never to attack unless attacked. He is to defend his fatherland. This is a sufficiently remarkable code for a child of seven to scheme out. Another childish note is characteristic of the later man. His mother once was sportively talking to him of his future wife. The child, conscious of his own marred and scarred visage, said that the fair unknown must not look too curiously upon his outward seeming, but that 'what was within should prevail over what was without.' The baby Mirabeau was prophetic of those future conquests, when, as in the case of Wilkes, his seamed countenance did not prove any serious disadvantage.

The mind of Mirabeau's father varied after the most weathercock fashion concerning young Gabriel Honoré. Now he praised him, now dispraised, struck by the stubborn forcefulness of the boy's character and irritated by the unyielding spirit which tangents from his own. In the end the queer, unwholesome dislike prevailed over all other emotions in the heart of the Friend of Man. He resolved to send the unlucky lad out of his sight, to place him under some rule more iron than his own; nay more, he would not even let this flesh of his flesh bear the paternal name. The burly, troublesome, terrible lad of fifteen was packed off to the correction school of the Abbé Choquard, a stern, bitter taskmaster, the very man, as old Mirabeau conceived, to break his wild colt for him. But the sacred name of Mirabeau was not to be inscribed upon the Abbé Choquard's registers. There was an estate of the mother's in Limousin; from that estate the Friend of Man borrowed the name of Buffière, prefixed to it the Christian name Pierre, and sent Gabriel Honoré Mirabeau thus metamorphosed into Pierre Buffière off to Paris and his merciless master. But the merciless master was more malleable metal than the father. The young Buffière's astonishing capacity for doing everything he put his hand to easily, and doing it well, was in itself a quality difficult even for the sternest and severest taskmaster to resist. The catalogue of Mirabeau's accomplishments in those Choquard days is sufficiently comprehensive. He knew no less than four languages, Italian, Spanish, German, English, as well as mathematics, music, fencing, dancing, and riding. He was a very Crichton.

As the Choquard school did not prove to be a taming school quite after the heart of Victor de Mirabeau, he began to cast about for some sterner discipline, and decided upon the army. To the army accordingly Mirabeau was sent, but still not as a Mirabeau, only as Pierre Buffière. In the army, as elsewhere, Buffière-Mirabeau made himself conspicuous and won golden opinions from all kinds of persons, and got into all manner of scrapes and quarrels. He fell in love, like the typical young soldier of a thousand tales, with a young lady on whom his superior officer had already looked with eyes of affection. The romance ended in a row, a flight to Paris, discovery, capture, a lettre de cachet, and a dungeon in the Isle of Rhé. After a while, and after much entreaty, Buffière came out of Rhé to take to the army again, and this time to the wars in good earnest. There was much going on in Corsica. Pasquale Paoli, after knocking the Genoese about, had taken to knocking their successors the French about, and the French were determined to put him down at any cost. Troops were being poured into the island, and now, with some of these troops, with the Legion of Lorraine, Buffière was to march and do battle. In the absolute fitness of things it would be natural to expect to find a Pierre Buffière, a Gabriel Honoré de Mirabeau, fighting on the side of Pasquale Paoli instead of against him; but the sub-lieutenant in the Legion of Lorraine had to do as he was told—always a difficult thing for him—and so he fought against Paoli.

It is curious to think that in that very year 1769, in which Buffière-Mirabeau was fighting against the Corsicans, a child was born to an officer of Paoli's insurgent army, a child whose birth was one of the most momentous that the world has witnessed. On Paoli's side no better soldier fought than Carlo Buonaparte, and no soldier in the world had ever a better or braver wife than Letitia Ramolino. The wife accompanied the husband in all his dangers, was taken with the pains of labour in Ajaccio in the August of 1769, and a male child was born to her, as the story goes, on a piece of tapestry which represented some of the battle-scenes of the Iliad. Thus in the midst of battle, and surrounded, as it were, by the symbols of battle, Napoleon Buonaparte was ushered into Corsica and into the world. That little strenuous island was indeed a theatre for Titans in that year, when within its girth it held the almost unknown young man who was destined to be the greatest man in France of his age, and the baby boy who, in his turn, was destined to be the greatest man in France, and to fill the world with the gloom of his glory. Both were of the kin of the demigods; the lives of both were brief; the lives of both were destined to be the most momentous ever lived in France, among the most momentous ever lived in the history of the world. So, for the first time and the last, the two greatest names of the French Revolution came together unwittingly; the young Mirabeau beginning the work which the baby Buonaparte was to make and mar thereafter.

The struggle in Corsica did not last long. Before the swelling French reinforcements Paoli gave way, broke, fled. Many and many were the *Voceri* wailed for the gallant dead; many a Corsican widow or bereaved mother sighed,

> E per me una doglia amara
> D' esser donna e poveretta.

Paoli himself with difficulty escaped from Corsica, and made his way to England to enjoy the friendship of Mr. James Boswell, of Auchinleck, and to be presented to Dr. Johnson. 'They met with a manly ease, mutually conscious of their own abilities and of the abilities of each other.' Was there ever a happier account of the meeting of two distinguished men? To Johnson we are glad to think that 'General Paoli had the loftiest port of any man he had ever seen.' That lofty port will loom upon us again in stranger society. For the moment the national cause of Corsica was extinguished; the fact that a child had been born to an obscure Corsican general, that a young sub-lieutenant in the Legion of Lorraine was free to come back to France with a whole skin, were events that seemed not of the slightest moment to any living soul. Decidedly, decisively, the spirit of prophecy was wanting on the earth, for either of those two slight events was of vaster importance than the subjugation of a thousand Corsicas. Anyhow, Corsica, which had been swayed turn by turn by the Carthaginians, the Romans, the Saracens, and the Genoese, had found its fate at Ponte Nuovo. The island was subjugated, Paoli was in exile talking to Dr. Johnson, Napoleon Buonaparte was born, and Buffière-Mirabeau was coming home again.

It would almost have seemed at first that this stormy young Buffière was coming back to something like peace, something like tranquillity. He had an interview with his uncle, the Bailli, and won the Bailli's heart; he had an interview with his father, who seems almost to have softened for a little, who lectured him a great deal in the dreary 'Friend of Man' manner, and finally consented to allow his son to, as it were, un-Buffière himself, to become again Gabriel Honoré de Mirabeau. Gabriel Honoré de Mirabeau would have liked exceedingly to follow the career of arms in which Pierre Buffière showed such promise, but here, as in most things, the Marquis barred the way to his son's ambition. That the son should desire anything seems always to have been sufficient reason for making the father obdurately, obstinately opposed to it. The Marquis resolved accordingly to temper his Achilles once again in the Stygian stream of Paris. But whereas Pierre Buffière was drilled and schooled and domineered over in Paris, tasting of the terrors of the Choquard system, Gabriel Honoré de Mirabeau might ruffle it in the houses of the great as became a gentleman of his blood. To Paris accordingly Mirabeau went, to the very delightful, perilous Paris of 1770; and in Paris, as elsewhere, won the hearts of men and women. He made one friend with whom he was destined to work much in later days, the young Duke de Chartres, ambitious then to appear the most immoral man in Paris—a difficult, a daring ambition. He was to become ambitious of graver things by-and-by.

Unhappily this halcyon hour was brief. The

mad old ruffian Friend of Man seemed physically and mentally incapable of keeping on good terms with his son for long. In 1772, when Gabriel Honoré was only twenty-three years old, his father goaded him into making a marriage as unlucky as his own. The young Mirabeau wooed Marie Emilie de Covet, the only daughter of the Marquis de Marignan, and, as was generally the way with any woman he wooed, he won her and married her. But, though the young lady was an heiress, she was allowed very little money while her father lived. Mirabeau was not a business man; he got deeper and deeper into debt. Some fraudulent servants whom the Friend of Man employed to spy upon his son reported to him that Mirabeau was cheating him; the imbecile old man believed it, and by virtue of a fresh lettre de cachet—he revelled in lettres de cachet—confined him in the little town of Manosque. Here, with wife, child, and an allowance of fifty pounds a year, he devoted himself to study, wrote his 'Essay on Despotism,' quarrelled with his wife, quarrelled with many people, quarrelled with his father, who vented his indignation by sending Gabriel Honoré, by virtue of a fresh lettre de cachet, to a sterner and surer imprisonment. The stranger who visits Marseilles always asks to be shown, and always eyes with curious emotion, a certain solid tower on a little rocky island in that stormy harbour. That solid tower was famous for two of its prisoners, one a real man, one the scarcely less real creation of a great

man's genius. The solid tower is the historic Château
d'If: the fictitious prisoner was Edmond Dantès,
afterwards Count of Monte Cristo; the real prisoner
was Gabriel Honoré de Mirabeau. Here in this
dreary place he was kept for some time; here, as
elsewhere, he won the heart of his gaoler, Dallegre.
In the following year, 1775, he was transferred by
his father's orders to the fortress of Joux, near
Pontarlier, in the mountains of the Jura, and here we
may say that he met his fate in the person of Sophie
de Monnier. This charming and beautiful young
woman had been married at eighteen to a mean,
dismal old man more than half a century her senior.
Mirabeau became acquainted with Madame de
Monnier and fell deeply in love with her; she,
naturally enough, fell deeply in love with him. But
she had another admirer in the Count de Saint-
Mauris, the Governor of Joux, a man whose passions
had not been calmed by seventy years of a misspent
existence. His fury on discovering the loves of
Mirabeau and Madame de Monnier prompted him to
write to the Friend of Man calumniating his prisoner.
The Friend of Man wrote back that Mirabeau should
be yet more strictly confined and never suffered to
leave the castle. Mirabeau, hearing of this, escaped,
and after some months of weary wanderings in Switzerland, hunted by his father's emissaries, he induced
Sophie de Monnier to fly with him to Holland.
Moralists not a few have denounced Mirabeau for
his conduct in this regard, and yet here, if anywhere

in his vexed, unhappy life, the extenuating circumstances were many and great. The persecutions of a fanatic old madman like the Friend of Man are not the kind of arguments best calculated to lead a fiery young man along the paths of virtue. As for the woman, when we think of her girlhood prostituted in most unnatural marriage, when we reflect that her lover was a man whom no woman ever was able to resist, we may feel that it is not too hard to pardon her. That the love of these two was deep and genuine it is needless to doubt. Their joint life in Amsterdam was one of severe hardship, yet they seem to have been perfectly happy in the bitter poverty which allowed them to be together. But the happiness did not last long. Their retreat was discovered, and they were arrested just as they were on the point of flying together to America. What a different history France might have had if only the foolish, brutal Friend of Man had allowed his unhappy son and the unhappy woman he loved to go in peace to the New World! Sophie was imprisoned in Paris in a kind of asylum for women. Mirabeau was shut up in the donjon of Vincennes. In that donjon he remained for forty-one months, from 1777 to the December of 1780. From that donjon he wrote the famous letters to Sophie which have filled the world with their fame and which occupy a curious place in the literature of human passion. In that donjon, being allowed books and paper, he wrote indefatigably, if only to keep himself from the persistent thoughts of suicide. He translated the exquisite 'Basia' of Johannes Secundus; he wrote all sorts of essays and treatises, including the celebrated one on 'Lettres de Cachet and State Prisons.' At last there came a term to his sufferings. His child died, and the Friend of Man, fearing lest the name of Mirabeau should perish, resolved to suffer the hideous resolution which he had formed and callously records, 'to keep the father in prison and even to destroy all trace of him,' to be relaxed. Mirabeau's other child, his daughter by Sophie, also died. This event fostered the Marquis's resolution, and after entreaties from all manner of persons, from Mirabeau's wife, from Sophie, who wrote taking upon herself all the blame of their love and flight, from his daughter Madame de Saillant, after many expressions of humility which it must have cost Mirabeau much to utter, he graciously consented that the prison doors should be opened. So, after a captivity of more than three years, Mirabeau was again a free man. He stood his trial at Pontarlier for the rape and seduction of Madame de Monnier, and was acquitted in 1782. He was free but penniless: his father would give him nothing; in a desperate effort to please his father he brought an action against his wife to force her to live with him and lost his case, and a decree of separation was pronounced between them. They never were reconciled, but the time came when she was proud of the name of Mirabeau, and the last years of her life were to be passed in the house where he lived, surrounded by all the objects that could remind her of him, and she was to die in the room in which the greatest of the Mirabeaus died. Separated from his wife, Mirabeau was also separated from the woman he loved. Poor Sophie! Mirabeau grew jealous of her, saw her only once after his liberation from Vincennes, and then only to quarrel with her. His breach with Sophie is the greatest blot on Mirabeau's career, but his love had cooled, and his desperate futile desire to be reconciled to his father governed all his purposes. Poor Sophie! Her old husband died, and she lived in her convent for some years, loved by all who came in contact with her. Then, unhappily, she fell in love and was about to be married, when her lover died, and she killed herself in the September of 1789, when the Old Order was reeling to its fall before the blows of her old lover. Poor Sophie!

It seems to have been hardly worth Mirabeau's while to have humiliated himself so much, for he failed in the purpose for which he strove; his father remained practically as hostile to him as ever. He did indeed allow his son to breathe the liberal air, but he still held over his head the royal order which permitted the Friend of Man, who was the enemy of his son, to compel that son to live wherever his father pleased. The privilege of breathing the air was indeed the only privilege the elder Mirabeau did accord the younger Mirabeau.

If he could have lived on the chameleon's dish, our Mirabeau might have had more reason to be grateful. The Friend of Man refused all provision to his son, and the son, striving desperately to make wherewithal to feed and clothe himself, complains bitterly that his father hopes to starve him to death since he cannot hope to make him rob on the highway. Mirabeau struggled hard for life in Paris, where so many men of genius, from François Villon to Balzac, have struggled for life, and found the fight a desperate one. Then, in a despairing way he drifted across to London to struggle for life there, and to find the fight harder than in Paris. Thinking that on the whole beggary in Paris was preferable to beggary in London, he returned to France in 1785, found the public mind much occupied with finance, and flung himself at once into the thick of the financial controversy. People began to talk much of this brilliant pamphleteer; Minister Calonne even employed him for a season. Then he drifted off to Germany, to Berlin; drifted back to France again; wrote more pamphlets against agiotage, which brought him into antagonism with the Government; got into a financial controversy with Necker, in which he made allusions to the need of summoning the States-General and giving France a constitution. When the Notables were convoked, Mirabeau hoped to be made the secretary of the Assembly, but his hope was disappointed; the place was given to Dupont de Nemours. Mirabeau was now an indefatigable writer, living much in the public eye. In days which had no newspapers as we understand newspapers, in days when there were no public meetings, no parliamentary institutions, it was no easy task for a poor ambitious man of genius to force himself and his views upon public attention. But Mirabeau was determined, and Mirabeau succeeded. Pamphlet after pamphlet, political treatise after political treatise teemed from his pen, and their brilliancy, their daring, their fierce energy, aroused and charmed the attention of the reading world. France was waking up to an interest in the political life which had been so long denied : questions of political liberty were in the air; the salons, where philosophy and poetry had reigned, were now echoing chiefly to discussion of the rights of man and the ideals of constitutions. Naturally a man so gifted as Mirabeau, capable of expressing the growing feelings of love for political liberty in such burning words, was hailed with enthusiasm by the new politicians. When the States-General were summoned he was eager to be elected to it. He hurried to Aix, only to be met by the Nobles with a stern hostility and a formal exclusion from their body as not possessing any fief of his own. Very well, Mirabeau practically said, you exclude me from the nobility. I will try the people. He did try the people ; he stood for Aix, in Savoy, and for Marseilles as a deputy for the Third Estate. He was elected at both places ; he chose to represent Aix, and he came back to Paris as to the conquest of a new world. We are told that he was received with no show of welcome on that famous Fourth of May in the church of St. Louis. We are told that when he answered to his name on the yet more famous Fifth of May the plaudits that had greeted other names were changed into hisses. Mirabeau was not the man greatly to be moved by such cheap expressions of opinion. He knew well enough that his wild life had been made to seem yet wilder in popular report: he was content then, as he had always been, to fight his fight for himself, and to trust to his own stubborn genius and his unconquerable heart. But even he, with all his ambitions, with all his prescience, could scarcely have foreseen what a fight was awaiting him as he sat with his colleagues on the opening of the States-General.

There was another Mirabeau in that place, a younger child of the house, destined to inglorious immortality as Barrel Mirabeau. The friend of Rivarol, the friend of Champcenetz, he was, like them, an impassioned Royalist; like them, a wild spirit enough; like them, and surpassing them in this, a mighty lover of good eating, and especially of good drinking. Born in 1754, and made a Knight of Malta when he was but one year old, Boniface Riquetti, Viscount Mirabeau, had eaten and drunk and fought his wild way to these his thirty-five years like the barrack-room ruffler he was. The mad, bad, old Friend of Man had been as lenient to his younger son as he was barbarous and brutal to his eldest son.

Boniface entered the army in 1772; he had served with distinction at Malta; he had lent his bright sword to Mr. Washington and the American colonists in company with Lafayette; he distinguished himself, and earned the Order of Cincinnatus. In 1780 he came back to France, said a light farewell to the Order of Malta, and married, but can hardly be said to have settled down. Now the nobility of Limoges had sent him to the States-General, and from his place among his peers he could glare with a coppery hatred at his elder brother, whose rumoured amour with Madame Lejay pained his virtuous heart. The hatred that the Friend of Man entertained for Gabriel Honoré was shared to the full by Boniface Barrel Mirabeau. One day among the days soon to be Gabriel Honoré will reproach Boniface Barrel for coming drunk to the Assembly, to which Boniface Barrel will practically reply, 'Mind your own business; it is the only vice you have left me.' Boniface was the hero of the Rivarols and Champcenetz, the Peltiers and the Suleaus; his unwieldy bulk was the delight of the caricaturists; the sword he drew for General Washington and Lafayette was ever ready to leap from its scabbard in the duello.

CHAPTER XXX

THE MAN FROM ARRAS

THERE were few men present on that great day whose presence was more dangerous to Louis XVI. than the Anglomaniac, dissolute, Freemason Duke of Orleans. The Duke of Orleans was one of the best known men in all that strange gathering. He was the centre of all manner of intrigues. He was hated by the Queen. He was adored by the mob partly on account of that very hatred. He was the figure-head of a party that brought into more or less veiled association men of all manner of minds and all manner of purposes. He was among the most conspicuous figures in that day's pageant. Perhaps the very least conspicuous figure in the day's pageant was that of a young man from Arras, who had been sent as deputy from his native town, and about whom Paris and Versailles knew nothing and cared nothing. Yet the insignificant young man from Arras, with the meagre, unwholesome face and the eager, observant eyes was, if King and Court and Third Estate could but have guessed it, infinitely more important than the Duke of Orleans or than a dozen such Dukes of Orleans, infinitely more important than any man in the whole Assembly, with the single exception of Gabriel Honoré Riquetti de Mirabeau.

It is said that, long years before the meeting of the States-General, it came to pass that Louis XVI. visited the famous college of Louis le Grand in Paris. Flattered authority brought forward its model boy for august inspection and gracious august approval. What seeds, elated authority no doubt whispered to itself, might not be sown in the youthful, aspiring bosom, by a word or two of kingly commendation. In this way, the son of Saint Louis and the son of an Arras attorney were brought for a moment face to face. The leanish, greenish young man no doubt bowed in respectful silence; the monarch no doubt said the civil words that were expected of him and went his way, and no doubt forgot all about the matter five minutes afterwards, forgot that he had ever met the most promising pupil of Louis le Grand, and that the promising pupil's name was Maximilien Robespierre. What seeds, we may wonder, were sown in that youthful aspiring bosom by the word or two of kingly commendation. Did the most promising pupil of Louis le Grand have any prophetic glimpse of the strange, almost miraculous ways by which he and that complimentary, smiling, foolish king should be brought again into juxtaposition? Assuredly not; and yet history, in all the length and breadth of its fantastic picture gallery, hardly affords to the reflective mind a more astonishing interview than that—the patronizer and the patronized, the plump, comely, amiable king, the lean, unwholesome, respectful pupil. So strangely did destiny forge the first links of enduring union between these two lives that might well seem as inevitably sundered as the poles.

We may fairly assume that when Louis XVI. looked with angry scrutiny upon the hatted heads of the audacious Third Estate he did not recognize that one lean, greenish face under its black felt was familiar to him. The promising pupil of Louis le Grand had scarcely dreamed that the next time he stood in the royal presence he would dare to assert a noble privilege and cover himself in the presence of a king. The taking off and the putting on of a hat may seem a simple matter, on which little or nothing of any moment could possibly depend. Yet that insignificant process, rendered in this instance so significant, may first have assured the young deputy from Arras of the vast gulf that lay between him and the promising pupil of the old days. There was a greater gulf yet to be fixed between that insignificant young deputy, audacious with the audacity of force of numbers and a common encouragement, and the man who bore his name a year or two later. Of that, his colleagues had little notion then. There was no man in the Third Estate, there was no man in the world, wise enough to predict the future of, or indeed any future for, that obscure, unhealthy young lawyer. Were there no readers of hands, no star-gazers, no pupils of Lavater there to discover their master in the humblest of them all?

He had come from pleasant Arras, in the leafy Artois land, where Scarpe and Crinchon flow together. The smiling land had seen many strange and famous faces. It had seen the wrinkled baldness of Julius Cæsar in the days when he overcame the Atrebates. It had seen the lantern jaws of the Eleventh Louis when he came to beat Burgundy out of the Arras hearts, and sought, as kings before and after sought, to change facts by changing names and to convert Arras from its errors by re-baptizing it Franchise. It had seen the bearded Spaniards hold their own for many generations and leave their traces permanently behind them in the architecture, which makes the wanderer rub his eyes and wonder if, by chance, he has not somehow strayed into Old Castile. Latin and Gaul and Frank, and Burgundian and Hidalgo from Spain, of each and all the leafy Artois land held memories; but of all the faces that had come and gone there was none it more needed to remember than the pale youthful advocate to whom all these memories were familiar, and who now was representing Artois in the States-General. The fair old square of Arras, with its glorious old Town Hall, its cool Castilian colonnades, and all the warmth of colour and gracious outline of its Spanish houses, had been crossed a thousand times by young Maximilien de Robespierre, and no man had taken much heed. But the Robespierre footsteps were going to sound loudly in men's ears, the Robespierre face to become the most momentous of all the Arras gallery.

He was still very young. He was born in Arras on May 6, 1758, and had now just completed his thirtieth year. Of his ancestors we know little or nothing; the genealogy of the family is uncertain. They seem to have stemmed from an Irish stock planted in France in the sixteenth century. The name Robespierre is certainly not Irish, but it is suggested that the name of the original immigrant may have been Robert Spiers, a possible, if fanciful derivation. Some strain of nobility is suggested by the courtly prefix of 'de' which Robespierre himself wore for a time; but his immediate kin, his father and grandfather, belonged to the middle class, and followed the profession of advocates to the Provincial Council of Artois. It is said, and it certainly matters very little, that the family name should be Derobespierre, all in one word, and it is indeed so written in the act of birth of Robespierre preserved in the baptismal register of the parochial church of the Magdalen for the year 1758. When he dropped the prefix is not quite certain. There came a time when such prefixes were dangerous indeed, smacking of adhesion to the Old Order, treason to republicanism, and the like. In the list in the 'Moniteur' of the deputies of the Third Estate the name is simply given Robespierre. The point is unimportant; that familiar creature History has settled the matter, and Maximilien Marie Isidore de Robespierre is known to us and to all time simply as Maximilien Robespierre.

When he was only seven years old, his mother, Jacqueline Carrault by her maiden name, died, and the death seems to have broken the heart and the life of the elder Maximilien Robespierre. He left Arras abruptly, and, after wandering in a purposeless kind of way about the world, drifting through England and through Germany, died in Munich, leaving his four children, two boys and two girls, unprovided for. Mr. Lewes cynically throws doubts upon this sensibility. All things considered, he thinks the painful associations of Arras much more likely to have had reference to some unsettled bills. Men do fly from creditors; but they seldom leave their native town, their profession, and their children, from grief at the loss of a wife. However this may be, the Robespierres' father did go away from Arras, did die away from Arras, leaving his children to the mercy of the world. The relations came to the rescue. Maximilien was educated for a time at the College of Arras, and after a while, thanks to the patronage of the Bishop of Arras, M. de Conzie, he got a purse at the College of Louis le Grand in Paris. Here he had for colleagues Camille Desmoulins and Fréron, Desmoulins the Picard and Fréron the Parisian. The simple bond of scholastic studies and scholastic emulation was to be exchanged in its due time for a closer and a bloodier bond. The grave, prim, patient lad from Arras, schooled by poverty in perseverance and the ambition to do well for his brother and his little sisters, dreamed that the wild, vivacious Picard was to be his victim and the turbulent, energetic Parisian his judge. Here it was, too, at this College of Louis le Grand, that the King came and saw for the first time, in the face of the model boy of the school, the face of his own fate. There is a kind of tragic completeness in the way in which the lives of all these children of the Revolution, the doomed and the dooming, are kept together, which recalls the interwoven strands of some Greek tale of destiny. To Robespierre, however, just then, the only destiny apparent was the destiny to scrape some money together, and provide as a model brother should for his poor next-of-kin. With this end always in view, he worked hard and he worked well. After finishing his classical studies he studied the law, still under the wing of the College of Louis le Grand; he worked at the same time in the office of a procureur named Nollion. This procureur had a first clerk named Brissot, then at work upon his 'Theory of the Criminal Laws,' and exciting himself exceedingly about the sufferings of the blacks in the American Colonies. He and the young student from Arras may have often exchanged sympathies on the injustices of this world, happily unconscious of an 8th Brumaire and a 10th Thermidor.

When the time came for Robespierre to sunder his connection with the College of Louis le Grand, the college authorities, to mark their sense of admiration for his 'conspicuous talents,' his good conduct, and his continued successes, accorded him in a formal and sonorous document a gratification of six hundred livres. Thereupon Maximilien Robespierre returned to Arras, having succeeded, it would seem, in obtaining the succession in his studies for his younger brother. We learn, in an uncertain legendary way, that while he was still in Paris he made a kind of Mecca pilgrimage to Rousseau, then drifting swiftly on towards his mysterious death. One would like much to know what passed between the Apostle of Affliction and the prim, pertinacious young collegian who adored the 'Contrat Social' and the 'Vicaire Savoyard,' and how far the Self-torturing Sophist saw in the livid Artois lad, with his narrow purposes and inflammable sentimentalism, the proper pupil of his own philosophies. What a subject for a new Landor such a conversation offers.

The new Landor can hardly be said to have presented himself in the person of the anonymous author of what purported to be an autobiography of Robespierre, published in two volumes in Paris in 1830, and really the work of M. Charles Reybaud. Yet there is a good deal of cleverness in this pretended autobiography. The remarks Robespierre is made to utter concerning his admiration for Rousseau are such as seem singularly appropriate to his mouth, and the final determination to visit the philosopher is quite what Robespierre might have written. 'I set out alone for Ermenonville on a fine morning in the month of June. I made the journey on foot, the reflections that preoccupied me not permitting me to find it long. Besides, at nineteen, when one is mastered by an idea, a fine road before him and the head full of the future, he soon arrives at the end. A youth of my age would have made, to see a woman's eyes, the same journey which I made to see a philosopher.' This last touch is well worthy of Robespierre. The interview with Rousseau is charming enough to make us wish it were real. The pair wander together for two delicious hours, discussing botany and philosophy; they part with an appointment to meet again the next month; but when the appointed day arrives Rousseau is dead. At least the interview is one which might very well have taken place: those who desire to cling to the belief that Rousseau and Robespierre did meet may dwell with pleasure upon the words of Charlotte Robespierre: 'I know not on what occasion it was, but it is certain that my brother had an interview with Jean Jacques Rousseau.'

Once back in Arras, Maximilien seems to have settled steadily down to a most exemplary, industrious, methodical life. . He was devoted to his family, to his studies, to his profession, content for highest relaxation with the simple pleasures and amusements of a small country town. There was an Academy in Arras, of which the young advocate was a conspicuous and diligent member. For this Academy he wrote a eulogium of Gresset, in which he ran full tilt against the Voltaireans, and a eulogium of the President, Dupaty. There was also in the little town one of those amiable harmless associations of a cheaply æsthetic kind, of which the grotesque Arcadians of Rome had set the fashion, called the Rosati. The Rosati seem to have delighted in a good deal of innocent tomfoolery in the ceremonial receptions of members, who had, it seems, to draw three deep breaths over a rose, affix the flower to their button-holes, quaff a glass of rose-red wine, and recite some verses before they were qualified to inscribe their names on the illustrious roll of the Rosati. For the Rosati Robespierre wrote a masterpiece, now forgotten, called the 'Preacher's Handkerchief,' and the curious can read with no great difficulty a madrigal of the gallant and poetic advocate, offered to a lady of Arras whom he addresses in a simpering vein as the young and fair Ophelia, and whom he adjures, in spite of her mirror, to be content, to be beautiful without knowing it, to ever preserve her modesty. 'You will only be the better beloved,' says the rhyming rose-wearer, 'if you fear not to be.'

Was Ophelia, we may wonder, the fair being

whom legend asserts that Robespierre loved but who proved inconstant? Was she the woman to whom the motto on an early picture of Robespierre is said to allude? Robespierre in the picture has a rose in his hand, and the motto runs, 'Tout pour mon amie.' How the lady liked the faded graces of the poet we do not know. But we may rest at least convinced that the world, whatever it gained or lost by Robespierre's adherence to politics, did not lose a great poet. It was but a cast of the dice in Fortune's fingers, and Maximilien Robespierre might have gone on to the end of his days, cherishing his family, studying his books, addressing his Academy and penning frigid gallantries for the amiable noodles of the Rosati. But he had another cup to drink than the rose-red wine of the provincial poets.

Yet this brother of the rose guild was imbued with a sensitiveness which was more than feminine. We learn from his sister of the agony of his grief for the death of a favourite pigeon. Birds appear to have been at all times a weakness of his. A letter of his has been preserved, to a young lady of Arras, in which he discusses with an elaborate and somewhat awkward playfulness the conduct of some canary-birds which appear to have been presented by the young lady to the Robespierre family. Could there possibly be a stranger preface to the Reign of Terror than this quiet provincial life, with its quiet provincial pastimes and studies, and its babble about roses and canary-birds and Ophelias, and its gentle air of domestic peace? There need be nothing very surprising in the contrast. History delights in such dyptichs. But it is a far cry from the poet of Ophélie to the killer of Olympe de Gouges.

Life was not indeed all canary-birds and roses to the young Maximilien. Let Mr. Morley, who perhaps more than any modern writer possesses the art of telling a difficult truth delicately, speak. 'He was not wholly pure from that indiscretion of the young appetite about which the world is mute, but whose better ordering and governance would give a diviner brightness to the earth.' How that better ordering and governance is to be brought about, Mr. Morley does not hint. Robespierre and his revolutionary familiars thought on this matter very much as Mr. Morley thinks, and did their best in their strange way, when the world seemed shattered to bits, to remould it nearer to their heart's desire. Among the many heroic virtues upon which Robespierre in later years sought to base his astonishing system, purity had its prominent place. Burke's criticism on systems based on the heroic virtues proved as well founded here as elsewhere. Wild schemes which sought to abolish love and substitute friendship had their inevitable reaction in the naked orgies of the Directory. The governance and ordering of the young appetite is the first and last of world problems. That that indiscretion should number the cold, passionless, methodical Robespierre among its victims is not the least remarkable proof of the difficulty of the problem.

Those strange revolutions of what the Persian poet calls the Wheel of Heaven, which brought the young Robespierre again and again in contact with the men who were to be his familiars, his victims, and his executioners in the great drama, brought him, on his return to Arras, in juxtaposition with a young officer of engineers named Carnot. Young Carnot had a lawsuit. Robespierre pleaded it for him. Young Carnot was a member of the Rosatis, and shared in its delicate follies. In one of his verses written for the Rosatis, Robespierre asks:

> Qui n'aimerait à boire
> A l'ami Carnot?

Here, again, is one of those brilliant contrasts in which the story of the Revolution is so fecund. A young lawyer and a young engineer-captain sit side by side in affable amateur gatherings with rosebuds in their button-holes and recite verses or listen to the recitals of others. A twist in the kaleidoscope, and they are still sitting side by side in organized fellowship, but this time their names are the most famous in France, and their fellowship is the Committee of Public Safety. The son of the Organizer of Victory, in his memoirs of his father, would wish it to be understood that there was little or no friendship between the young Robespierre and the young Carnot. But they were in the same town, members of the same social guild; they may not have been close friends, but it is difficult, especially with Robespierre's familiar allusion in our ears, to believe that they were not brought into some degree of familiar relationship.

Robespierre's legal career at Arras was sufficiently distinguished. He pleaded the cause of science when he defended the cause and won the case of a citizen of advanced views who had mounted a lightning-rod upon his house, to the alarm of less educated municipal authority. He fought for an old woman who had got into a quarrel with a powerful Abbey. He held his own against the Bishop of Arras, his old patron, M. de Conzie, and his courage pleased his old patron and prompted him to a fresh act of patronage. He appointed him as judge of his civil and criminal tribunal. All the world knows and marvels at the reasons which induced Robespierre to resign this office, which, while he held it, he employed manfully to uphold popular rights against the edicts of Lamoignon. One day the necessities of his office compelled him to record a death sentence against a murderer, convicted by overwhelming proof. His sister Charlotte relates how he came home positively crushed by despair at the act which he had just committed. It was wholly in vain that she strove to console him, pointing out with sisterly solicitude that the man he had condemned was a scoundrel of the worst kind, unfit to live. All the answer she could wring from the despairing Robespierre was, 'A scoundrel no doubt; but think of taking a man's life!' He thought of it till he could bear it no longer, and then he formally resigned the office which forced him to such terrible, such heart-breaking horrors, and returned to his career at the bar. Time was to make him less squeamish.

A competition was opened by the Academy of Metz in 1784 for an essay 'Sur les Peines Infamantes.' Robespierre entered the lists with an essay which won the second place. The first was gained by Lacretelle the elder, then a lawyer in Paris, afterwards destined, with his brother the historian, to struggle against Robespierre in a far more serious competition. Robespierre published his essay in 1785. It is an earnest, even eloquent protest against the prejudice which inflicts upon the families of criminals some stigma of their punishment. The way which Robespierre sees out of the difficulty is curious, as showing the survival of one of the old noble privileges and the gradual working of Robespierre's mind. Death by the scaffold was reserved solely for criminal offenders of noble blood. Robespierre proposed that this distinction should be swept away, and that punishment by the scaffold should be the lot of criminals of all classes. By thus equalising the punishment he considered that the stigma attaching to the families of condemned criminals was minimised. The Sansons were swinging their headsman's swords in those days, and Robespierre's Parisian colleague in the States-General had not yet conceived the immortal instrument which was to be so strangely efficacious in carrying Robespierre's theory into practice.

When the year 1789 set France fermenting, Robespierre was Director of the Arras Academy. He seized upon the opportunity offered by the convocation of the States-General to fling himself into the agitation of political life. He formulated his political creed, or so much of it as had as yet taken shape in that narrow, laborious mind, in an 'address to the Artois nation,' in which he insisted upon the need of reforming the states of Artois. In Artois, as elsewhere in France, there was a kind of farce of representation. In most cases the representation was a fiction, as the members who composed the States had not been freely elected by their fellow-citizens. In Artois the states were theoretically made up of representatives of the Three Orders, the Nobility, the Clergy, and the Third Estate, but practically none of them were seriously represented. Robespierre, with his keen, quick perceptions, saw that the happy moment had come for reforming all that, and in his thorough way he was for reforming it altogether. He denounced the existing order of things, painted a vigorous picture of the miseries which injustice and inequality gave rise to, and called upon his fellow-citizens, with a passion which was none the less real because its stream ran a little thin, to tumble the sham old Estates of Artois overboard altogether. Robespierre had the discernment to perceive that now or never was the moment for those of his inclining to assert themselves. The Estates of Artois were eager to bolster themselves up again with the aid of the National Assembly. They claimed the right themselves to send the deputies to the States-General. Robespierre assailed these pretensions fiercely; he urged the people to appreciate the importance of the hour, to send those in whom they could trust to represent them, and to be no longer juggled by the trickeries and treacheries of the privileged classes.

In this pamphlet Robespierre practically put himself forward as a candidate; it stimulated public feeling and made him a marked man. People read his vehement appeal, thrilled at its indignation, and resolved that Robespierre should be the man for Artois. He followed up this first blow by another in an address to the people of Artois, in which he painted a skilful picture of the sort of deputy the Third Estate of Artois really needed. The picture needed a name no more than the picture in the Salon of 1791 needed other label than 'The Incorruptible.' Having painted his picture of the ideal deputy in such a way as without mentioning his own name to present his own image, he spoke directly of himself. He did not think himself indeed worthy of the honour of representing his fellow-citizens, but he did modestly think that he might be of some service with advice and counsel in that trying time. 'I have a true heart, a firm soul,' he declared. ' If there is a fault to urge against me, it is that I have never known how to cloak my thoughts, to have never said yes when my conscience bade me say no, to have never paid court to the powerful, to have preserved my independence.'

Robespierre was duly elected an Artois deputy, and set off in the spring weather from Arras, where he was known, to Paris, where he was utterly unknown. In those days, when communication between the capital and the provinces was slow and difficult, it was perfectly possible for a man to enjoy quite a little reputation in his own locality and be wholly ignored a hundred leagues away. Robespierre left Arras as a very distinguished person, the admired of the people, the disliked of the privileged classes, an able lawyer and author, a too susceptible, too humane judge. He arrived in Paris, where no whisper of his provincial fame had preceded him, where nobody knew who he was or cared to know who he was. He was not, like Mirabeau, the man to command attention in places where his name was unknown. His small ungraceful body, his ungainly limbs, lent few advantages to his presence. A physiognomist might perhaps have discerned much in the face, with its pointed chin, its small projecting forehead, its large mouth and small nose, in the thin drawn down lips, the deeply sunken blue eyes, over which the lids drooped languidly, the almost sinister composure of the gaze, whose gravity was occasionally tempered by a not unpleasing smile. But there were no physiognomists idle enough in Paris just then to give their attention to an obscure stranger's face, and so Robespierre came and went unheeded—and now sits unheeded, looking at the King.

If Robespierre was little understood, little known at the time of which we treat, he scarcely seems to be much better understood or much better known to-day. France, in the persons of its writers, may be said to divide itself into two hostile and wholly irreconcileable camps. On the one side we have M. d'Héricault, who looks upon him as a fiend in human shape; Michelet, who holds much the same opinion, but expresses it with greater art; M. Taine, who has invented the 'Crocodile' epithet, which is as wearisome as that of 'Sea-Green Incorruptible.' On the other side we have Louis Blanc, who greatly admires Robespierre; M. Hamel, who adores him; M. Vermorel, who does the like. Hovering between the two factions flits M. Scherer, desperately anxious to be impartial, succeeding on the whole fairly well. But if France is divided in opinion, so too is England. There are only four important expressions of opinion that have been uttered upon Robespierre in England, only four serious studies of his life made in England. These are Bronterre O'Brien's 'Life of Robespierre,' of which only one volume was ever printed and which is now an exceedingly rare book; George Henry Lewes's 'Life,' also exceedingly rare; Mr. John Morley's essay in the first volume of his 'Miscellanies,' and of course Carlyle's 'Revolution.' Of these four works, the first two may be classed as for Robespierre, the second two as against him.

What astonishing differences of opinion these four men represent! Carlyle, writing less than half a century after the meeting of the States-General, sees only that a 'stricter man, according to his Formula, to his Credo and Cant, of probities, benevolences, pleasures-of-virtue, and such like, lived not in that age,' sees only 'a man fitted, in some luckier settled age, to have become one of those incorruptible barren Pattern-Figures, and have had marble tablets and funeral sermons.' Wild Bronterre O'Brien, impassioned Chartist that he is, sees in Robespierre little less than divinity. 'The more virtuous, the more magnanimous, the more god-like I prove Robespierre's conduct to have been, the greater will be the horror in which his memory will be held by the upper and the middle classes.' Mr. George Henry Lewes does not share this passion, but he counts as an admirer, a warm admirer of Robespierre. From among the turbulent spirits of the Revolution he sees three men issuing into something like sovereignty—Mirabeau, Robespierre, Napoleon. To him Robespierre is the man 'who in his heart believed the gospel proclaimed by the Revolution to be the real gospel of Christianity, and who vainly endeavoured to arrest anarchy and to shape society into order by means of his convictions.'

Mr. John Morley's judgment jumps rather with that of Carlyle than with the greater and the less enthusiasms of Bronterre O'Brien and of Lewes. Mr. Morley seems to be endowed with a fatal unreadiness to admire anything or anybody in the past except the writings of Mr. Burke and Mr. Burke himself. He is particularly bitter against Robespierre, partly, we cannot help feeling, because, having been so often himself accused of revolutionary sympathies, he wishes to show how scrupulously impartial, how finely analytical he can be in dealing with a great revolutionary. To Mr. Morley, Robespierre is only a man of 'profound and pitiable incompetence,' a man without a social conception, without a policy. He finds a curious study in 'the pedant, cursed with the ambition to be a ruler of men.' He sees in Robespierre 'a kind of spinster' in whom 'spasmodical courage and timidity ruled by rapid turns.' Finally, Robespierre is always and ever present to Mr. Morley's mind as the man of the Law of Prairial. It is the great defect of Mr. Morley's method that it is entirely lacking in dramatic sympathy. Dramatic sympathy is one of the most essential qualities, if it is not the most essential quality, for the proper appreciation of history. Mr. Morley is curiously without it. If a man does not act under all circumstances as Mr. Morley thinks he ought to have acted, as Mr. Morley thinks that he himself would have acted, then Mr. Morley has no patience with him and vituperates him from a severe vocabulary. Let us hope that we may at least try to get nearer to the real Robespierre, the man who is neither the god of Bronterre O'Brien, the fiend in human shape of D'Héricault, nor the pedantic 'spinster' of Mr. John Morley.

CHAPTER XXXI

SOME MINOR CHARACTERS

THE two most conspicuous figures in that assembly were, as we have seen, Mirabeau and Equality Orleans. The least conspicuous, most important figure was that of the respectable advocate from Arras, who is looking at the scene with short-sighted blue eyes that peer through spectacles, Maximilien Robespierre. Between these two extremes are clustered the rest of the dramatis personæ, the minor characters of the play, some of whom are to play very important parts, some of whom do little more than carry a banner or bring on a letter. Certain of these we are already familiar with, Mounier for example and Malouet, whom we have met at Vizilles; these are among the important: others that are of much less importance we shall meet with later on as they rise up to take their cues in the great tragedy. But there are some few, half a dozen or so, whom we may as well become acquainted with at once—most notably a certain good-looking young man of grave, reserved bearing who is sitting among the Third Estate. We have heard of him before down in Dauphiné; his name is Barnave.

Among those present there was no one of nobler nature than the young Barnave. Still very young, the gravity and stillness of his life had marked him out as a man from whom much was to be expected. He was in many ways a typical representative of that semi-Pagan philosophy which preceded the Revolution, and which modelled itself upon the wisdom of Greece and the composed austerity of Rome. We have seen already the part he played down in Dauphiné by the side of Mounier in that minor Revolution which by its example and its inspiration was so momentous. He knew now that he is appearing on a greater stage; he longed to play a greater part. We can even read his thoughts in those early hours. 'My personal position,' he has written, 'in those first moments resembled that of no one else. While I was too young to dream for a moment of guiding such an august assembly, that very fact gave a greater security to those who aspired to become leaders. No one discerned in me a rival; everyone might detect in me a disciple or a useful ally.' But the young Barnave was ambitious. He wished to be neither the disciple nor the subservient ally. He chafed against that title of aide-de-camp of Mounier which public opinion gave him. As he sat there, gravely stoical of exterior, internally restless, wondering, and aspiring, his eyes must have rested now and again upon the Queen's face, rested, and no doubt admired, and read nothing there of her fate and of his.

Barnave, Mounier's colleague in the Dauphiné deputation, was born at Grenoble on October 22, 1761. His family were of the middle class; his father a well-to-do and respected lawyer. From his earliest years the young Barnave was trained to a high morality, to a grave and noble survey of life. His father and mother were Protestants, and Barnave was educated in the Protestant faith; but his own religious convictions appear to have been finally moulded by a kind of medley of the philosophy of the old classic world and the philosophy of his own time. An episode of his childhood had a curious effect upon the direction of his life. His mother one day took him to the theatre. There was but one box vacant, and Madame Barnave entered it. Presently the director of the theatre came to Madame Barnave, informed her that the place she occupied was wanted for a friend of the Governor of the province, the Duke de Tonnerre, and asked her to withdraw. Madame de Barnave, a woman of firm principle, a woman not easily alarmed, refused to go. The director retired and gave place to the officer of the guard, who repeated, peremptorily, the Governor's order. Madame de Barnave quietly, steadily refused to obey. The officer, in obedience to the Governor's order, returned with a reinforcement of four fusiliers to eject Madame Barnave by force. By this time the theatre was in an uproar. The occupants of the pit, furious at the insult that was being offered to one of the most prominent and most popular citizenesses of Grenoble, were menacing the soldiers, and there was every prospect of the theatre becoming the scene of a serious riot when Barnave, the father; who had been communicated with, arrived. He took his wife by the arm and left the theatre, saying in a loud tone of voice, 'I go by the order of the Governor.' The public immediately espoused the quarrel. It was solemnly agreed that the theatre should be taboo until the offence was atoned for. Taboo accordingly the theatre was, until at last, tired of months of empty benches, the manager came to Madame Barnave, and by his entreaties persuaded her to appear once more at the play-house, and so restore to it its lost credit. The episode made a profound impression upon the mind of the childish Barnave. He saw his mother publicly insulted by the representative of the dominant order, the inequality of social life was revealed to him, and he swore his oath of Hannibal that he would never rest until he had 'raised the class to which he belonged from the state of humiliation to which it appeared to be condemned.' So the influence of a ludicrous and offensive Duke of Thunder had its share in moulding the destinies of the Revolution. The child in the theatre, shamed and angry at the unwarrantable insult offered to his mother, grew into the man who at Dauphiné laid the axe to the root of the tree, who at Versailles watched it tremble to its fall.

From father and from mother the young Barnave inherited a proud courageous nature. As a lad of sixteen he fought a duel for the sake of a younger brother, whom he tenderly loved, and was wounded, well-nigh killed. A little later the brother for whom he had fought so chivalrously died, and Barnave expressed for him a profound regret which breathes much of the antique spirit, an Attic sadness of final separation. 'You were one of those whom I had set apart from the world and had placed the closest to my heart. Alas! you are now not more than a memory, than a passing thought; the flying leaf, the impalpable shadow, are less attenuated than you.' These might be the words of some plaintive threnody in the Greek Anthology, in their resigned despair, in their sombre recognition of the nothingness of life.

The gravity which characterized Barnave set the seal of manhood upon his youth when that youth was still little more than boyhood. He had always sought the companionship, the friendship of those who were older, wiser than himself. The ordinary pleasures of youth seem to have had but few attractions for him. He was serious, with a kind of decorous gravity which might have belonged to some Roman youth; he was ambitious; he was completely master of himself. His thoughts turned to literature, but it was his father's wish that he should study law, and in obedience to that wish he worked hard and well. Constitutional law attracted him profoundly; he studied all questions of government with zeal; in the year 1783 he delivered an address upon the necessity for the division of powers in the body politic. When the struggle began in Dauphiné the young Barnave was ripe to take his share in the struggle.

Near to Mirabeau according to pictured history, not near to him in fact, shows a man of forty years who was beginning to be talked about, the Abbé Sieyès. Emmanuel Joseph Sieyès, born at Fréjus, in the Var, on May 3, 1748, had lived these first forty years of his life without making any profound impression upon the world, or even upon France. At forty a man might, most unreasonably, begin to despair of fame, if he has as yet worn no feather from her wings. It certainly would have been most unreasonable for Sieyès to despair; for, though he knew it not, his life was not half lived yet, and fame was waiting for him at the next turning. Some keen eyes had noted him already; the keen eyes of the young Barnave especially. It was the earliest dream of the young Barnave during those first days of States-General to bring Mounier and Sieyès into alliance—a desperate enterprise, as easy as to solder close impossibilities and to make them kiss. The young Barnave was strong and patient, but the strength of the Titans and the patience beloved of the gods could not suffice to bring a Mounier and a Sieyès into union of thought and union of action. During his forty years of pilgrimage he had moulded his own mind, and mapped out, as far as man may, the steerage of his course into the future. Sprung from an honest bourgeois stock, his youth promptings made him eager to enter the military service, either in the Artillery or the Engineers. But he was sickly of body, and his family, in his own angry words, 'doomed him' to enter the Church. Trained in his childhood by the Jesuits, he was sent when scarcely fifteen years old to Paris to complete his theological studies at Saint Sulpice. At Saint Sulpice he worked hard, grappling with strenuous, inquiring spirit at all sorts of topics that were not set down for him in the scheme of Saint Sulpice. In fact, the youthful Sieyès was not a persona grata in the eyes of Saint Sulpice authority. He went in for advanced philosophical speculation, studied profoundly without accepting his Encyclopædists and his Rousseau, read much and wrote much, and in his writings permitted himself much freedom of opinion. At length Saint Sulpice, shifting from tacit to pronounced disapproval, suggested plainly to the philosophic Sieyès that there must be on the face of the earth other institutions more suited to his peculiar temper than Saint Sulpice. At all events, Saint Sulpice cared to shelter him no more, and Sieyès, acting upon the hint, withdrew himself to the Seminary of Saint-Firmin, and there completed the period necessary for the Sorbonne degree. In time he obtained a canonry in Brittany; later, he was made Vicar-General and Chancellor of the diocese of Chartres, and became a member of the Council of the Clergy in France. It was in 1788 that he first came conspicuously forward as a politician. His famous pamphlet, 'Qu'est-ce que le Tiers État?' had a tremendous success. 'What is the Third Estate?' asked Sieyès, and answered himself, 'Everything.' 'What has been till now?' 'Nothing!' 'What does it desire to be?' 'Something!' Such a politician was naturally too advanced for the clerical order; they did not elect him to the States-General. But the Paris electors had Sieyès in their eye and in their mind, and when they were electing their deputies they included him in the number. Some slight discussion was raised when his name was proposed. 'How,' it was asked, 'could a member of the clerical order be properly chosen to represent the Third Estate? The point was not pressed. The services Sieyès had rendered and his advanced liberalism were his best advocates, and he was elected the twentieth and last deputy for Paris.

A grave, respectable man of nearly fifty years of age, and wearing them well, with a certain, steady dogmatism in his bearing, such was Malouet, who had been many things and done many things in his half-century. Malouet was born at Riom, in Auvergne, on February 11, 1740, of a family of humble provincial magistrates. Educated by an uncle, an amiable and accomplished Oratorian, at the College of Juilly, there was at one time a chance that Malouet might have entered the priesthood—and indeed he actually wore the ecclesiastical habit for a season, but only for a season. Then he turned to law and to literature, passed his legal examinations, wrote a chilly classical play and a couple of chilly comedies. When he was only eighteen years old he was attached to the embassy of the Count de Merle at Lisbon, and in Lisbon he passed eighteen fruitful months, learning much of the ways of statesmen, and confirming in his young mind that judicial way of estimating men and things which was all his life his characteristic. When the Count de Merle came back to Paris, Malouet was for a time attached in a kind of nominal post to the Marshal de Broglie's army, and saw battles lost and won. In 1763, when peace was declared, Malouet's friends found for him another post, newly created, that of Inspector of Embarkations for the Colonies. For two years he filled this office at Rochefort, always acquiring tact, always forming profound judgments—always methodizing his mind and adding to his store of knowledge. By this time De Choiseul had started his mad scheme for a European settlement in Guayana, which was to cost France fourteen thousand men and thirty millions of money.

Malouet was sent to Saint Domingo as a subcommissioner, and for five years struggled with an impossible colonial system. By his desperate determination to be impartial he pleased neither the blacks nor the planter class. It was always more or less his lot, says Sainte-Beuve drily, to please nobody. After five years, Malouet, who was now married and well to do, found the climate too bad for his health, and he returned to France, where he exercised much influence in the Admiralty departments. After three years he set out again in 1776 for French Guayana. Those three years were important years for Malouet. He mingled much in the society of men of letters, was on intimate terms with D'Alembert, Diderot, Condorcet, and the eccentric, diffuse Abbé Raynal. By his marriage Malouet gained, through the Chabanons, the happiest insight into the most cultured literary society of the hour, and gained also that certain measure of literary skill which characterizes his own writings. He left this pleasant literary life in 1776, to return to Guayana; he passed two years there, and was on his way home when he was captured by an English privateer and carried to England, where he was well treated and not detained long. In 1781 he was made intendant at Toulon, and at Toulon he remained for eight years an ideal man of affairs. Here it was that the Abbé Raynal, paying him a flying visit, finally stopped for three years, and might have stopped longer, so Malouet declares, if he had wished it. When the elections for the States-General began in 1789, the electors of Riom chose him for their delegate, and he was seated now in the great hall watching his colleagues, feeding his suspicions of Mirabeau.

A man of whom we have heard already is Joseph Mounier, who handled the agitation in Dauphiné so skilfully, and whose name was so influential in the days when the States-General were being elected. His intimate interest in England, his knowledge of the English language and of English institutions, seem to have lent something of an English character to his face, which would have seemed almost more appropriate at Westminster than at Versailles. Jean Joseph Mounier was born on November 12, 1758, at Grenoble, in a house in the Grande Rue, where a not altogether accurate tablet now commemorates the fact, and describes him as having been the President of the National Assembly. His father was a cloth merchant, with a modest fortune and seven children. An uncle, a curé of Rives, took charge of young Joseph's education, and the story goes that the very severity of the curé's ideas of education planted in the boy's mind the ideas of liberty. He went afterwards to the Collège Royal-Dauphiné at Grenoble, where the gravity and stillness of his youth earned him the nickname of Cato. But for all his Cato gravity he did not escape expulsion from his college. He had the audacity to write ' Nugæ sublimes' at the head of a page of metaphysics. This trifling with great things was not to be tolerated ; the outraged spirit of Royal-Dauphiné could only be pacified by the withdrawal of Mounier. A fanciful legend has it that Mounier, after leaving college, dreamed of the career of arms, and finding that that career was practically closed to one who was not of noble birth, he swore his oath of Hannibal against the privileges of the noble classes. Anyhow, he took up the law, married under somewhat romantic conditions a sister of one of his friends, Philippine Borel; and in 1783 settled down to what promised to be a peaceful country life. But a chance meeting with some English tourists led to a friendship, to a correspondence, to a study of the English language, of the English constitution. Mounier began to follow with impassioned interest the debates in the British House of Commons. He studied the theories of government and its practice in many countries. When the difficulty broke out in Dauphiné, Mounier was ready, an experienced and thoughtful man, to come to the front and to take his part. As he sat now in the States-General, he thought that destiny reserved for him still greater deeds. He had to eat the bitter fruit of the tree of disappointment.

Yonder soldierly man of two and forty, with the large body and the wide smiling eyes, the curled hair and commanding profile, is Dubois-Crancé, who is yet to be much heard of. He lives again for us in David's likeness. We see the great neck, powerful under the loose shirt that is opened as if to allow him freer play, the great forehead from which the curling hair goes boldly back, the firm mouth, the large, shapely nose, the resolute chin, the commanding eye. He was evidently a man meant for much. There were plenty of Dubois or Duboys in France, according to a biographer of Dubois-Crancé, but this Dubois came from Champagne, and inherited the fine and slightly mocking spirit which was said to be a Champagne birthright. He was an eager, even excitable speaker, foaming up like his native juices, that 'foaming grape of Eastern France' which an English poet has celebrated, and settling down speedily again as the sparkling champagne settles down after its first petulant exhilaration. Born at Charleville on October 17, 1747, the youngest son of the Intendant Germain Dubois, de Crancé received his education from the Fathers of the Charleville College. Child of a warlike breed, Edmond Louis Alexis Dubois-Crancé longed to follow the career of arms.

When he was little more than fourteen years old he was allowed, by a special dispensation as to age, to enter the first company of those Musketeers of the King's Guard whose name is chiefly dear to the world for the sake of d'Artagnan. In the ranks of the Musketeers the young Dubois-Crancé learned his trade, endured the badinage of his brother-officers over certain attacks upon the family right to titles of nobility, and slowly formed his character, very much as an armourer might forge the sword he wore at his side. He had a modest fortune from his father, which was lucky, for in an age when all advancement went by favour, Dubois-Crancé was the last man in the world to advance. He could not and did not curry favour. He made a rich and happy marriage in the December of 1772. In 1775, when the Musketeers were disbanded, he retired on a pension and with the title of officer. In 1776 he retired to Châlons, busy and happy with the cares of his books, and the joys of his well-stored library and his literary labours. In 1789 he was chosen Deputy of the Third Estate for the bailiwick of Vitry-le-François, and came up to Paris in the end of April prepared to act in all obedience to the cahier which set forth the remonstrances, plaints, and griefs of the people of Vitry-le-François—a cahier which owed its shape and purport largely to his own inspiration. It has been no less happily than truly said of him that while he was at this time Voltairean in mind, Deist by conviction, Catholic by education, Gallican like Richelieu and all the great Frenchmen of the eighteenth century, Royalist by habitude, Dubois-Crancé was a Republican unawares, like all the Constitutionalists, who were anxious to set the nation and the law above the monarchy while still preserving the concord between them. Before all things Dubois-Crancé was a patriot—the patriot as defined by Brissot de Warville, the man who wishes absolute liberty for all men.

One other interesting figure we may pause for a moment to glance at, a unique figure.

In Augustin Challamel's curious and interesting book, 'Histoire-Musée de la République Française,' we get a portrait of Michel Gérard, the only man in the whole Third Estate who insisted upon stumping about Versailles in his native peasant garb. He looks a sturdy, honest fellow, with his solid, shaven face and long hair, and his simple farmer's clothes in their quaint Bas-Breton cut. He was an honest, sturdy fellow, with no great admiration for the bulk of his colleagues, with no overweening admiration for himself. His fifty-two years of life had scarcely prepared him for the things to be, but he faced all things coolly.

There are many others in that brilliant crowd on whom the mind lingers, men distinguished already, or who shall yet be distinguished. But they will come before us in their due time: for the moment our eyes, as fanciful spectators of that great scene, have looked upon some of the most important of its players.

CHAPTER XXXII

PEOPLE IN THE STREETS

LET us believe that it is in our power, after having witnessed in imagination that eventful assembly in the Salle des Menus, to pass out from thence and wander off to Paris, and make acquaintance with one or two persons whom we may assume to have been abroad that day. The people in the Salle des Menus at Versailles were vastly important people, and yet there were some walking in the streets that day who were destined to play the leading parts in the great drama upon which the curtain had just been rung up.

One of the strange chances of history associates a momentous name with the time. At the very time when the States-General were thus coming together, to mix but not to combine, there appeared in Paris a volume of verse. The volume had no connection with the new political movement: it had no literary success; it did not deserve any. It may be doubted whether a new Iliad, a new 'Hamlet,' or a new 'Avare' would have attracted much public attention in the week which saw the assembling of the States-General. And yet the volume had its importance, for it brought before the world, for the first time, a name that was to be heard much of in the succeeding years. It is possible that some of the members of the States-General may have carried a volume of the book in their pockets as they lay at Versailles. Mirabeau may have glanced scornfully at it; it may have stirred for a moment the spoilt blood of the Duke of Orleans, or been smiled at by the Bishop of Autun. It was called 'Organt.' It was a coarse, dreary imitation of Voltaire's abominable 'Pucelle.' It professed offensively to be printed 'Au Vatican;' it bore for preface the simple words, 'J'ai vingt ans: j'ai mal fait: je pourrai faire mieux.' It's author's name was Saint-Just.

'Organt' is now one of the curiosities of the bibliophile; it is scarcely sufficiently well known to be called a curiosity of literature. It is scarce—few people possess it; it is dull—few people have read it: even its cold licentiousness is not sufficiently animated to make it attractive to the swillers at the pornographic sty. It is not worth wasting half an hour or half a minute over. There are, indeed, some thick-and-thin admirers of Saint-Just, hagiologists of the mountain, fanatical worshippers to whom all the deeds of their hero are alike heroic, who profess to find grace, charm, humour, in this frigid, drear indecency. Critics of such a temper would consider that Richelieu was eminently qualified for the drama, that Cicero was a fine poet, that Frederick the Great was the literary peer of Voltaire. It might, we should imagine, be possible to admire Saint-Just without of necessity admiring 'Organt.' But the preface was a kind of pithy 'apologia pro vita sua,' a memoir in little. He was twenty years of age; he had done badly, very badly indeed, but there was the stuff for better things within him. It behoves us to be careful, in estimating the career of such a man as Saint-Just, not to let ourselves be led away too much by the actions of his youth. His morality was not of an elevated kind. But youth is not too often moral, and neither the traditions nor the literature of the time were very favourable to a high Roman morality.

There was some excuse to be made for Saint-Just. He was a very young man, of the kind whom Shakespeare's Aristotle sets apart from moral philosophy; he lived in an age which had a marked tenderness for the lightest, even the loosest of verse. At this very time an English nobleman, Lord Pembroke, then abiding in Venice, could think of no better way of employing his means and leisure, and delighting his friends, than by reprinting the poems in Venetian dialect of the famous or infamous Giorgio Baffo. As a rare book, as a curious book, Lord Pembroke's Baffo is eagerly sought after by collectors, and its four volumes are seldom met with. To us it is curious because it bears a date destined to be most memorable in history. On the title-page, opposite to the leering, pimpled visage of bad old Baffo, is the superscription 'Cosmopoli, 1789.' To the nice observer of mankind there is something peculiarly significant in the juxtaposition of literary events. In the same year the representative of an ancient house—a sufficiently typical representative, too, of the Old Order—devoted a portion of his princely revenues to the reprinting of an exceedingly profligate, indecent old rhymer; and a young daring, penniless democrat, a representative of the New Order in its most advanced form, made his appearance before the world as the author of an indecent poem. Saint-Just and Lord Pembroke appear before the world in the same volcano year as the patrons of the lewd.

Over Saint-Just, as over Robespierre, the wildest disputes have arisen. The lovers of the fiend-in-human-shape theory have held him up to the execration of the human race: his impassioned admirers have exalted him, endowed him with the attributes of a young archangel. M. Ernest Hamel, the enthusiastic biographer of Robespierre, has written also an enthusiastic biography of Saint-Just, much of which is devoted to contradicting the biography of M. Edouard Fleury, in his work 'Saint-Just et la Terreur.' M. A. Cuvillier-Fleury, the Academician, sees in Saint-Just only a politician over-estimated by the misfortune of the time, a man of letters gone astray in great affairs, a rhetorician playing at the tribune, an artist of phrase, of language, of attitude, who might say, like Nero dying under the dagger of Epaphroditus, Qualis artifex pereo. It is not now the time to estimate the character of Saint-Just. He has hardly stepped upon the political stage; he is, as it were, waiting at the wings to take his call : let it be enough to see what his life has been up to this time. Louis Antoine de Saint-Just was born on August 25, 1767, at Decize, a little village of the Nivernais. His family was old, but plebeian and not noble. His father was a veteran soldier who had earned the cross of Saint Louis, a signal distinction, which did not, however, bring nobility with it. In 1773 the elder Saint-Just came to Blérancourt; in 1777 he died, leaving a wife who was still young, two little daughters, and Saint-Just, then ten years old. Madame de Saint-Just was devoted to her son, who seems to have cordially returned her affection. From her he got that melancholy which was always characteristic of him; from her that sweetness of manner which even his enemies recognised and made use of to attack him. A little later Saint-Just was sent to Soissons, to the college of Saint Nicholas, kept by the Oratorians, where he seems to have been unhappy, turbulent, even mutinous, but an ardent lover of learning. Plato, Montesquieu, and Rousseau were his favourite authors. When he left college, he went for a time to study law at Rheims; but he did not complete his studies, and he returned to his own village to devote himself to literature. Here he wrote the 'Organt,' which was published towards the end of 1789, after which Saint-Just himself came to Paris. Whatever opinion may be formed about the character of Saint-Just, it would be difficult to differ about the charm of his personal appearance. If the portrait given by M. Hamel, from the pastel belonging to Madame Philippe le Bas, be faithful, he had a face of singular beauty, with an almost feminine charm of outline, and an air of melancholy sweetness. The large, fine eyes seem full of tenderness; the mouth is delicately shaped; the thick hair, parted in the middle and coming low over the forehead, frames the almost girlish comeliness of the face in its mass. It is certainly a most attractive face.

There was a man in Paris at this time who was destined to be even more wildly adored in his time, and even more wildly execrated by posterity, than Saint-Just, or even than Robespierre. Probably no name, not even Nero's, suggests to the unreflecting mind more images of horror than the name of Marat. It is a kind of synonym for insane crime, for the mad passion for blood, for mere murderous delirium. What we said of Saint-Just we must say again for Marat; the time has not come for us to attempt an estimate of his character. He, too, waits his chance to make an appearance in the great drama. What it behoves us to do is to learn what the man's way of life had been until this year, in which for the first time he thrust himself into the great game of politics.

Jean Paul Marat was born on May 24, 1743, as well as can be ascertained, at Boudry in Neufchâtel. His father was Jean Paul Marat, of Cagliari in Sardinia ; his mother was Louise Cabrol, of Geneva. He was fortunate enough—we have it on the evidence of his own record—to receive a good and careful education at home. Part of his description of his early youth reads like a similar statement made by a very different man, Marcus Aurelius Antoninus : ' J'ai eu l'avantage de recevoir une éducation très soignée dans la maison paternelle, d'échapper à toutes les habitudes vicieuses de l'enfance qui énervent et dégradent l'homme, d'éviter tous les écarts de la jeunesse et d'arriver à la virilité sans m'être jamais abandonné à la fougue des passions : j'étais vierge à vingt-et-un ans.' We learn also from Marat's own words that his health was very feeble in his early years, that he had none of the petulance nor the playfulness of ordinary children. Even those who are entertained with Mr. George Henry Lewes by thinking of Robespierre as a gambolling infant, would find it hard to think of Marat as a playful child. He was docile and industrious : his schoolmasters could always, he says, manage him by kindness. Once a master beat him, and anger at an unjust humiliation filled the young Marat with a resolute determination never to return to that master's tuition. For two days he refused food rather than obey ; then when his parents, in an attempt to regain their compromised authority, locked him in his room, he flung himself from the open window into the street, and carried, in consequence, a scar on his forehead for life.

He was always consumed by a thirst for glory, to make a great name, to be famous somehow, some way, but at all events to be famous. The various phases which this thirst for fame took are curious enough. When he was five years old his ambition contented itself with the modest desire to be a schoolmaster; at fifteen he had augmented his desires, and longed to be a professor; at eighteen he wished to be an author; at twenty to be a creative genius. 'I was reflective at fifteen,' he says, 'an observer at eighteen, a thinker at twenty. From the age of ten I contracted the habit of the studious life; the labour of the mind became for me a veritable necessity, even in my illnesses, and I found my dearest pleasures in meditation. Such Nature made me, Nature and the teachings of my childhood: circumstances and my reflections have done the rest.' Marat seems to have been much attached to his mother, and her death while he was still young was a deep grief to him. His father, a medical man of ability, seems to have had little of the softer parts of life. He wished his son to be a learned man, and in a great degree he had his wish.

At the age of sixteen Marat found himself well prepared for the struggle of life. His mother was dead, he felt that he should be no longer a burden on his father, on his younger brother and two sisters. He went out upon the world like the heroes of the fairy stories, and drifted all over the greater part of Europe. He lived two years in Bordeaux, ten in

London, one year in Dublin, one year at the Hague, Utrecht, and Amsterdam, nineteen in Paris. He acquired in the course of these varying habitations a large number of languages—English, Italian, Spanish, German, Dutch, as well as Greek and Latin—and his scientific knowledge was extensive and profound. He sighed and sought for literary glory. In 1775 appeared at Amsterdam his book on 'Man, and the principles and laws of the influence of the soul upon the body, and the body on the soul.' An English version had come out two years earlier. The book is forgotten now; we may doubt if here and there half a dozen stray admirers of Marat read it in the days that pass; it made no profound mark upon its time. But it was attacked by Voltaire in 1776, which was in itself a kind of immortality. Camille Desmoulins and Marat shall yet quarrel over the sneers from Ferney. Marat was not, however, the kind of man to be easily abashed, even by a Voltaire. He kept on writing books—books on light and electricity, essays on optics and translations of Newton's 'Optics,' pamphlets on the balloon catastrophe of June 1785, which caused the death of the aëronauts Pilâtre de Rosier and Romain. It seems certain that he was a sincere and eager man of science, that he earned a fairly distinguished name, that he interested Franklin, and that he was desperately in earnest about his theories. His last scientific book, published in 1788, on 'Light and Optics,' bore the enthusiastic epigraph, 'They will survive in spite of wind and wave.' There lies before the curious, too, a romance given to the world by the Bibliophile Jacob, dealing with the 'Adventures of the young Count de Potowski,' which is said to be by Marat, and which is accepted as Marat's by his devoted biographer, Alfred Bougeart. Veritable or not, it does not rank its author among the great romancists of the earth.

There was busy work before the Gallicized child of the Cagliari doctor. Good-bye to proposals to establish the existence of a nervous fluid as the true vehicle of union between soul and body; good-bye to attacks upon Helvétius; good-bye to honorary membership, for 'Chains of Slavery' literature, of patriotic societies of Carlisle, Berwick, and Newcastle; good-bye to that illustrious position of brevet-physician to the Guards of the Count d'Artois, which has oddly earned him, from Carlyle and others, the grotesque title of a horse-leech. Marat now became the impassioned political pamphleteer. The M.D. of St. Andrews University, the man of science whose rejection by the Academy aroused angry indignation in Goethe, the disciple in the 'Plan de Législation Criminelle' of Beccaria was to begin his strange career of fame and infamy as the author of the 'Offrande à la Patrie' in 1788 and the flood of little pamphlets which begot the 'Ami du Peuple' in 1789. As we watch him here, on the threshold of his new career, we must at least admit that there never was a man in more deadly earnest, that there never was a man in his wild way more upright or more sincere. It is pleasant to read, it is pleasant to be able to cordially endorse, the very sane words of an English writer in the 'Encyclopædia Britannica': 'Whatever his political ideas, two things shine clearly out of the mass of prejudice which has shrouded the name of Marat—that he was a man of great attainments and acknowledged position, who sacrificed fortune, health, life itself, to his convictions; and that he was no "bête féroce," no factious demagogue, but a man, and a humane man too, who could not keep his head cool in stirring times, who was rendered suspicious by constant persecution, and who has been regarded as a personification of murder because he published every thought in his mind, while others only vented their anger and displayed their suspicions in spoken words.' We shall have much to do with Marat: it is very well to keep these temperate thoughts and words in mind during the course of our relations with him. Here, however, before we grow into too grim and deep a knowledge of the man, we may as well put on record the profound regret of all bibliophiles that Marat's little 'Essay on Gleets,' published in London in 1775 for the 'ridiculously small sum' of eighteenpence, is absolutely unfindable—gone like the 'snows of yester-year'; gone, perhaps, to the moon, where, according to Ariosto, all thing lost on earth do go, but certainly gone; gone as if it had never been. That pamphlet was fourteen years old now in the year 1789, and Marat had other and more momentous matters to think of.

There was all this time a man at the Paris bar who took no part in the opening of the play, but who was yet to act a leading part in the performance, Georges Jacques Danton. The business yet to be of the Bastille, which brought into juxtaposition such men as Marat and Marceau, Santerre and Thuriot de la Rosière, did not bring forward the name of Danton. The Cordeliers club, that centre and hotbed of all that was most extreme in the revolutionary movement, had not yet made Danton its chief and illustrious. But there was Danton in this Paris of 1789, a man of thirty summers working away at his profession, and watching everything that happened with his keen, wide eyes.

Georges Jacques Danton was born at Arcis-sur-Aube on August 26, 1759. His father, Jacques Danton, procureur in the bailiwick of Arcis-sur-Aube, died in 1762, when Georges Danton was three years old, leaving a widow, who married again, and who lived till the October of 1813. He left also two girls and a boy. Danton grew up a strong, sturdy, largely-made country boy. Never very comely, a series of mishaps left their successive marks upon his massive features. He was tossed by a bull in his boyhood, and one of the horns of the bull gave him a hare-lip for life. This disagreeable experience, instead of deterring him from frequenting the society of bulls, seemed only to have tarred him on to becoming a sort of amateur bull-fighter, and on a second occasion he got into an argument with a bull, which ended in his being badly gored in the face, and his nose being flattened and nearly destroyed. Afterwards he got into a quarrel with a savage boar, which tusked him badly. Later still he caught the small-pox, and the disease still further disfigured his countenance. But in spite of all these misfortunes there was a commanding quality and rugged charm about his face which generally commended it to those with whom he came in contact. He was sent to school at Troyes, and while there in 1775, hearing of the approaching consecration of Louis XVI., he formed an unconquerable desire to see how kings were made. He borrowed some money from his schoolfellows, ran away from school by scaling the wall, walked the whole twenty-eight leagues, and saw the consecration. It did not apparently impress him in the least, and when he came back to school he made very merry over the solemn pomp of king-making which he had been at such pains to witness. There is hardly a more interesting episode in history than this of the wild country lad of sixteen standing in that cathedral at Rheims, and watching with ironical attentiveness the making of a king. Did the scene come back to him, we may wonder, in later years, when he was to play so prominent a part in undoing what that ceremony did? His relatives had some idea of his adopting the clerical calling; but the proposal did not appeal to the young Danton. He decided for the law, came to Paris, entered a lawyer's office somewhere about 1779. He worked hard at the law, and tasted poverty for some years. In 1787 he married Antoinette Gabrielle Charpentier, the pretty and well-endowed daughter of M. Charpentier, who kept the Café de l'École in the Palais Royal. Such was the record of the man who now, as advocate in Paris, watched what was going on and waited for his opportunity.

One future actor in the great play, one future victim of la Sainte Guillotine, followed eagerly all that is going on, but followed it sadly, from afar, like Ovid in Pontus. A picturesque young poet was over in England, in London, a secretary in the French Legation. He was only twenty-seven years old, but already his unpublished poems had made the name of André Chénier decently illustrious in circles of the politely lettered: his passion for Madame de Bonneuil was familiar gossip to the socially scandalous. He was the most Grecian of young men, talked, thought, wrote nothing but Sappho, Greek Anthology, and Theocritus. He was born, appropriately enough, in Constantinople, for his Greek spirit was more Byzantine than Athenian. He was very miserable at being away from Paris, and longed to return. Patience, young Franco-Anglo-Hellene. You will return too soon: there is a day waiting you, a July 25, 1794, when you will ride with a couple of counts, your fellow-poet Roucher, and that most famous of adventurers Baron Trenck on their and your last adventure. But the young man saw nothing of all this through the dusty London summer as he drove his diplomatic pen and dreamed of Paris and the blue Sicilian sea and the brown-limbed shepherds of Theocritus. His brother was in Paris, the eager, strenuous dramatist and eager, strenuous republican politician, Marie Joseph. We shall meet with both again.

One other figure we may perhaps note. It is that of a man of some forty-three years of age, a man with a peaked face, a large hard mouth, and large hard eyes. He was a Picard. He had been educated in Paris, and had known what it was to be poor. He had been a procureur at the Châtelet, and had sold his office. He had been a widower, and had recently married again a wife who was devoted to him. He had many children. He had written some enthusiastic verses in praise of Louis XVI. His name was Antoine Quentin Fouquier-Tinville.

CHAPTER XXXIII

THE OVERTURE ENDS

NECKER himself read out the recapitulation of this long discourse, and stimulated a little the flagging spirits of a wearied assembly. They might well be excused for feeling a certain weariness. The opening speech of the Keeper of the Seals had not been over-lengthy, but it had been practically inaudible, as M. de Barentin's voice was weak. The financial statement of M. Necker was exceedingly long. It occupies thirty closely-printed columns of the 'Moniteur' and it depressed its audience. It was, of course, could good M. Necker only have known it, so much waste time ; as well might a philosopher attempt to stay the progress of a conflagration by reading a paper on the inflammable nature of tinder. However, useful or useless, the speech did come to an end, like all things, French monarchies and French revolutions included ; Necker made his bow, papers were rolled up, the King rose up and departed, with his glittering Court about him, amid shouts of 'Vive le Roi!' from the assembly, shouts which we may imagine to have come with greater volume of enthusiasm from the noble and clerical throats than from the throats of the Third Estate. It was half-past four of the May day, and the Versailles streets were still light, when the great States-General, for the first time brought together, spread itself abroad in all directions, chiefly needing refreshment. Hunger is imperative even upon saviours of society, whether reactionary or revolutionary, and we need scarcely doubt that the most prominent thought in all men's minds after that lengthy speech of Necker, which M. Broussonet, Perpetual President of the Society of Agriculture, prosed out, was dinner. But over all those dinners that day, whether in the stately palace or the humblest lodging in which the modest member of the Third Estate found himself, in the inn which sheltered the provincial priest of narrow purse, or in the château where one noble offered princely hospitality to another, nothing was talked about but that day's work and that day's congress. But no one of them all, not Mirabeau the Magnificent, nor loyal Cazalès, nor scheming Talleyrand-Périgord, nor young Roman Barnave, nor obscure, unnoticed Robespierre, had any dream of the tragic character of the drama to which they had just played the overture. Nor did they dream of the rapidity with which the ball was to be set rolling. Louis XVI., going to sleep that night, would have scarcely slept, or would have dreamed bad dreams, if he could have guessed that little royal document, to be made public on the morrow, accompanied by a little dexterous

royal manipulation of the great triune puzzle of the
States-General, would be the first little insignificant
move which should end for him and so many of his
in the Place de la Grève. If we were superstitious,
we should like to imagine the ghosts of the great
kings of the House of Capet crowding into the royal
room that night, gazing in mute despair upon their
most luckless descendant and vanishing, ominous, into
air. But Louis, who recorded many things in his
strange diary, has not, disappointingly, recorded the
dreams that visited his tired brain that night.

Necker's speech was, naturally enough, not regarded with universal favour. It seemed curiously
unworthy of the great occasion in the eyes of the
democratic leaders. Here was an historical assembly called together from all the ends of France, and
Necker could find nothing more momentous to offer
it than a dreary discussion upon the finances. The
finance question was important, but not the most important, to men who were eager to reform the Constitution, to men who carried their new zeal so far
that they thought Louis XVI. should have, as it were,
consecrated the occasion by resigning his royal
authority and receiving it again as the free gift of a
free people.

The chief immediate effect of the great opening
of the States-General was to spread abroad a profound sense of disquiet. Punctilious deputies, irritated
by the petty humiliations inflicted on the Third
Estate by de Brézé and his kind, suspected that

these slights were but the marks of graver purposes. Undoubtedly there was much to justify suspicion of sinister intentions on the part of the Court. There were mysterious movements and massing of troops. A battalion of Swiss and two new regiments, the Royal-Cravate and the Burgundian Cavalry, had just entered Paris, and rumours came thickly of fresh troops marching on the capital. Was not all this a covert but distinct menace to democratic Paris; was not the Court preparing to manipulate a troublesome Third Estate by the strong hand?

CHAPTER XXXIV

THE EIGHT WEEKS

On the very day after the opening of the States-General the strain was felt and the struggle began. By posted placard, by heraldic proclamation, the King had made it known to his three orders that they were to assemble again at nine of the clock on the morning of May 6. At the appointed hour, therefore, the deputies of the Third Estate presented themselves duly at the Great Hall, only to find that they had the hall all to themselves. The place looked a little lugubrious, a little vacant and desolate. There was not the brilliant crowd of yesterday; there was not the courtly colour and glitter. The six hundred deputies of the Third Estate did not seem a great body in the vast hall; their uniform attire, which aroused the wrath of Mirabeau, showed sombrely, almost funereally. The two other orders had not arrived, did not arrive: it was soon obvious that they were not going to arrive. It presently came to the knowledge of the expectant Third Estate, naturally suspicious and wisely watchful, that the two other orders were at that present moment abiding in special halls of their own, and busily engaged in verifying their powers by themselves. The deputies of the Third Estate were ready at once to proclaim their opposition to any such process. To them, or at least to the wisest amongst them, it seemed vital that the States-General should be regarded as a composite body; that if separate verification of powers were admitted, the separate vote by orders might come to be admitted too, and the most important privilege for which they had struggled be thus whistled down the wind. It must have been a curious sight, that great hall with its six hundred sober-habited deputies, excited, angry, courageous, determined not to concede any of the points for which the will of the people had called them into existence, yet anxious too, naturally enough, not to proceed too fast, not to be premature, not to be rash nor unpolitic.

After waiting for some time without any sign of the advent of either the nobility or the clergy, it became obvious that the assembled deputies ought to do something. The only question was, What was best to do? The first thing and the simplest seemed to be to introduce some element of order into their excited, murmurous ranks. The oldest deputy present, the father, as we may say, of the Third Estate, M. Leroux, whilom mayor of the bailiwick of Amiens, was called upon by some process of popular acclaim to maintain order among his children. They were not yet, with their unverified powers, a properly constituted body; but, like all human societies, they could, of their own will, establish a sort of social comity among themselves. This social comity M. Leroux was to preserve, aided in his efforts by the six oldest deputies next in age to himself. So much having been resolved upon, the next matter in hand was to decide upon what step the semi-coherent Third Estate should now take.

The first recorded speech that rises clearly out of the unexpected chaos is that of Malouet. Malouet's proposition was to send a deputation from the Third Estate to the two other orders inviting them to join their colleagues in the common hall. Mounier argued the point. He was more prudent, more deliberate; he thought nothing was lost by sitting still. It may be, he suggested, that the other orders are at the very moment deliberating upon some such proposition; it would be therefore better to wait and let the other orders speak. A great deal of discussion followed, which we should like to hear—every word of that first fluctuant democratic assembly would be curiously interesting—but which is lost for ever to human ears. In the end it was decided that for the time being the best possible action was inaction: the Third Estate resolved to sit still and do nothing. With a quaint formal logic they argued that, as their powers were not then verified, they were still only a mere aggregation of individuals come together to form the States-General, but as yet unformed. They could—they admitted this much—discuss things amicably among themselves, but in themselves they recognised no power whatever to act—to, as a body, do anything whatever. Characteristically they pushed their logic so fine that they refused even to open any of the many letters addressed to the Third Estate. As they could, however, discuss 'amicably,' they discussed the other orders, and agreed that these should have time to reflect upon the unwisdom of the course they were pursuing. In the midst of all this, at about half-past two, a deputy from Dauphiné—he remains nameless, a mystery—came in with the news that the two other orders had resolved upon the separate verification of their powers. Thereupon the sitting, such as it was—for in the eyes of logical democracy an unorganized body could hardly even sit—came to an end, and its units parted, perplexed but patient, to meet again on the morrow at nine of the clock.

Meanwhile the clergy and the nobility had in their own insane way been pretty busy. The clergy, with the Cardinal de la Rochefoucauld for provisional president, had decided, after a brisk debate, that their powers should be verified within the order. One hundred and thirty-three votes were given for this decision as against one hundred and fourteen opposed: not much of a majority after all. The majority was greater among the nobles, where the debate was even keener. Under the provisional presidentship of M. de Montboissier, the oldest noble present, the question whether the verification should be special or general was fought out. The advocates of special verification argued that the deputies elected in the noble order should submit their powers to commissioners chosen from that order. They held that the nobility could not recognise the legitimacy of the powers of the members of the other orders, and could not therefore submit their own powers to them; that the order of nobility was alone qualified to investigate the titles by which their deputies claimed to be included; and, finally, that it really was not worth while to waste time about the matter, as the main thing was to get verified somehow, and so proceed to business. This last argument was sufficiently specious, but it did not delude the democratically minded nobility. Lafayette, the Duke de Liancourt, the Vicomte de Castellane, gallant Count Crillon from Beauvais, the deputies of Dauphiné, of Aix in Provence, of Amont, and some others, to the number all told of forty-seven deputies, argued that it was the right of the States-General, as composed of all three orders, to verify the powers through commissioners of the three orders, seeing that the elections had been sanctioned by the three orders of each district, and that the deputies had taken the oath in presence of the three orders. But their arguments were thrown away: the democratic forty-seven were out-voted by one hundred and eighty-eight nobles, blindly anxious to invite collision and accelerate catastrophe. In accordance with the decision of the majority, twelve of the oldest nobles were nominated as commissioners to verify the powers of the order. Thereafter, as M. Freteau urged that no deliberation should take place until the election of the deputies of Paris, the nobles raised their sitting and adjourned to the following Monday, under the impression, as far as the triumphant majority were concerned, that they had done an exceedingly good day's work. Of that fact, Lafayette and the rest of the protesting forty-seven were, we may well imagine, less serenely assured.

On the following day, Thursday, May 7, Malouet repeated his proposition of the previous sitting. He thought that they ought to allow nothing to delay the m in purpose for which they were called together. They might have to reproach themselves bitterly if any disaster followed upon their inaction. In any case, no harm could come of his proposal. The mere invitation to the two other orders to come and join them could not possibly, as some seemed to fear, constitute them into an organized body. It would only show their eagerness to begin work, and would throw the blame of delay upon the clergy and the nobility. Then, for the first time that we have any knowledge of, the lion voice of Mirabeau was lifted in the debate. Mirabeau was altogether opposed to Malouet's suggestion. He held that the Third Estate should persist in its policy of masterly inactivity. It did not exist as an organized order, and had not, therefore, the right to send any deputation. His words, we may imagine, were fierce, vehement, eager : it is tantalizing to have them only preserved in the dry and dusty brevity of the 'Moniteur.' Mounier endeavoured to steer a medium course between the anxiety of Malouet and the indignation of Mirabeau. He was as opposed as the latter to any formal deputation ; he was as unwilling as the former to risk any danger by unnecessary delay. His advice, therefore, was at least ingenious. The Third Estate, not being organized, could not formally address itself to either of the two other orders. But—and here the ingenious Mounier revealed his tact—there was nothing whatever to prevent individual deputies of the Third Estate from lounging, in a casual way, into the rooms where the other orders were assembled, and suggesting, still in a casual way, that it would be on the whole rather a good thing if the two orders were to join themselves to the third order, as the King had ordered. These casual deputies might further intimate, still in that ingenious casual way which committed them to nothing, that the deputies of the Third Estate would do nothing, and intended to do nothing, until the two other orders joined them. Mounier's plan took the fancy of his hearers and was adopted by an immense majority. Twelve members were chosen—how, we are not informed—and these twelve went, in their casual way, to have a look in upon the clergy and the nobility. Presently the twelve deputies came back again with the results of their casual embassy. They had found the room of the nobility deserted, except for its twelve commissioners of verification, who informed their visitors that the nobles would not meet again till the Monday. The clergy they had found in full session, and the clergy had replied that they would think over the proposition made by the Third Estate. There was nothing for the Third Estate to do now but to wait a bit. Wait they accordingly did, and in about an hour the Bishops of Montpellier and of Orange, with four other ecclesiastics, came into the hall, where we may assume that their entry created no small sensation.

The clerical deputation had not much to suggest, however. All that they had to offer was the proposal that each of the three orders should nominate commissioners who might deliberate together as to whether the powers of the three orders should be verified in common or no. Having discharged themselves of their mission, the bishops and their four followers withdrew. A confused, vehement debate sprang up on the proposal. The debate came to nothing. The matter was too important for hasty, ill-judged decision, and the sitting came to an end, as it had begun, in doubt, but also in determination not to give in.

That same May 7 was an eventful day for other reasons. It saw a deadly blow struck—and parried—at the liberty of the Press. On the previous day the King's Council of State had issued an order calling attention to the issue of periodicals which had not received the usual legal permission, and declaring that the existing law would be enforced against the publishers of all such periodicals. The next day made plain the meaning of this rescript. Another order of the Council of State appeared formally suppressing the periodical entitled 'Etats Généraux,' of which the first number, dated from Versailles, May 2, had already appeared. The King, according to this precious Order of Council, had felt himself bound to mark particularly his disapproval of a work as condemnable in its nature as it was reprehensible in its form. His Majesty, therefore, discovering that this print was 'injurious, and bearing, under the appearance of liberty, all the characteristics of license,' ordered its immediate and comprehensive suppression. It was typical of the unlucky Court and the unlucky King that such a time should have been chosen to play so desperate a game, and that the selected victim should have been a Mirabeau—should have been the Mirabeau. Mirabeau was the author of the 'Etats Généraux'; Mirabeau was not the kind of man to be daunted by the royal fulmination. His letter to his constituents concerning this edict is a masterpiece of eloquent indignation. 'It is true, then,' he says, 'that, instead of enfranchising the nation, they seek only to rivet its chains; it is in the face of the assembled nations that they dare to produce these Aulic decrees.' But Mirabeau was not to be dismayed, not to be intimidated. He was careful to exonerate the King from complicity in the ill-advised decrees. It was not the monarch who was culpable, but his audacious ministers who had presumed to affix the royal seal to their criminal edicts, and who, while they tolerated and fostered the lying prints of the Court party, sought to destroy with an antique prerogative the right of the deputies of the nation to make known to their constituents the doings of the States-General. Mirabeau announced, as it might have been expected that he would announce, that he intended to continue the condemned publication, and continue it he did under the title of ' Lettres à mes Commettants.' So much the Court gained by their move. Nay, they gained more than this, and worse for them.

The assembly of the electors of Paris was still sitting, working at its cahiers, when the news of the royal edict reached them on this very May 7, while the Clergy and the Commons were exchanging ideas. The Elective Assembly immediately interrupted its task to formulate a solemn protest against the decree of the Council. For the first time Paris interfered in public affairs, and it made a good beginning. From that moment the freedom of the Press was assured in France. The Court party in their desperate game had made a rash move, and lost heavily at a moment when they could not even afford to lose lightly. The mad attempt to conceal from the nation at large what was going on in the States-General that represented it, or only to let it know as much as it seemed good to the Court party to allow to filter through the courtly prints, was completely checkmated. From that hour the whole population of France was almost as much in touch with the States-General, or rather with the Third Estate, as Paris was itself. For Paris, for the people, lived now in close and daily communion with the Third Estate. Into the great Salle des Menus, where the Third Estate daily collected together, the populace poured daily, first come first served, to listen to what the Third Estate said, to witness what the Third Estate did. Paris was in feverish, electric communication with Versailles through the endless procession of comers and goers who, as it were, linked the two centres together.

Every day more and more the course of events was dividing the State into two parties, the party which was represented by the Third Estate, and the party which was represented by the King, or rather by the Court. The differences which divided the Court itself were being obliterated in the face of what the Court regarded as the common danger represented by the attitude of the Third Estate. The Court had for its prop the support of the majority at least of the two privileged orders. It had also, or thought that it had, the support of the troops it was massing around Paris and Versailles. The Third Estate, knowing itself menaced by the attitude of the privileged orders, knowing itself also to be menaced by this massing of troops, had on its side only the popular Press, and the voice of public opinion. But every day as it went by gave the members of the Third Estate clearer assurance that the people were with them. They were shown so much by the daily crowds who thronged from Paris to witness their debates. They were shown so much by eager, excited Paris, holding its own kind of irregular National Assembly in the gardens of the Palais Royal. There day after day the crowd grew greater, and the news from Versailles was more eagerly sought, more and more excitedly canvassed. They knew so much in the action of the Elective Assembly of Paris, which swelled their number with democratic deputies, and which so boldly fought for them the battle of the freedom of the Press.

On Friday, May 8, the Nobles did not meet at all. The Clergy met to do little or nothing. The Third Estate assembled to discuss some system of police, some organization for its anomalous position. The debate was interrupted by the arrival of the Bishop of Mans and four curés of his diocese with the news of the death of M. Héliaud, deputy of the Commons of that province, and with the request that the Third Estate would assist at the interment that night. He had got 'out of the scrape of living,' perhaps a little too soon. The next day, Saturday, May 9, the Third Estate continuing its debate of the previous day, resolved for the present to adopt no elaborate regulations, but to leave the order of the assembly provisionally in the hands of their dean. The Clergy busied themselves with the nominations of its commissioners and the composition of the mooted conciliatory deputation. The Nobles did not meet at all. Sunday intervened, a Sunday that must have been tremulous with excitement, and on the Monday the extraordinary game began again. To the eyes of all France, of all the world, was presented the astonishing spectacle of a States-General which could not or would not take shape, of a Third Estate which sat with folded arms and did nothing, of two privileged orders doing worse than nothing. Through the long succession of May days from the 11th to the 24th, nothing was done, nothing that can be called anything.

The Commons still adhered to their determination to regard themselves merely as an assembly of citizens called together by legitimate authority to wait for other citizens. Malouet and Mounier made occasional suggestions of various kinds with reference to some further possible action or decree of organization, suggestions which were generally rejected. The Clergy and the Nobility occupied themselves with deputing representatives to attend the service held for the late King Louis XV., a deed sufficiently characteristic. It seems cynically fit that while the world was fermenting with new ideas the two privileged orders should be busying themselves with the memory of the monarch who in his own person may be said to have incarnated the Old Order, with all its vices, and whose cynical indifference to what might come after him had been in so great a degree the cause of what had come to pass and what was yet to come to pass. On Wednesday, May 13, a deputation from the Nobility, headed by the Duke de Praslin, entered the hall where the Third Estate assembled, announced that they had duly organized themselves, and expressed their willingness to meet, through a commission of their own order, with any commission appointed by the Third Estate to confer with them upon the matter. This suggestion was promptly backed up by a similar proposal from the Clergy through a deputation headed by Gobel, Bishop of Lydda. Rabaut-Saint-Etienne, who had not learned intolerance from the old lessons of the Cevennes, advised the Third Estate to hold the proposed conference with the two privileged orders. On the other side, Chapelier, urged thereto by his fiery Breton blood, proposed a kind of angry protest against the action of the Clergy and the Nobility. The debate lasted over the next day and many days; was not ended until Monday, May 18, when the proposition of Rabaut-Saint-Etienne, slightly modified, was accepted, and it was agreed to nominate a commission from the Third Estate to confer with the two other orders. On the next day, Thursday, May 19, the commission was appointed. It consisted of sixteen members—namely, Rabaut-Saint-Etienne, Target, Chapelier of the hot Breton blood, Mounier the fertile of suggestions, d'Ailly, Thouret, Dupont, Legrand, de Volney, Redon, Viguier, Garat l'Aîné, Bergasse, Salomon, Milscent, and, best of all, Barnave. While all this was going on, the Nobility had been busying itself chiefly with the election of the Count d'Artois. The Count d'Artois had been elected for Tartas, and had declined the election, in obedience to the orders of the King. The Nobility sent a formal expression of its regret to the Count d'Artois, and the Count responded in a high-flown epistle in which he acknowledged with gratitude the courtesy of the Chamber of Nobility, and talked of the blood of his ancestors, and assured the Nobility solemnly that, so long as a drop of that blood rested in his veins, he would prove to the world at large that he was worthy of the privilege of being born a French nobleman. No premature prophetic inkling of shameful flight marred the effect of this rhetoric.

While the Commission of Conciliation, most ironically misnamed, was meeting, one or two things occurred in the hall of the Third Estate which deserve to be recorded, especially as both of them served to bring Mirabeau conspicuously forward. On Saturday, May 23, Target's demand for a record of their proceedings was rejected, and with it the petition of Panckoucke to be allowed to print the proceedings as supplement to the 'Mercure de France.' Then a letter was read to the assembly from Court Usher de Brézé. De Brézé wished to inform the Third Estate that the King, willing to accord the honour of reception to such deputies as had not come to Versailles on the 2nd, would receive them on the following day, Sunday, in the Hall of Hercules at six in the evening. When the letter was read to its conclusion, which expressed a 'sincere attachment,' Mirabeau called out, ' To whom is this "sincere attachment" addressed ?' The reader of the letter answered that it was addressed to the Dean of the Third Estate. Mirabeau answered that there was no one in the kingdom who was entitled to write so to the Dean of the Commons, and the Commons, approving of Mirabeau's words, instructed that same dean to let Court Usher de Brézé know their mind in this matter. The other event belongs to the sitting of Monday, May 25. On that day the dean read out a motion which had been submitted to him. This proposed that the deputies should only attend in black clothes, or, at least, should only speak in black clothes; that strangers should only be allowed to sit upon the elevated grades at the two sides of the hall, while the deputies occupied the middle; that the benches should be numbered and drawn for by lot, and the deans changed every eight days; that the benches of the Clergy and Nobility should be always left empty. The quaintest debate arose on these propositions. Some members thought the whole motion ridiculous at a time of such gravity. Others, profoundly philosophic, approved of the black clothes rule as a significant lesson to the ridiculous vanity of the rich. Mirabeau declared that the whole thing proved the immediate necessity of some sort of regulations in order to keep their debates in becoming order. To this Mounier retorted that when he proposed the same thing a fortnight earlier Mirabeau had opposed it, and caused its rejection. As Mounier, in speaking, made considerable use of the expression 'Count Mirabeau,' an indignant deputy whose democratic name is lost in oblivion protested against the incessant repetition of ranks and dignities in an assembly of equal men. Mirabeau replied that he mocked himself of his title of count; that anyone might take it and wear it who liked; that the only title he cared for was that of the representative of a great province, and of a great number of his fellow-citizens. To this the democratic deputy replied that he cordially agreed with 'Count Mirabeau,' and added that he called him count in order to show how little importance he attached to such a title, which he was ready to give gratis to anyone who liked to wear it. After this odd little discussion, in which the first note of the later war against titles of all kinds was thus sounded, Mirabeau's proposition for the better regulation of debates was carried by a large majority.

On May 23, and also on May 25, the Commission of Conciliation met and did not conciliate. The Nobility and the Clergy stuck to their guns. They would have the special verification by each order of its own powers. They would not hear of a verification in common. The Third Estate, on their side, would not yield. A suggested compromise, by which the orders should be verified by commissioners of the three orders, was emphatically rejected by the Nobles, who acted all through the negotiations with a haughty intolerance that did not characterize the Clergy. The Clergy, much more divided among themselves, far more deeply imbued with the democratic spirit, had not acted with the impetuosity of the Nobility. They did not, as the Nobility did, complete their verification after the Commission of Conciliation was resolved upon. On the contrary, they suspended their verification, and declared themselves not constituted until the result of the commission should be made known. So things stood on Wednesday, May 27, when the Commons assembled in their hall and listened to the reading of the final decision of the Nobility, in which they insisted upon adhering to the separate verification, leaving it to the States-General to decide what rule should govern the verification of the powers of future States-General.

On this provocation Mirabeau asserted himself more strongly than he had yet done. Camusat de Belombre proposed to send a deputation to the Clergy, calling upon them to join themselves to the Commons. This proposition Mirabeau supported with all the strength of his eloquence, with all the influence of his dominating personality. Even we of to-day who read the speech over in the chill livery of black and white, seem as we read to hear what Carlyle has so happily called 'the brool' of that lion voice, seem to see the splendid figure dominate that confused, unorganized assembly, the marred, magnificent face glow with its patriotic passion. It would be rarely curious to know the exact impression which such a speech, so delivered, made upon such hearers as sensible Mounier and sensible Malouet, who always remind us of the strong Gyas and the strong Cloanthes in the Virgilian epic ; upon pallid, portentous Robespierre; upon a hot-hearted Barnave; upon many others. The individual effect we can never know ; the general effect was electric. In scornful, scathing words he assailed an insolent nobility. He held up to derision their preposterous claims to recognition as a 'legislative and sovereign chamber.' In words of mingled conciliation and menace he reviewed the vacillating conduct of the Clergy. Let us, he said, send a most solemn and a most numerous deputation to call upon the Clergy in the name of the God of Peace to rally to the side of reason, justice, truth, and join the Commons in a last appeal to the intelligence or the discretion of the Nobility. Amidst wild applause the suggestion was accepted. Target was bidden to turn once more to the chamber which sheltered the deliberations of the Clergy ; and at his heels trod a deputation consisting of some of the ablest and the most enthusiastic of the assembled Commons.

The appearance of Target, the expression of Mirabeau's words, had a profound effect upon the Clergy. A general enthusiasm appeared to be spreading among the more enlightened and the more impressionable, which was highly distasteful to the reactionaries. Lubersac, Bishop of Chartres, whose name deserves to be remembered, was one of the first to propose that the Clergy as a body should, at that very moment of time, rise and betake themselves to the Commons' Hall, and forthwith unite themselves with their brethren of the Third Estate. This proposition was received with rapturous delight by a large body of the Clergy present, but the reactionary prelates pleaded, counselled, finally prevailed; at least, that is to say, they succeeded in delaying the wholesale exodus of the clergy from the Clergy Chamber. It was decided to postpone the reply until to-morrow. To-morrow and to-morrow and to-morrow had crept at this petty pace now for some time, and the anti-national prelates hoped for further procrastination. Could not influence be brought to bear upon the Court? could not the Polignac party press and be pressed? On the next day, May 28, the Clergy solemnly decided to suspend all discussion upon the proposition of the Commons until the result of fresh conferences. The anti-nationals were well content. They knew that a letter had been written, or rather accepted by the King, which was at that moment being read in the Commons. That letter would effect much: so they hoped, and devoutly believed.

The royal letter had different fates in different quarters. It called in set terms upon the Commissioners of Conciliation to meet again on the following day, in the presence of the Keeper of the Seals, in order to try once again to cause a fusion. When this letter came to the Chamber where the Nobility were assembled, the Nobility were in a state of white heat of excitement. Cazalès and d'Antraigues had just been making flaming speeches, in which they insisted that the division of orders and the respective vetos should be declared constitutional. The session, stimulated to giddiness by the clattering and rattling inanities of the fiery Cazalès and the fiery d'Antraigues, did accordingly vote and decide, by a majority of two hundred and two to sixteen, that 'the deliberation by order, and the prohibitive faculty which the orders have separately, are constitutional to the monarchy,' and that it, the Noble Estate, 'will adhere abidingly to those guardian principles of the throne and of liberty.' As those high-sounding words were greeted with acclamation, no doubt that Cazalès felt, and that d'Antraigues felt, that they had between them deserved very well of their country, and had preserved the monarchy from its most dangerous enemies. The Duke of Orleans indeed, and Count Crillon, protested against the declaration, but nobody heeded them. All was excitement, enthusiasm, high-flown devotion to the monarchy and their order. It was in the midst of all this passionate effervescence that the Marquis de Brézé handed the president the letter from the King, open and unaddressed, as was usual when such a document was sent to a chamber not yet constituted. But effervescent Nobility would have none of it. They were not an unconstituted Chamber, they were a duly constituted Chamber. Cazalès and d'Antraigues had not harangued for nothing; the blood of the Nobility was up; the letter must needs be returned, and sent again more orderly. M. de Brézé accordingly withdrew, taking his letter with him, and returned with all despatch, bearing the same document duly arranged according to the wishes of the punctilious Nobility. It was characteristic of them, in that hour, to think that a scrupulous adherence to fine formalities might really serve to stay the course of democracy and discontent.

In the meantime the Commons were no less animated, no less excited. Their proceedings had opened with a message from the Clergy, announcing the receipt of the royal letter, and in consequence the postponement of any decision in reply to yesterday's Target demonstration. Then came the reading of the royal letter, a sufficiently foolish letter.

'I could not see without sorrow,' the poor King wrote, 'and even without inquietude, the National Assembly, which I had convoked in order that it might occupy itself with me in the regeneration of my kingdom, given over to an inaction which, if it were to be prolonged, would dissipate those hopes which I have formed for the happiness of my people and for the prosperity of the state.' The King was wrong. The regeneration of his kingdom was being worked out in that very inaction which he so much deplored. His people, for whose happiness he was so concerned, were slipping away from his royal, paternal authority; and it was not the eloquence of Cazalès and d'Antraigues, the Rosencrantz and Guildenstern of this sorry episode, that would keep them in their place at the foot of the throne. However, Louis thought, it would seem, that the best thing was to try again. The Commissioners of the three orders should meet again on the morrow, in the presence of the Keeper of the Seals, and certain other commissioners that the King would send, and no doubt with a little deliberation the 'harmony so desirable and so urgent' would be realized.

As soon as the letter was read, Malouet, always prudent, always cautious, made a very characteristic proposition. He proposed that the discussion should be carried on in secret, and that strangers should be ordered to withdraw. Thereupon up rose and thundered at him a strange figure. Thundered or tried to thunder rather, with one of the weakest voices in the world. The new speaker had several names. His family name was Chassebœuf. For this his father had substituted Boissirais. He was now known by the name he had adopted as Count Constantin François de Volney. Volney's 'Ruins of Empire' are still a name, and little more than a name in literature. Few people, we fancy, read them now, and are perturbed or pleased by their reflections. At this time they were not even written. Count de Volney was only a young man, a little over thirty, who knew Arabic, and had written a book of travels in Egypt and Syria, recently published.

What! the fiery, impetuous, weak-voiced Volney screamed. Strangers! Who talks of strangers? Are they not our friends and brothers? Are they not our fellow-citizens? Is it not they who have done us, done you, the honour of electing us as deputies? We have entered upon difficult undertakings; let then, in Heaven's name, our fellow-citizens environ us, inspire us, animate us. They will not, indeed, add one jot to the courage of the man who truly loves his land, and longs to serve her, but they will force a blush to the cheek of the traitor or the coward whom the Court or cowardice has already been able to corrupt. Thus, or in some such wild and whirling words, did Volney harangue the Third Estate, and dissipate prudent Malouet's proposal to the thin air. The strangers remained to listen, with due profit, to the rest of the debate, which was finally adjourned without any decision being arrived at.

The next day heard more discussion, still undecided, undefined. Among the Nobles, an energetic Lally Tollendal, Paris deputy, friend of Necker, son of the famous, unhappy Governor of India, made various suggestions, of no great importance and with no great effect. Lally Tollendal was not an unremarkable man. The speech he made was not a bad speech. It was perhaps as good a speech as could be made in favour of so bad a case. It is not to be found in the 'Moniteur,' where indeed so much is missing. It is not to be found in that 'Histoire parlementaire de la Révolution Française' of Buchez and of Roux, to which Carlyle has paid somewhat scornful compliments. It is to be found in that magnificent series of 'Archives Populaires' which is being brought out in Paris by order of the National Assembly, under the direction of MM. Mavidal, Laurent, and Clavel, a series of inestimable value to the student of the French Revolution. We have seen already that he had, after long and unwearying assiduity, succeeded in upsetting the judgment passed upon his father. He passed his time in these early days of the States-General in alternately encouraging the Nobles to resist and recommending them to yield. He was yet to be the friend of Madame de Staël, an exile in England, and at last a peer of France. He was not the man for the rough work of revolutions. We need not see or hear much more of him.

CHAPTER XXXV

SLOW AND SURE

In the Hall of the Third Estate the lion voice was again heard thundering. Mirabeau was every day asserting himself more and more. Every opportunity that arose only brought him into clearer eminence as the strong man of the Third Estate. He read the royal letter, with its clumsily concealed purpose, and he rent it with his angry eloquence. ' This is a snare, only a snare!' he cried to the listening Commons. But with ready skill he exonerated the King from conscious share in the duplicity. Yet why did the King interfere at all? he asked. There was no reason, no justification for his interference. The Third Estate was engaged in legitimate negotiation with the two other orders. It had practically succeeded in winning the Clergy to its side, and might reasonably count upon soon persuading the Nobility to follow the clerical example. Was that the moment for interference? And what was the meaning of this royal letter? An act, indeed, as far as the King personally was concerned, of goodness and of patience and of courage, but none the less a snare planned by the hands of men who had given their royal master an inexact picture of the state of affairs, a snare woven by the hands of Druids. It was a snare if they acceded to the demands of the King. It was a snare if they refused. It was a snare every way. If they accepted everything would finish as in 1589 by an order of council. If they refused, the Throne would be besieged with clamours against their insubordination, and new strength would be lent to the absurd calumnies that the constitution was in peril from the democracy. Mirabeau proposed, therefore, that an address should be presented to the King, that the commissioners should do everything in their power to effect the meeting of the conference in the common Hall, the Salle des Menus, and that they should seek to restore concord between the three orders without touching upon any of the principles which the Third Estate represented.

After a long debate the meeting adjourned at half-past three, to meet again at five o'clock, when the debate was resumed and protracted until half-past ten at night. It was then finally resolved that the Commons accept the proposed conference under three conditions. Firstly, that a deputation should be sent to the King to assure him of the respectful homage of his faithful Commons. Secondly, that the conference should be held on the day and hour that his Majesty should indicate. Thirdly, that a formal report should be drawn up of each sitting, signed by every member who was present.

This decision to accept the proposed conference marks a fresh crisis in the constitutional struggle, marks off a fresh point of departure. The three orders, separated for so long, were brought as it were face to face again, through their commissioners, and watched each other warily like gladiators in the arena. So far, the Third Estate, upon the whole, had had the best of it. It seemed upon the point of success when the royal letter came. The manner in which it accepted the royal proposal was in itself a point in its favour. On the other hand, the Nobility were as arrogant, as self-confident, as overbearing as ever, and the Clergy, who had vacillated under the steady, persistent pressure of the Third Estate, were beginning to swing back into their old pronounced sympathy with the other privileged order. The action of the Court in forcing the hand of the King had encouraged the reactionaries in the two camps. They now thought that continuous firmness was alone necessary to dissipate the resistance and display the weakness of the Third Estate. Under such conditions of wary antagonism the conference was to begin.

In the meantime the Commons had some ado to get their address presented to the King. On the day after the address was resolved upon, May 30, the Keeper of the Seals informed the Third Estate that the King, being about to depart, could not receive the Commons' deputation, but would fix a day and hour when he would receive it. This reply meant a good deal more than it said. It was the time-honoured custom that such an individual as the representative of the Third Estate would be on this occasion should address the King on his knees. This was the sort of venerable ceremonial to which the Third Estate in their present mood were scarcely likely to allow any representative of theirs to submit. It seemed, therefore, to the courtly mind the simplest plan to postpone the troublesome matter on the good old courtly principle.

On May 30, when the letter of the Keeper of the Seals was read out to the Third Estate by their dean, a point of some difficulty was immediately raised. Although the King had postponed the reception of the deputation, yet the first meeting of the joint commissioners was to take place that same evening. Now, some of the members present argued that if the commissioners of the Third Estate attended the conference, they would, by so doing, stultify the resolution at which the Commons had arrived on the previous day—namely, that the conference should only be resumed after the royal reception of the deputation. Hereupon other members arose and declared no less confidently that the resolution of the previous day decided upon the deputation and the renewal of the conferences, but did not, by the use of the word 'after,' make the conferences conditional upon the reception of the deputation. There was quite a lengthy wrangle over this point, which it was found impossible to settle, as no official record of any kind of the proceedings was kept. The memories of different members clashed. The notes which different deputies took for themselves in their private pocket-books, on being consulted, were found to clash also. Luckily, the Marquis de Rostaing found a solution of the difficulty. Let us, he said, go on with the conferences, but let us also resolve not to conclude them until our deputation has been received by his Majesty. This suggestion was accepted unanimously by the Commons, who were very keen about their deputation coming to pass. That it was undoubtedly the original intention of the proposers of the deputation that it should precede the renewal of the conferences is, however, made perfectly clear by a study of the text of the address drawn up for the deputation to present to the King, an address which was read to the Third Estate on this very May 30 by their dean.

There was indeed some excuse for the unwillingness of the monarch to welcome the deputation from his faithful Commons. His eldest son, the young Dauphin of France, was sick, sick unto death. Poor little Louis Joseph Xavier of France: he had been ailing now for nearly three years, his puny body wasted, and his scant strength sapped by slow and weakening disease. The luckless life that had been so eagerly looked for, that had first fluttered its faint flame on October 22, 1781, was now waning rapidly to its close. Scarcely eight years all told of childish life, and now it was about to flicker from a world that was growing too stormy for princes. There had always been anxiety about the Dauphin. In more than one of her letters to her brother Joseph of Austria, Marie Antoinette speaks with evident anxiety of the child's health. In a letter written in the September of 1783, she speaks of the folly of the physicians in not wishing the little Dauphin to make the journey to Fontainebleau, 'although he has twenty teeth and is exceedingly strong.' In the December of the same year she wrote again: 'My son is marvellously healthy; I found him strengthened and speaking well.' A little later in the same month she wrote: 'Everyone is amazed at the splendid condition in which my son came back from La Muette.' Now the end of the little life had come. 'She should have died hereafter,' says Macbeth in the bitterness of his heart when he hears of his consort's death in the stormy hours of struggle which leave no time for tears. Something of the same kind might have been said over the dying Dauphin. There was no time for tears then. France, in the first throes of its great constitutional travail, scarcely noted the drooping of the little royal head. It dropped at last, tired of life, on the night of June 3. He had been a-dying through all the angry days from May 28, and the sorrow of the father pleaded its defence for the reluctance of the King to receive the deputation.

In their address, in language of the utmost respect for the sovereign, the Third Estate set forth its own case with considerable, indeed with sufficient boldness. It shared the royal regrets at the inaction of the States-General, but threw the blame of that inaction entirely upon the shoulders of the Nobility. With a certain cautious irony the address assured the King of the confidence which the Third Estate felt in his fairness and reason to prevent any attempt or encroachment upon the liberties of the assembly. By a bold stroke the address endeavoured to ally the King in common cause with the Third Estate against 'those different aristocracies whose power can only be established upon the ruin of the royal authority and of the public weal.' It finally assured the monarch that when the Commons had the duly constituted right to address him, he should speedily be able to judge of their fidelity to the honour and dignity of the Throne and the credit of the nation. Such was the remarkable document which was to be submitted to an astonished King as soon as might be.

On the evening of May 30 at six o'clock the conference began at the Chancellery of Versailles. The Keeper of the Seals was accompanied by the commissioners named by the King—the Duke de Nivernois, de la Michodière, d'Ormesson, Vidaud de la Tour, de Chaumont de la Galaisière, the Count de Montmorin, Laurent de Villedeuil, the

Count de la Luzerne, the Count de Puységur, the Count de Saint-Priest, Valdec de Lessart, and Necker. To these august presences, to these shadows of great names, came the commissioners of the Third Estate with their minds pretty clearly made up, came the commissioners of the Nobility with what they were pleased to call their minds quite made up, came the commissioners of the Clergy with their minds in a more or less vacillating and perplexed condition. Probably a more hopeless, more meaningless conference was never yet attended by men.

The conference opened with a well-meant attempt on the part of one of the Clergy to propose a plan of conciliation. This plan, or rather this proposal of a plan, was promptly set aside in favour of a preliminary discussion of principles and facts. Then d'Antraigues, the stormy petrel of his party's suicide, got up and made one of the most imbecile orations that ever yet fell from a foolish mouth. He began by declaring that the action of the Nobility was just the one right, just, reasonable, and, as it were, Heaven-inspired course of action which they were bound to take. This fine theory of noble infallibility he proceeded to back by a long string of arguments founded on the actions of previous States-Generals. What other States-Generals had done they might do—such was the drift of his argument—but not a jot more.

There is something piteous, something pathetic in this desperate wooden-headed way in which the champion of the claims of the Nobility meets a wholly new condition of things with a string of musty usages and rusty traditions. Fiery-hot d'Antraigues might almost as reasonably and pertinently argue that because Clovis split the skull of one of his soldiers on a memorable occasion, therefore his Sacred Majesty the sixteenth Louis of the line of Capet would be justified in braining, with a battle-axe swung in his own royal hands, the contumelious and audacious instigators of the Third Estate. There was a brawling, wrangling debate upon meaningless d'Antraigues' meaningless speech, which lasted for some four hours. A member of the Third Estate, whose name fame does not appear to have very jealously preserved, replied to d'Antraigues. He argued that at the time of the States-General of 1560, of 1576, of 1588 and 1614, the powers were verified, not by order but by Government, and that therefore the Nobility could not even invoke ancient usages in favour of its pretensions. To this an indignant noble retorted that it was the right and privilege of nobles to be judged only by their peers. To this a champion of the Commons replied that there was in the matter under discussion no question whatever of judgment of a crime to which the pretended privilege referred. Then one of the nobles carried the war into the camp of the

Third Estate by contesting their right to style themselves 'Commons,' an 'innovation of words which might lead to an innovation of principles, if indeed it had not done so already.' The discussion, if discussion it can be called, was finally adjourned until June 3, over the days of festival.

CHAPTER XXXVI

ON AND ON

IT was worth while to follow with so much attention the delays and doubts, the vacillations and strivings, the tentative endeavours of the curious agglomeration of human beings from all the ends of France which was known for a season to the world as the Third Estate. For since history began to be recorded no more remarkable process of growth has been inscribed upon its pages than the gradual growth or even crystallization of the inchoate mass of simple members, unverified deputies to the States-General, unorganized members of a new and bewildering Third Estate, into a National Assembly which was to change the fate of France. As we follow the slow process day by day we can well-nigh witness the steady quickening of the almost inert mass into a consciousness of its own strength, of its own possible power. We can note its stubborn determination to be, and to have not merely its right of being but its actual being recognised, waxing stronger with every coming together in the Salle des Menus. We can watch too with interest how there, as in all assemblages of men, the stronger come to the front; how a Mirabeau, with no official position, yet naturally takes distinct and persistent headship; how even the thin small voice of an obscure and unheeded Robespierre also asserted itself at the right time and made its due claim upon the attention of fellow-men. It was not merely a National Assembly or a new constitution that slowly fermented during those lingering hours of disappointment and delay. It was a new France, and a new world.

To us of to-day, with our knowledge of what was in the future for these men, there can scarcely be much grimmer or more pathetic reading than the reports in the 'Moniteur' or elsewhere of those early meetings, of the early speeches, and of their speakers. The shadow of death is over it all. As we are confronted with name after name of each of those men, the brilliant, the ambitious, the well-intentioned, the hopeful, the heroic, we think of the fate of each, and can scarcely avoid a shudder. It is a very necrology, the list of those eager Parliamentarians. The words 'was guillotined,' with the date, affix themselves in our fancy to name after name as we read. A few, it is true, escape the guillotine. Some die too soon like Mirabeau. Some die too late like Sieyès, refusing in his dotage many a long year later to receive Monsieur de Robespierre, whose ghost had long since wandered by Cocytus. Some live to be a Councillor of State like Mounier, or to die poor like Malouet. But for the rest, all the more important figures are like forest trees marked for the inevitable axe. The ingenious machine to which their latest colleague, Doctor Guillotin of Paris, will give a name must be the doom of so many of them who then thought of no such thing, who feared if at all only the attacks of a despotism, and who dreamed of liberty and a Saturnian age. If any one of all those deputies had been gifted with that strange Scottish power of second sight which environs with a misty veil those destined to untimely and violent deaths, the most conspicuous heads in that assembly would have been so veiled that day.

While the conference was going on, the discussion over the deputation to the King was going on too. The Third Estate had resolved to elect a dean every eight days. The dean who was elected when the deputation was proposed happened to be M. d'Ailly. M. d'Ailly resigned his functions almost immediately after being invested with them on the ground of bad health. It became necessary to choose a new dean, and by a large majority Bailly was elected to the post. This was the first important appearance upon the scene of a figure destined to be conspicuous and unhappy. There are few sights more melancholy than that of a man of quiet scholastic life suddenly flung into the strife of fierce political life at some moment of great national struggle. Jean Sylvain Bailly was eminently in his place at the Academy of Sciences, eminently in his place in his astronomical observatory outwatching the stars, eminently in his place at his familiar desk writing prize treatises on Leibnitz, and an excellent, even brilliant history of astronomy, ancient and modern. It was unhappily not enough for Bailly to be the only Frenchman save Fontenelle who had the honour to be a member of the three great academies of Paris. He must have his share of civic life, must serve his country as a good citizen should, must needs be ambitious, most honourably ambitious to play a part in politics. An appreciative Parisian public voted him to the States-General, and handed him over to the headsman. He was an honourable, high-minded man, a scholar, and a gentleman, but he was more in his element among the wheeling worlds of space than in the wheeling humanities of a revolution. Better for him if he had kept his eyes among the stars, like the hero of Richter's exquisite story. He could indeed help the Revolution on its way. His simple noble nature was one of the ornaments of the Third Estate. But he could not guide the Revolution, or largely help to guide it, and he certainly could not stop it, as he tried in vain to do. As well might he have hoped by stern concentration of his astronomer's mind to play the part of a new Joshua, and stay the revolutions of the sun, as to stay the revolution of the forces around him. Under happier conditions, and in more tranquil times, he might have earned a distinguished place among a nation's representatives, but the stormy tides of an insurgent and desperate democracy were too strong for him. His mild, intelligent face was not the face of a man born to sway the multitude. His high forehead sloping back from an exceedingly aquiline nose, his large benign eye, the full cheeks and slightly heavy lower face, the mobile mouth, sensuous rather than sensual, all these were characteristics of intelligence, of delicacy of mind, of qualities excellent in a scientific man who was also a man of letters; excellent even for a statesman in serene hours, but not strong enough to dominate the Carmagnole of Sans-culottes into which the destinies were driving France.

There was a good deal of small altercation going on in these days in the chamber of the Third Estate. The refusal of the King to receive the Commons' deputation was in especial a fruitful theme of debate. On June 2, M. d'Ailly, as dean of the Third Estate, proposed to make some modifications in the address to the King, as resolved upon at the session of May 30. The proposed alterations were not accepted by the bureau, which adhered to the original address with some slight modifications. A rather sharp debate arose over these modifications, which according to some members of the bureau were purely nominal, and according to one of the members of the bureau were of a nature highly prejudicial to the Assembly. Some of those present called for the re-reading of the original address, that the exact nature of the changes introduced might be made known. Others demanded the reading of the second address proposed by M. d'Ailly and now withdrawn. Others were opposed to any re-reading as useless and profitless. Others again urged that if there were to be any re-reading, all strangers present should be compelled to retire. Some were for placing implicit confidence in the wisdom and discretion of the gentlemen of the bureau. Some thought that to do so was to endow the bureau with far too much authority. In the end a decision against re-reading was carried by 185 votes to 114.

On the next day, June 3, the deputation question came up again. By this time, as we have seen, M. d'Ailly had resigned his deanship—possibly that rejected second address may have had something to do with it—and Bailly had been chosen dean in his place. There was much complaining against the action, or rather the inaction, of the King. Susceptible constitutionalism pointed out that while the deputations from the Clergy and the Nobility had been received with alacrity and enthusiasm, the most meaningless delay was placed in the way of the deputation from the Third Estate. Even the sickness of the Dauphin was not admitted to be a valid excuse. In such a moment, it was argued, a sorrowing monarch ought to have all the more need and desire for the support and sympathy of his faithful Commons. Under all which considerations it seemed quite clear to the susceptible constitutionalism of the Third Estate that further pressure must be put, and that promptly, upon the King. Bailly declared that, though it was exceedingly difficult to get admission to the King, still he was entirely in the hands of the Third Estate. If they bade him, he would do all in his power to get into the presence of his sovereign. Thereupon Mirabeau, looking as usual straight to the heart of the matter—not, perhaps, we may imagine, without arousing even already some slight jealousy in the less impetuous and also less masterly mind of Bailly —proposed that Bailly should request the King to name a time when he would receive the deputation of the Commons. This motion was easily carried unanimously, but Bailly found it hard to carry out.

It was hard for the Commons to get at their King. He was more and more in the hands of the Nobles, and the policy of the Nobles as a body was the policy of the feather-headed d'Antraigues. Count Henri de Launai d'Antraigues was the hero of the hour with the gentlemen of the noble estate. Young, handsome, ambitious, frothily eloquent, he was eminently skilful, for a time at least, in winning the hearts of men and women. Perhaps, even while he was making his flaming harangues to a delighted Chamber of Nobility he had against his heart some latest love-letter of the beautiful Saint-Huberty, the exquisite Anne Antoinette, whose acting delighted

Paris, and whose generous heart was now entirely at the feet of the rhetorical young noble from Languedoc. The eloquent Languedocian gentleman, the much-beloved, much-loving, Magdalen Saint-Huberty, bound together for the hour by the bonds of a facile passion, were bound together for a dreary destiny and a dismal end. For the moment, however, d'Antraigues was flushed with pride of his fair mistress. For the moment the Saint-Huberty, forgetting all predecessors from Sieur Croisilles, her rogue of a husband, downwards, was rapturously devoted to her shining politician lover. For some time the young d'Antraigues had been quite a conspicuous figure in Paris. He boasted an illustrious descent. He claimed as an ancestor the distinguished gentleman and soldier to whom, when he was wounded, Henri Quatre wrote uttering the most royal and chivalrous wishes for his speedy restoration. Parisian society not altogether unreservedly accepted him at his own estimation. There were not wanting sneering sceptics who denied him all patent of nobility. His name, said these sceptics, was not d'Antraigues at all; it was Audanel, the anagram of de Launai, and the name which he signed as a pseudonym to some of his political pamphlets. Envious tongues even went so far as to insinuate that he had been, as it were, drummed out of a regiment of Vivarais for poltroonery in some affair of honour. It is true that Barau, in his history of the families of Rouergue, cited by M. Edmond de Goncourt, declares that the House of Launai owned among others the seigneury of Antraigues, and that the land was invested with the privilege of carrying the title of Count by letters patent of September 1668 for the benefit of Trophime de Launai, granduncle of our 'young Languedocian gentleman.' At the same time, Barau admits that when our d'Antraigues came to Paris and solicited the honours of the Court he could not completely furnish the necessary proofs. It is certain that when Mirabeau assailed him in his pamphlet, 'Lettre de M. le Comte de Mirabeau à M. le Comte d'Antra'gues,' for his sudden adhesion to the cause of the noble order and his attacks upon the Third Estate, the Provençal rallied the Languedocian upon his sham nobility. Mirabeau declared that the Vivarais deputy had converted himself into a d'Antraigues to the great astonishment of his worthy parent, who had never considered himself to be descended from that noble house, but had simply written himself 'd'Entraigues,' taking that name from a little house built in a marsh. It is curious in confirmation of this, that M. de Goncourt cites letters from the son of d'Antraigues and the Saint-Huberty, in which the son always signs himself d'Entraigues.

Whether illustriously noble or not, d'Antraigues passed for illustriously noble with a not too critical Parisian society. He carried himself like a gentleman of a good house; his mother was a Saint-Priest;

he had sufficient means to move with ease in the capital; he had travelled considerably; he was regarded in certain circles as a very rising man. In a world of actors and actresses, of men of science and men of letters, of philosophers and wits, of thinkers and triflers, he passed for brilliantly accomplished—destined to great things. He was supposed to be an ardent advocate of the rights and claims of the people—rights and claims which it was daringly popular to talk about and to recognise. His ready meridional flow of speech, his easily fired imagination, his swiftly roused, slightly meaningless warmth of words, all profoundly impressed an easily impressionable audience. Then he was very good-looking. A portrait of him exists by Carmontelle, the dramatist and painter. The young count is represented in the company of Montbarré, listening to the minister with his sword at his side, seated across a chair, with one arm hanging on the back, while his fine profile, his bright eye, the magnificence of his dress, and the elegant nonchalance of his bearing, says de Goncourt, make a perfect portrait of a graceful courtier. He had been Madame de Saint-Huberty's lover for some five years before he came at all conspicuously before the political world by his very revolutionary 'Memoirs on the States-General.'

Luckless, unreliable d'Antraigues was perhaps the most foolishly feather-headed gentleman who ever came from Languedoc. We may meet with him again, it may be once or twice, but we may as well glance over the rest of his unlovely career now, and say good-bye to him. He belonged to that strange, perplexing, impulsive, imaginative, unreliable breed which has enriched modern literature with a Numa Roumestan and a Tartarin de Tarascon. We should prefer that he might linger in our memory—if he lingered there at all—as the sentimental lover of the Saint-Huberty, addressing his opera-house deity in the high-flown sentimentalisms of Rousseau, and as the eloquent champion of popular rights, but that is unhappily not possible. He was a renegade and turn-coat; the moment he found himself among the noble order of the States-General, he swung round upon the political circle and became the impassioned, we might say the vulgarly impassioned, champion of the Old Order and all its works and ways. We need not accuse him of being grossly insincere in his conversion. Such a feather-head had no real principles, no real opinions. He was swept away by the impulse of the moment, the emotion of the hour; he had never been true to a friend, man or woman; he could not be true to any cause. As it had stimulated his excitable southern imagination to pose as the champion of an oppressed people, so in the heated atmosphere of the noble chamber it pleased him to play at serving an assailed monarchy, and lending his bright eloquence to the cause of an ancient nobility.

He was intoxicated by the flow of his own words, by his own cheap tinselled ideas, by his conviction that he was a great statesman. It was certainly in an evil day for the nobility of France and the supporters of the Old Order when they came to have such a champion. It is, however, consolatory to reflect that d'Antraigues rendered better service to the cause of liberty by his opposition to it than he could ever have rendered it by his support. His renegade popularity was of brief duration. It is written concerning him that he will presently emigrate, that he will marry the Saint-Huberty, that he will drift from European Court to European Court, offering his worthless services against his own country. He will become member of the Russian Legation at Dresden, and betray the secret papers of his master the Emperor Alexander to England. He will be regarded by royalists and émigrés as le beau conjuré, and considered as a kind of Royalist Marat, ready on the return of royalism to ask for four hundred thousand heads. He will be reported, if not believed, to have accused himself with pride of getting rid of sympathisers with the Revolution by poison. He will settle down in England, near London, at Barnes Terrace. He will write doleful and pitiful complaints against his wife, and maundering regrets for his marriage. He and she will finally perish by the knife of an assassin, a dismissed servant and suspected spy, Lorenzo the Piedmontese, who killed himself after the double murder. He and she will lie together in an English grave, somewhere in the grey St. Pancras region. Could there be a more dismal, more tragic ending for two lives that had begun so brightly?

CHAPTER XXXVII

DRIFTING

STILL the slow debates dragged on; still Bailly made his unceasing, unsuccessful efforts to see the King; still met the commissioners in conference. On June 3 the Nobles wasted time in profitless and purposeless investigations into the custom of deciding by order in the most distant days. They made a brave show of pedantry in citing capitularies of Charlemagne and a letter of Hincmar, 'De Ordine Palatii,' in discussing the existence of orders among the Franks of the time of Tacitus, and in wrangling over the term 'Commons' as applied to the Third Estate. In this apparent deadlock Necker developed a plan and produced it on June 4. He proposed that each order should verify separately its own powers, that contested points should be brought before the commissioners of the three orders, and that in any case of final disagreement the matter should be left to the judgment of the King, a judgment without appeal. On June 5, the Clergy decided to accept the Necker proposal. If the Nobility had been as astute as the

Clergy, and had acted as they acted, the Third Estate would have been caught in a very ingenious trap. But, luckily for the Third Estate and the cause it represented, the Nobles, guided by such spirits as d'Antraigues, Cazalès, d'Eprémesnil, and their kind, were less politic. They declined to accept a proposal, fashioned, had they but been wise enough to know it, entirely in their interests—declined to accept it except with amendments of a kind which the Third Estate was not likely to tolerate. Indeed, the Third Estate, long tolerant, was growing desperately impatient. On June 5 an indignant deputy proposed boldly what no doubt many were desiring, that the Third Estate should have done with temporizing for good and all, and should form themselves at once into a National Assembly. Mirabeau once more rose to the situation, dominated and directed the fluctuant assembly. All the efforts of the ministers, he declared, had been directed to sowing the seeds of division, while they pretended to preach union. Forced against their wills to convoke the States-General, they hoped by dividing them and setting them against each other to minimize their power, and to reduce them to the necessity of accepting the ministry as the final arbiter of their differences. They should not hide from themselves, he said, that the verification of powers prejudged the question of the manner of voting, since to verify the powers was in itself to deliberate upon the legality or illegality of those same powers. Since it was the same question, by what right could any tribunal whatever, other than the States-General, dare to decide in this particular? He wound up by declaring that to adopt the proposals of the royal commissioners would strike at the rights of the nation, and wound alike justice and expediency. It would paralyse with the chill of death the National Assembly before it had even manifested its existtence, and it would destroy the last hope of the nation. It was finally decided, by four hundred votes to twenty-six, that the Third Estate would not consider the ministerial proposals until after the close of the conferences.

On June 5, Bailly had announced to the Third Estate that he had been unsuccessful in his efforts to obtain an audience of the King and Queen, and he had proposed to the Commons that they should resolve to go as a body to sprinkle holy water upon the body of the dead Dauphin. This proposal was carried unanimously. Now, on June 6, Bailly was able to announce to the Third Estate that the King had at last consented to receive the long-deferred deputation, would, in fact, receive it that very day. Received the deputation accordingly was, though only to the number of twenty members, a smaller number than the Commons had originally proposed to send. The Commons deputation was composed of the following deputies: Bailly, Redon, Thouret, Bouillote, Chapelier, Volney, Target, d'Ambézieux, Rabaud - Saint - Étienne, de Luze,

Milscent, Tronchet, Ducellier, Prévôt, Mounier, Mirabeau, Lebrun, Legrand, Aucler, Descottes, Mathieu de Rondeville, Pélisson. The twenty were solemnly received by the afflicted King. The antique ceremonies of abasement which the Keeper of the Seals had talked over earlier with Bailly were, most wisely, not insisted upon. The Keeper of the Seals had suggested to Bailly that it certainly was the ancient usage for such an individual as an orator of the Third Estate to speak to his King on his knees. 'We do not wish, of course,' said the Keeper of the Seals, 'to insist upon an old ceremony which might wound the feelings of the Third Estate, but still, if the King wished it——' 'And how if twenty-five millions of men do not wish it?' Bailly boldly interrupted, after which no more was heard of the ancient usage.

Now, at last, without kneeling, the Commons deputation got into the royal presence. Now the bland, weak face of the King could survey, among those twenty men who trod gravely at Bailly's heels, with other notable faces the face most notable of all, and probably most distasteful to him of all, the face of Mirabeau. In that face no doubt Louis thought he saw the most dangerous enemy of the monarchy; only a little while and that face shall be thought of as belonging to the best friend of the monarchy. While such speculations as might be were passing through the muddled, angry, afflicted, royal mind, Dean Bailly gravely read the long-prepared address, to which he had neatly tacked a little condoling sentence about the poor dead Dauphin. The King then, having to say something, said as little as possible. He accepted with a cold satisfaction the expressions of devotion and attachment of the Third Estate. He assured them that all the orders of the States-General had an equal claim upon his goodness. He finally, with an undertone of menace, advised them above all things to second promptly, wisely, and peacefully the accomplishment of the good which the sovereign so anxiously desired to do for his people, and which the people no less anxiously and confidently expected from him. With these words the King dismissed the deputation, convinced, no doubt, that in uttering the words set down for him he had played a very statesmanlike part indeed. The deputation returned immediately to the Salle des Menus to give an account of their interview.

That June 6 was to be an eventful day in the Commons' Chamber. Bailly and his twenty colleagues had scarcely returned from the royal presence when a deputation arrived from the Clergy with a very remarkable proposition. The Clergy had been busy in their chamber that same morning. Decoulmiers, curé of Abbecourt, had moved the hearts of all his hearers by a pathetic harangue on the poverty of the people and the scarcity of grain. Fired by a somewhat tardy sympathy with the sufferings of the poor, the Clergy resolved to petition the King to order the strictest investigation in order to discover the monopolisers of the corn that belongs to the country. They further resolved to send a deputation to the Third Estate, calling upon the Commons to join with them in a conference having for its aim and object the alleviation of the popular suffering due to the scarcity of food.

.Here was a trap with a vengeance, and one of the most ingenious kind. The prelate who held up in the eyes of the Third Estate and the thronged benches of spectators a horrible hunch of black bread, and asked them with a tearful voice to look upon the food of the peasant, had calculated very skilfully upon the result of his dramatic appeal. If the Assembly yielded to the appeal, and took action of the kind demanded, it would by so doing practically sanction that very separation of the orders against which it had striven so long and so patiently. If, on the other hand, it rejected the appeal now made to it, it afforded its enemies the opportunity of saying that it set a technical and legal question far above the well-being of the people it pretended to represent.

The Third Estate parried this subtle stroke very skilfully. Bailly, as dean, replied to the deputation, that the ardent wish of the representatives of the people was to come to the people's help, and that in the action of the Clergy they hailed a hope of that speedy union without which the public misfortunes could only increase. · As soon as the deputation had withdrawn, carrying with them this craftily qualified reply, a vehement debate arose. Populus, a comparatively obscure member, a lawyer from Bourg-en-Bresse, declared energetically that the action of the Clergy was merely a most insidious political move. A member still more obscure followed Populus in a maiden speech. The new speaker was almost unknown in the Assembly: his appearance was not of a kind to attract. A face deadly pale, veins of a greenish hue, insignificant features, a sinister expression, an uneasy unwillingness to look anyone straight in the face, a continual and painful winking of the eyes, an almost childish nervousness which made him tremble like a leaf on rising to address the Assembly, such were the most conspicuous characteristics of the new speaker. But if the appearance of the man was insignificant, the words were full of significance; if the expression of the face was repellent, the expression of his thoughts captivated the audience; if the manner was nervous, the matter was bold, daring, and decisive.

'Let the Clergy,' he said, 'if they were indeed so impatient to solace the sufferings of the people, come into that hall and ally themselves to the friends of the people. Let them retard no longer by meaningless delays the duty of the Third Estate. Let them no longer seek by paltry devices to turn the Commons from the resolutions they had adopted. Nay, more, and better still, let them remember that the primitive privileges, the ancient canons of the

Church justify the sale even of the sacred vases in so excellent a cause. Let them, as ministers of religion and worthy imitators of their great Master, renounce the luxury which environs them. Let them put aside that pomp which is only an insult to poverty. Let them return to the modesty of their origin. Let them dismiss the stately servants who escort them. Let them sell their splendid equipages and convert this vile superfluity into food for the poor.' This energetic speech was received with a general murmur of the most flattering approval. Everyone was eager to know who the young orator was who had so adroitly seized upon arguments so skilful: nobody seemed to be aware who the orator was. It was not until some minutes of eager inquiry that men began to pass from mouth to mouth, through the body of the hall and all along the galleries, the name of Robespierre. The young Arras lawyer had made his first appeal to popular favour, and had not made it in vain. It is curious to note that Robespierre was so completely unknown at this time that his name does not appear in the columns of the 'Moniteur' which records the debate of June 6. A fragment of his speech is indeed given, but it is set down by the perplexed reporter or recorder to a mysterious and meaningless 'N———.' The speech is not mentioned at all in Buchez and Roux' 'Histoire Parlementaire,' and even the excellent 'Archives Parlementaires' only follow the 'Moniteur' in according it to a nameless speaker. Fortunately, however, the fact is recorded and a fuller summary of the speech given by Etienne Dumont of Geneva, the Protestant pastor who was the friend of Bentham, of Romilly, and of Mirabeau. He was present at the sitting of the 6th of June and described the impression it produced upon its hearers.

Malouet rose in support of the motion of Populus, that the Clergy should be invited at once to join the Third Estate in the Salle des Menus. The discussion was interrupted by the arrival of a deputation from the Nobles informing the Third Estate of the determination to which they had arrived with regard to the Necker proposal. The Third Estate gravely assured the deputation that its information would be duly considered, whereupon the deputation withdrew, and the debate upon the proposal of the Clergy continued. It was finally decided to send this message to the Clergy: 'Swayed by the same duties as you, touched even to tears by the public sorrows, we entreat you, we conjure you to join us at this very moment in the common hall, in order to consider the means of ameliorating those sorrows.'

CHAPTER XXXVIII

THE TENTH OF JUNE

IN all constitutional movements, in all tentative agitations, there comes a critical moment when the irresolute becomes resolute, when inertia becomes action, when a number of scattered forces become homogeneous, and union arises out of chaos. June 10, 1789, was such a critical moment in the history of the French Revolution. Up to that time, if we anticipate and amplify a simile of Sieyès, the new ship of state, the Tiers État, had been rocking meaninglessly at her moorings, and in the gathering storm there seemed every prospect that she might be wrecked while riding at anchor and actually in port. But with June 10 came Sieyès and his simile. 'Let us cut the cable,' he said, 'it is time.' And he proceeded to cut the cable, and set the ship free for her famous voyage and her amazing shipwrecks, a voyage and shipwrecks which that adventurous constitutional mariner Sieyès shall survive and sorrow over.

The Third Estate had fought hard for the true rights of the States-General. It had battled for the common scrutiny and the common vote. It had found leagued against it the overt hostility of the noble order, the covert animosity of the Court, the vacillations and chicanery of the clerical order. The conferences had come to nothing. The Commons were face to face with a tremendous alternative—either to yield ignominiously or to persevere in what might almost seem a desperate course. As was natural, it was Mirabeau who helped to decide the action of the Third Estate. Scarcely had the Commons assembled on June 10 when he rose and called the attention of the Assembly to the grave danger involved in further delay. There was, he believed, a member of the Third Estate, a deputy of one of the Paris divisions, who had a very important proposal to make to the Third Estate, and he solicited the best attention of the Commons to that proposal. Naturally the Commons, who, as a body, were beginning to regard Mirabeau as their natural leader, were only too eager to listen to any proposal which came to them thus heralded. Mirabeau sat down, and the Abbé Sieyès arose. This was Sieyès' first appearance before the Commons; this was Sieyès' first speech, it was his first decisive step in public life. He naturally addressed a favourable audience. His pamphlet was in every man's mind, in every man's hand, that famous pamphlet whose initial question was in every man's mouth. 'What is the Third Estate? Everything. What has it been till now in the body politic? Nothing.'

The priest against his will who had so long abstained from preaching or confessing, who had devoted his hours to the study of philosophy and the laws of applied politics, was well commended in the eyes of the expectant Commons; the big proposal he had to make was listened to with the greatest enthusiasm.

In brief, this proposal was that the first two orders should be immediately summoned to join the Commons, that they should be informed that the call of the constituencies would be made in an hour, and that the members of either of the orders who did not obey the summons would be condemned by default. Here was a serious, a daring proposal. It fired the Assembly with enthusiasm. After a debate prolonged to an evening sitting, the proposal of Sieyès was accepted with some slight modifications. The next day, June 11, being a religious holiday, the Third Estate did not meet, but we may note, significantly enough, that a hundred curés of the clerical chamber assembled together, and solemnly agreed that, without waiting for the decision of their body, they would unite with the Third Estate for the common verification of powers. On the following day, Friday, June 12, the Third Estate assembled, and proceeded to carry into effect its resolution of the day before yesterday. It sent two deputations, one to the Nobility and one to the Clergy, calling upon them to join the Third Estate in the Common Hall, and proceed to the calling of the constituencies and the verification of powers. To this summons the Clergy responded, with more or less periphrase, that they would think about it. To this summons the Nobles in their turn responded, also with more or less periphrase, that they would think about it. The reply in the case of the Clergy implied a certain amount of uncertainty. The Nobles were not in the least uncertain. They intended to adhere to their original resolution.

The Third Estate occupied itself for a while in discussing an address to the King. A proposal of Barnave's carried the day over a proposal of Malouet's, which was too much sugared with compliments to please the taste of an Assembly that was rapidly passing out of its political childhood. Barnave put the case of the Commons with great strength and directness. He threw the blame of the defeated project of conciliation entirely upon the shoulders of the Nobility. There was nothing left, he contended, for the Commons to do save to get to work as speedily as possible without losing any further time in vain discussions. He wound up by requesting the King with a polite firmness to allow the Dean of the Third Estate an interview with his sacred person, in order that an account of the determination and the action of the Commons might be submitted to him. This address disposed of, the Third Estate began to set to work in good earnest. Upon the motion of one of the Paris deputies, Desmeuniers, a man of letters, who had at one time been private secretary to the Count de Provence, it was resolved to proceed at once to calling over the roll of the constituencies. Each deputy, as his constituency was called, was to submit his powers to the bureau to be registered. The machinery was fairly in motion at last; but on this first day no single representative of the two higher orders put in an appearance at the Salle des Menus. The hundred Clergy were evidently held in check.

The political machine was now in working order. It was, in fact, actually working. It only needed that important appendage of all machines, political or other—a name. On June 15 Sieyès proposed that it should be styled the Assembly of Known and Verified Representatives of the French Nation. Mirabeau proposed simply, Representatives of the French People. Mounier proposed, ' Majority deliberating in the absence of the Minority.' A deputy from Vendôme, to whom nobody paid any attention, suggested that the Assembly should consist of ' Representatives of their Constituents.' Pison du Galland, a well-esteemed Grenoble lawyer, whom destiny will preserve for a peaceful and dignified ending as a judge at Grenoble, had a notion that the title of all titles was 'Active and Legitimate Assembly of the Representatives of the French Nation.' Legrand struck well in the centre of the speculative target with the happy and simple suggestion that they should call themselves ' National Assembly.' Supplementary to this question of the nomenclature, and really more important, was the question of the authority of the body. Should the King have a veto or no? Mirabeau protested passionately in favour of a royal right of veto: 'I believe the veto of the King to be so necessary that I would rather live in Constantinople than in France if he had it not.' Camus, the Aristotelian scholar, the learned in ecclesiastical law, pertinently asked if any royal veto could prevent the Assembly from being what it was?

The protracted debate dragged on till the midnight of June 16. The later scenes were stormy. The vast majority of the Assembly were in favour of coming to a vote at once, of constituting themselves a National Assembly before the next morning dawned. But a minority was opposed—a very decided, persistent minority, some hundred deputies in all, headed by prudent Malouet, who fought vigorously against an immediate decision. With cries, protests, noisy interruptions of all kinds, they prevented the appeal by name, much to the indignation of the spectators. One of these was so excited by the scene that he ran from his place to show his disapproval of the action of Malouet by taking him angrily by the collar. The fiery citizen made his escape successfully after this astonishing breach of Parliamentary decorum. In the midst of all the hubbub, the Assembly as a body preserved its dignity. Strongly patient, it was content to wait until the warring minority had worn itself out in clamorous interruptions. At midnight, when the tumult was somewhat abated, when three of the deputies had withdrawn, when the composed majority found itself in tranquil possession of the hall, Gautier de Biauzat urged that so important a resolution should be carried in the full light of day, under the eyes of the whole nation. Biauzat was a sensible man, a Moderate Liberal, a lawyer at Clermont-Ferrand, for whom fate reserved a peaceful ending as a Councillor of State in the year of Waterloo. 'I am ready,' he declared, 'to vote that we should constitute ourselves a National Assembly, but this is not the hour. To-morrow I will be ready to sign that vote with my blood.' His suggestion was accepted. The Third Estate, after its Parliamentary baptism of fire, rose at one in the morning.

CHAPTER XXXIX

THE SEVENTEENTH OF JUNE

ON the morning of June 17 the Third Estate met again for the last time as a separate, disorganized order. A vast throng of spectators lined the hal. to witness the solemn celebration, the thought of which was in all men's minds, comment on which was in all men's mouths. For a moment, indeed, it seemed as if the daring deed would be again delayed. A message came to Bailly, summoning him to the Chancellery to receive a letter from the King. The royal letter was a warning to the audacious Third Estate, reminding it that it could do nothing without the association of the other orders. Such a letter at such a moment might have seriously interfered with the determination arrived at. The hundred malcontents might feel themselves stimulated to fresh efforts in the direction of delay, the less enthusiastic members of the majority might be either chilled or alarmed into inaction. Under the circumstances, the Assembly acted wisely in avoiding all possible dissension by adjourning the consideration of the royal letter, and by forbidding its dean to leave the hall until the conclusion of the sitting. By a vote of four hundred and ninety-one to ninety—by a clear majority, that is to say, of more than four hundred members—the amended motion of Sieyès was carried, and the chaotic Third Estate was metamorphosed into the ordered and organized 'National Assembly.'

It is well, it is even essential, here to read and to record the words in which the newly created Assembly, through the mouth of Sieyès, formulated its right to existence :

'The Assembly, deliberating after the verification of powers, recognises that it is already composed of representatives directly delegated by at least ninety-six hundredths of the nation. Such a large body of delegated authority cannot rest idle in consequence of the absence of the deputies of certain constituencies or of certain classes of citizens, for the absent who have been duly summoned cannot prevent those who are present from exercising the fulness of their rights, more especially when the exercise of those rights has become a pressing and imperious duty.

' Moreover, since it only belongs to duly verified representatives to carry out the popular wish, and since all the verified representatives ought to be in this Assembly, it is further indispensable to conclude that to it, and to it alone, belongs the right to interpret and to represent the general will of the nation.

' There cannot exist between the Throne and the Assembly any veto, any negative power.

' The Assembly declares, then, that the common work of national restoration can and should be begun without delay by the deputies present, and that they ought to carry it on without interruption as without obstacle.

' The denomination of " National Assembly " is the only title that belongs to the Assembly in the existing condition of things, whether because the members who compose it are the only representatives legitimately and publicly known and verified, whether because they are delegated by well-nigh the entire sum of the nation, or whether, finally, because, the representation being one and indivisible, no deputy, in whatever order or class he may be chosen, has the right to exercise his functions separately from this Assembly.

' The Assembly will never lose its hope of uniting in its bosom all the deputies who are absent to-day ; it will not cease to call upon them to fulfil the obligation imposed upon them of aiding in the work of the States-General. The Assembly declares in advance that, at whatever moment the absent deputies may present themselves in the session that is about to open, it will rejoice to receive them, and to allow them, after due verification of their powers, to share in the great labours which should bring about the regeneration of France.

' The National Assembly resolves that the reasons

for this present resolution shall be at once set forth in order that they may be presented to the King and to the nation.'

The Assembly, having thus formulated its act of birth, proceeded to swear a solemn oath : ' We swear and promise to fulfil with zeal and fidelity the duties which devolve upon us.' This oath, sworn by some six hundred deputies in the presence of some four thousand spectators, might well 'excite the greatest emotion, and form an august and imposing ceremony.' The echo of that oath would ring very unpleasantly in the ears of the King, still more unpleasantly in the ears of the Queen, most unpleasantly of all in the ears of the Polignac faction and the intriguers of the Bull's Eye. Its echo, too, would reach to those two chambers where the Clergy and the Nobility were so busily engaged in doing nothing, and would arouse most unpleasant emotions there—envy, hatred, malice, and all uncharitableness, but especially and most unpleasantly a sense of fear. The echo of that oath would resound all over France, and tell the long-silent, long-suffering millions that they need suffer and be silent no longer, for they have found a voice at last, and a loud one, that princes, and prelates, and even kings must perforce listen to. The fame of this great oath has been much obscured by the yet greater fame and moment of another oath, which has yet to be taken very soon under conditions even more urgent, more magnificently dramatic than these. But the memory of that solemn conjuration should be kept green, for it inaugurated the Revolution.

In order to prove their existence as an organized and constitutional body, the newly born National Assembly proceeded at once to certain enactments. It immediately took over to itself the right of taxation. The existing taxes it declared to be illegally levied, as they had not been agreed to or accepted by the nation. Nevertheless, and for the moment, it consented to ratify their levy provisionally, until—and here came in a very happy diplomatic stroke—'the first separation of this Assembly, from whatever cause it may arrive.' 'After that day the National Assembly orders and decrees that all levy of imposts and taxes of all kinds, which shall not have been duly, formally, and freely accorded by the Assembly, shall cease entirely in all the provinces of the realm.' By this daring act the Assembly guarded itself against some despotic stroke, by leaving behind it a freed nation, whose duty and whose interest it would be to carry on the work. To provide against possible bankruptcy, it placed the national creditors under the safeguard and the honour and loyalty of the French nation. It further announced its immediate intention of dealing with the dearth and the public misery. The Assembly having thus established its rights, and entered thus upon the exercise of those rights, sent Camus off post-haste to printer Baudouin at Paris, to have these important resolutions printed without delay, and scattered broadcast over the length and breadth of France. The National Assembly meant business.

So from the most chaotic beginnings the formless, powerless, meaningless Third Estate had grown into a great constitutional assembly, claiming the right to administer the affairs of the State. During all those weary weeks of waiting, of delay, of inertia, the Assembly had been slowly taking shape, slowly, surely growing into being, as in the hands of the Indian juggler the little seed he plants in the soil grows on miraculously into the sapling and the tree. The spectators hardly perceive the process of growth between the sowing of the seed and the existence of the tree; but the process has taken place, the seed has become the sturdy sapling; the Third Estate has become the National Assembly. A modern poetess says of a modern diplomatist, 'that he held his Piedmont up to the light, and she suddenly smiled and was Italy.' In something of the same way it might be said of Sieyès, that he held the Third Estate up to the light, and it suddenly smiled and was France. It was France, indeed, that that National Assembly represented. For all intents and purposes of government, and especially for the great intent and purpose of regeneration of the country, that National Assembly was France. To this amazing, most perplexing conclusion had Necker's easily manipulated Third

Estate arrived, much to Necker's disappointment, and even disgust.

The name of the King in the Sieyès manifesto had evoked loud and enthusiastic cries of 'Long live the King!' in the morning sitting of June 17. At the evening sitting, the King's name came again before the Assembly under less congratulatory conditions. That missive from the monarch which the Assembly had not in the morning allowed Bailly to go for had now come into Bailly's hands, and was by him now read to the Assembly. It was addressed to 'M. Bailly, Dean of the Order of the Third Estate,' and the body of the letter was quite as ill-advised and foolish as its address. After protesting plaintively against the use of the term 'privileged classes,' as applied by the Third Estate to the two other orders, it went on to say that 'the reserve which the order of Nobility had shown in its acquiescence in the overtures made on my part should not have prevented the Third Estate from giving an example of deference;' and wound up by assuring the Third Estate that the more confidence and attachment the Third Estate displayed towards their King, the better they would represent the feeling of the people whom the King loved, and by whom it was his happiness to be beloved. The Assembly took the letter very coolly. Unkingly maunderings of that kind were not likely to delay the onward course of the new constitutional body. Indeed, at that moment the constitutional body proceeded to discuss with great gravity an important question concerning the physical body. Learned Dr. Guillotin, of Paris, was much concerned in his medical mind by the condition of his colleagues in the National Assembly. It seemed to him that the air of a hall breathed, exhaled, and inhaled by some three thousand persons could not possibly be otherwise than bad for his brother-deputies. He thought further that the seats were too closely crowded together for either health or comfort; moreover, the seats, such as they were, were portentously hard and unyielding for sessions of twelve to fourteen hours. He earnestly suggested that they should be forthwith provided with cushions. We of a later time associate the name of learned Dr. Guillotin more with man's thinking apparatus than with man's sitting apparatus. It is gratifying to discover that the mind which devoted itself to the best means of removing the human head could also devote itself to the physical well-being of the other extremity. A grateful Assembly hailed with enthusiasm the suggestions of their scientific colleague, and promptly requested him to preside over all the necessary arrangements for the ventilation of the hall, the better arrangement of the benches, and the due cushioning. All of which good Dr. Guillotin would no doubt have been delighted to do, if only time and fate had permitted. But there were interruptions, interruptions of the most unforeseen kind waiting in the immediate future to interfere with the excellent sanitary intentions of Dr. Guillotin.

Arthur Young has recorded his experience of the Assembly on what he happily calls the 'rich day' of the 15th of June. 'We went immediately,' he says, 'to the hall of the States to secure good seats in the gallery; we found some deputies already there, and a pretty numerous audience collected. The room is too large; none but stentorian lungs or the finest, clearest voices can be heard. However, the very size of the apartment, which admits two thousand people, gave a dignity to the scene. It was indeed an interesting one. The spectacle of the representatives of twenty-five millions of people, just merging from the evils of two hundred years of arbitrary power, and rising to the blessings of a freer constitution, assembled with open doors under the eye of the public, was framed to call into animated feelings every latent spark, every emotion of a liberal bosom. . . . . In regard to their general method of proceeding, there are two circumstances in which they are very deficient: the spectators in the galleries are allowed to interfere in the debates by clapping their hands, and other noisy expressions of approbation: this is grossly indecent; it is also dangerous; for if they are permitted to express approbation, they are, by parity of reason, allowed expressions of dissent; and they may hiss as well as clap; which, it is said, they have sometimes done: this would be, to overrule the debate, and influence the deliberations. Another circumstance is, the want of order among themselves; more than once to-day there were a hundred members on their legs at a time, and M. Bailly absolutely without power to keep order.' Those words of Arthur Young's, which paint so vivid a picture of that new-born, turbulent Assembly, have in them a kind of allegory. All those excited deputies so vehemently striving to be heard at once, were typical of the conflicting theories of national regeneration that came into being with the dawn of political liberty. Those crowded benches where the public sat grimly approving or grimly disapproving, had a significance beyond what Arthur Young discerned. And that description of Bailly, 'absolutely without power to keep order,' seems to be written in words surcharged with prophecy.

CHAPTER XL

TENNIS

On Friday, June 19, 1789, the newly-created National Assembly sought rest from its labours in the serene belief that it was the ruling power in France. That same night the most desperate stroke was resolved upon by its enemies. The King was away at Marly, oscillating feebly between the imperious counsels of the Queen and the prudent commonplaces of Necker. At Versailles, where the popular passion stirred even the courtly air, Necker had more power. He could command from the King a respectful if bored attention. The best to be said for Necker's prudent commonplaces, and indeed it is saying much, is that attention to them might have put off the evil day a little longer. But at Marly the Queen had it her own way. The Polignac influence, the influence of the pitiful blood-princes, the influence of all the evil and all the imbecile counsellors who guided or who followed the Queen, were able to bear upon the weak King with irresistible force. The courtly talk was bloody. The insolent National Assembly must be crushed into the earth from which it sprang. If Versailles, if Paris protested, were there not troops, were there not foreign mercenaries, were there not cannon? Let a gallant King hold his own though he slaughter half his citizens. But the King, if he was not of the stuff of which kings are well made, was not of the stuff out of which scoundrels are well made either. He had not the wit to be wise and follow Necker or do better than Necker. He had not the will to be cruel with his Court, and to choke democracy with its own blood. He adopted a kind of despairing, ridiculous, middle course. He would blow neither hot nor cold; he did, perhaps, the very most foolish thing that under the conditions he possibly could have done. If he did not suppress the National Assembly out of hand, at least he would prevent it from meeting until the royal session of the coming Monday. This brave act was to have two great consequences. It was to humiliate and belittle the overweening Third Estate. It was to prevent the Clergy from uniting with the Third Estate, as the majority of them seemed now ominously inclined to do.

On the night of June 19 the King went through the process which he called making up his mind. On the morning of the next day, in the clear daylight of six o'clock on that summer morning, June 20, 1789, Versailles was placarded with the announcement of the royal session for Monday, and the closing of the Salle des Menus for necessary preparations until that date. To Bailly came an uncourteous letter from Master of Ceremonies de Brézé—uncourteous inasmuch as it should have been written by the King, and not by de Brézé—informing him of the shutting that had taken place, and the sitting that was yet to take place. Bailly, in the face of this astonishing news, displayed an unconquerable coolness, an unconquerable dignity. When the hands of his clock neared the appointed hour of eight, he made his way towards the Salle des Menus, as if nothing had happened, or could happen, to hinder the triumphant course of the National Assembly. It was not a pleasant morning even for a man speeding to an agreeable appointment. It drizzled depressingly with a fine persistent rain: the sky was grey, and most unsummerlike; it seemed as if the very elements were of the courtly faction, and frowned disapproval upon the Third Estate. Under that dismal sky, through that depressing rain, Bailly and a swelling concourse of attendant colleagues picked their way along the muddy streets to the Salle des Menus. At the Salle des Menus, Bailly made as if he would enter as usual, but he was instantly stopped by the sentinels on guard. Then ensued a colloquy between Bailly and the officer in command, while the attendant deputies hung about in groups, and sheltered themselves; those who were most prudent, under dripping umbrellas. The officer in command was reasonably polite, but absolutely peremptory in his refusal. Bailly urged with all the eloquence at his command that the sitting of the National Assembly had been convened, and that the King had no right to intervene. The officer only shook his head and pleaded his orders. Some of the younger deputies in their irritation talked from under their umbrellas of forcing their way into the hall. The officer replied to such menaces by an order to fix bayonets, more chilling than the rain. What was to be done? one deputy asked of another, as they stood there on the sloppy pavement, and peered into each other's faces, pale under the protection of the damp umbrellas. It is hard to be heroic under an umbrella; it is hard for the wet civilian to feel heroic in the face of a taciturn soldiery with fixed bayonets and no respect for persons. Yet those deputies wished to be heroic, and were in fact heroic. While Bailly and one or two others were permitted as a special favour to enter the Salle des Menus and collect the papers of the National Assembly, the indignant deputies, in the midst of a no less indignant populace, discussed, on the Paris Avenue, all manner of proposals. Some were all for hurrying off to Marly, and holding their Assembly under the very windows of the offending King. Others were for going to Paris, a suggestion which met with much popular enthusiasm, and which would have antedated the Revolution by some four weeks. Suddenly, ingenious Dr. Guillotin, ever a man of an alert, inventive mind, said his say. Was there not, he asked, a certain old tennis court in Versailles large enough to offer accommodation, and. considering the weather, agreeable shelter for a considerable body of people? Why should they not proceed in a body to this tennis court, and hold their menaced meeting there? No sooner said than done. Dr. Guillotin has more than one reason for being remembered by history.

Priests of the historic muse might well be pardoned for permitting themselves a certain hyperbolic passion, a certain lighting up and letting off of verbal fireworks over that marvellous session of the Tennis Court. To that ancient, tattered, dilapidated Tennis Court, where princes had played ball unheeded up to yesterday, where cheaply audacious, imbecile princes should feign a desire to play ball tomorrow, to that dusty paradise of nets and rackets, the National Assembly trooped, spurred by indignation, by need of shelter, by the advice of ingenious Dr. Guillotin. One member who was in bad health had to be carried in arms, and lifted about in a chair inside the court. Bailly came, still cool, still dignified, convoying his rescued papers. His immediate friends ranked about him, encouraging and deriving courage. Escorting the deputies and their dean came their masters, the attendant people, furious with the fury of awakened, suddenly slighted democracy, and bearing, as on stormy waters, the National Assembly to its haven and its fate. A few moments more, and the Tennis Court, whose dismal solitude had echoed unheeded that day-dawn, was choked with a mass of men who were making a revolution.

Many pictures have preserved for the curious eyes of later generations the exterior and interior aspect of that Tennis Court. We can see the indignant deputies entering amidst enthusiasm by the lofty door, surmounted by a kind of scroll or scutcheon, and framed in high flat pillars terminating in an arch that is merely decorative. We can see them again inside the court, with its walls painted black, in order that the balls may be seen more distinctly against them; with one wall lower than the rest, from which sprang pillars to support the roof. Here the open space gave light and air to the court; here, too, nets hung to prevent the balls from escaping. Round three sides of the court about midway up the wall projected a kind of pent-house roof structure which has its part in the 'pastime of princes.' There were a few wretched benches scattered here and there. With some difficulty a table was procured, and a commodious chair for Bailly, which, however, he declined to use. It was not for the Dean of the National Assembly, he argued, to sit while the members of the National Assembly stood.

'Ubi bene, ibi patria.' Wherever the delegates of the people were gathered together, there was the National Assembly, whether it were in the golden splendour of the Salle des Menus or the naked austerity of this Tennis Court. Bailly, with his clerks and papers, enshrined himself at a table, persistently cool and dignified. The assembled deputies thronged about him, all their various temperaments displaying themselves freely under the touchstone of that tremendous hour. Mounier was the fortunate man who made himself the mouthpiece of the hour. He proposed to the fluctuant Assembly that they should adopt by oath the declaration that, wherever it might be forced to unite, there was the National Assembly, that nothing could prevent it from continuing its deliberations, and that it should never separate until the completion and establishment of the Constitution. Such was the oath that Mounier proposed. Such was the oath that Mounier, looking back years afterwards, in exile, and in antagonism to the triumphant Revolution, still found it good to have proposed and sworn to. Bailly took the oath first. He was so calm, so collected, that his voice never faltered over the momentous words. His utterance was so loud and clear, that every man in that great audience, and many men outside that great audience, heard him and applauded him. Then followed that memorable scene which a hundred pictures and descriptions have rendered as familiar to most of us as remembered episodes in our own lives. Do we not know that eager rush of deputies concentrating around the table where Bailly stands? Can we not see the six hundred hands uplifted in solemn if slightly theatrical unison, the eager faces lifted up to a heaven beyond the bare roof of the Tennis Court, the eager faces peering down from galleries and apertures? Can we not hear the hubbub of wild voices repeating the oath, the clamour of spectators shrieking a more than Roman applause? It is a great scene, and the very thought of it makes the blood come quicker, though it is exactly a hundred years between this June in which we write and the June when that mighty oath was sworn. It was the greatest game of tennis ever played on earth, and the balls were the crowns, even the heads of kings. Swearing over, the turn came for signing. Every man who had lifted his right hand in support of Mounier's resolution should with the same right hand append his name to the written oath. This the deputies did, working hard, for it took time to inscribe those six hundred names, until four of the clock of that summer afternoon. One man, and one alone, of all that vast crowd had the hardiness or the foolhardiness to oppose the popular impulse. M. Martin d'Auch, of Castelnaudary, in Languedoc, emerged for the first and only time from obscurity to win for himself something of the same kind of fame obtained by the fool who set fire to the Temple of Ephesus. He wrote his name, and wrote after it the word 'opposant,' in token that he would have none of Mounier and Bailly and the wild ways of an audacious democracy. The luckless Languedocian deputy had indeed the courage of his queer opinions. He came very near to paying for his courage and his queer opinions with his life. Many of his colleagues insulted him. Furious spectators denounced him to the crowd outside, who began to yell for his blood, and to brandish weapons. That Languedocian life would not have been worth a copper coin if its owner had passed into the midst of that murderous mob. Bailly, who did not know what was going on, saw the scuffling, heard the clamour. He forced his way into the heart of the throng of furious deputies, leaped upon the table to command attention, and had Martin d'Auch brought before him. Martin d'Auch seems to have been, up to this point, if not cool, at least clear as to his purpose, and dogged in maintaining it. He could not swear to execute acts not sanctioned by the King. Bailly argued with him, reproved him severely even, in the hope 'of satisfying the general discontent.' Outside the clamour was increasing. Bailly ordered M. Martin d'Auch to conduct himself or be conducted away as quickly and quietly as possible. He was carried by the more kindly of his colleagues to a side-door. There, overcome by the whirlwind himself had raised, he fell fainting, and exclaiming, 'This will be my death!' Even at that side-door it would seem that he was only conveyed safely away on the assurances of his escort that his mind was unhinged. M. Boullé was much exercised by his colleague's conduct. 'Why,' he wrote plaintively, 'should this sublime moment be selected by one of our number to dishonour himself?' He goes on to say that 'what is strange is, he had not behaved badly up to that time, and he voted for the Constitution.' He adds: ' His name is now blasted throughout France. And the unfortunate man has children!' Blasted throughout France, indeed. The memory of poor puzzle-headed Martin d'Auch has earned an immortality of infamy for that solitary act of folly or less than folly. In that building which commemorates the Tennis Court oath, and where the names of the illustrious six hundred are duly inscribed, and each encircled by its wreath of honour, the space where the name of Martin d'Auch would come is left blank, as the space for Marino Faliero is left blank in the gallery of the Venetian Doges.

What seems to have most annoyed the deputies was not so much Martin d'Auch's refusal to swear as they had sworn, but his audacity in marring the fair unanimity of the document to which they subscribed by putting his own name thereto and adding the word 'opposant.' Some of the more vehement spirits were for erasing at once alike the name and the qualification. Others, more prudent, and more far-seeing, urged that it should be left upon the document untouched. They argued, or might have argued, that the very exception made the unanimity of the other deputies only the more apparent and the more important. These counsels carried the day, and proved at least that the new Assembly was capable of respecting liberty of opinion and the voice of the smallest minority.

This was the last of Martin d'Auch. I have not learned, I do not know if it is possible to learn, what became of him, bearing that 'name blasted throughout France.' One would like to hear his side of the story, like to learn the motives, clear or confused, which led him, one against so many, to do and dare on that famous day. The minority are always in the right, says the eccentric reformer in one of Henrik Ibsen's comedies. We may be permitted to think with Mounier and Boullé and most other people that the minority of Martin d'Auch was in the wrong in this instance. But his memoirs would be rare reading : his notes on the various phases of the Revolution, if he lived through them and made notes, as full of matter as the meditations of Jacques. The private opinion of a highly respectable 'crank' on that amazing panorama of method and madness, the French Revolution, could not fail to be curious and probably diverting. One may wonder, too, with a touch of pity, what became of those children, luckless bearers of a 'name blasted throughout France.' Did they rejoice in their stubborn old father, or slip away from him, and, later, change the branded name and seek oblivion as respectable Citizen This or Citizen That? Are there descendants still of that resolute irresolute? In all that full, instructive episode of the session of the Tennis Court there is nothing in its way more instructive, more significant, than the story of Martin d'Auch. It is bad to play the part of odd man out when one happens to be in a minority of one against six hundred gentlemen who are engaged, consciously or unconsciously, in making a revolution.

Before the Tennis Court meeting broke up the National Assembly had resolved that, when the meeting of the royal session of the 22nd concluded, the members should remain in the hall, their hall, to continue their deliberations. But the session was still to be delayed. The royal intelligence or lack of intelligence at Marly was being primed by Noble audacity. The Nobility Chamber sent a deputation of forty-three of its members to carry an address to the King, assuring him that the question now concerned him even more than them. He replied in a lofty vein, the mouthpiece of some abler inspiration than his own : ' Patriotism and love for their King have always distinguished the French nobility,' and so forth, and so forth. Louis declared that he expected, with a full confidence in the fidelity of the Nobles, that they would adopt the conciliatory measures with which he, for the good of his people, was busy.

It was not quite easy to see where the conciliation came in. Would that it were possible to have a full, exhaustive, and impartial account of everything that took place at Marly during the momentous hours of that Sunday. Would that we might follow, step by step and thread by thread, all the workings of the courtly plot, all the complications of the courtly intrigues. Whatever the deliberations of the Sunday were, they bore fruit in a further postponement of the royal session. A fresh proclamation put the ceremony off from Monday, the 22nd, to Tuesday, the 23rd. Once more the National Assembly found the doors of the Salle des Menus closed against them; once more they found themselves without a legislative home. They did not again go to the Tennis Court: why, is not absolutely certain; conflicting history offers two reasons. The first, and most dramatic is, that the Count d'Artois, in a fit of more than usually foolish bluster, had retained the court for his own use, intending to divert himself and his friends by playing tennis on the spot where the National Assembly had dared to assert itself. The second story, which is backed by the authority of Bailly, of de Ferrières, of Rabaut Saint-Étienne, and of the 'Two Friends of Liberty,' is that the populace, expecting a second Tennis Court sitting, had crowded into the place to witness the deliberations, and that the deputies did not think there was sufficient space left to them to work in comfort. Whatever the cause, we may be permitted to feel glad that history does not record a second Tennis Court meeting to dim the unique interest of the first. Whatever the cause, the place where they did meet was still more favourable to the fortunes of the Third Estate. The deputies tried to find asylum at the Récollets, but failed, as its members were afraid to commit themselves. But it now seemed that some hundred and forty-nine members of the Clerical Chamber, anxious to join the Third Estate, had taken up their quarters in the Church of St. Louis. The unlucky King's ill-advised delay brought about the very thing most essentially to be avoided by the King's party, the fusion between the clerical and popular orders. In the nave of the Church of St. Louis the National Assembly 'set in their staff.' A table was set for the President and his secretaries. A number of chairs to right and left represented respectively the natural places of the clerical and noble orders. The public were admitted, and the church was soon full. At two o'clock the ecclesiastics, who had assembled in the choir, entered the nave under the guidance of the Archbishops of Vienne and Bordeaux and the Bishops of Rodez, Coutances, and Chartres, and solemnly took their places with the National Assembly. 'The temple of religion,' it was happily said, 'became the temple of the country.' The fusion between the two orders was practically accomplished. A popular picture of the time represents a peasant leaving his plough to grasp the hand of a priest who greets him cordially: 'Touchez-là, Monsieur le curé ; j'savais ben que vous seriais des nôtres,' says the legend. The artist, either carelessly or ironically, probably carelessly, has represented these types of the two orders as offering each other their left hands. Left-handed or right-handed, the salutation had taken place. It would have been better for the King and his courtly counsellors not to have postponed that royal session.

On Tuesday, June 23, however, the royal session did take place. It began with sombre auspices for the Third Estate. Bailly was troubled in his mind by memories of a nocturnal visit from Baron de Menon, the Duke d'Aiguillon, and Count Mathieu de Montmorency, who came with tidings that Necker had broken with the Court and would not attend the session. Revolving many cares in his mind, like pious Æneas, Bailly came to the Salle des Menus to find fresh cares awaiting him. The old, tedious, ill-advised insults were repeated. The deputies of the Third Estate were kept outside the door in driving rain—it rained a good deal that June. The place and the environs were surrounded by a menacing display of armed troops. While the clerical and noble orders were afforded entrance by one door, the Third Estate was kept a long time dancing attendance at another door, until at last Bailly's declaration that the National Assembly would, as one man, bodily take its departure moved even the stolid officialism of M. de Brézé, and the indignant Third Estate came into the hall to find the two other orders seated. Save that the public was not present, the hall wore much the same aspect as it did on that day when the States-General opened. But if the public was not present, neither was Necker. His place lay ominously vacant, giving rise to much wonder. Those who were in the courtly swim knew why. Bailly knew why. The news soon spread to the less learned. Necker had his plan for meeting the difficulties of the situation. He had framed a scheme as ludicrously inefficient as Mrs. Partington's mop and pail, by which a kind of bastard imitation of the English constitutional system was to be grafted on to or superimposed upon most of the old evil system. He was for two Chambers. He was for a principle of voting by which the orders voted together on unimportant and separately upon important matters. He was for an establishment of provincial States or Parliaments. He was for non-publicity of meeting—for everything, in a word, which awakening France just then did not happen at all to want. But, paltry and peddling as Necker's scheme was, it was too much for the King, or rather for the wire-pullers behind the King. The kingly party would have no concessions. The King came down to Versailles on June 23, to meet the mutinous Third Estate, with an elaborate declaration of autocratic bluster. Necker resigned. He was a weak, vain man, incapable of appreciating or dealing with the great occasion, but he could not go with the kingly party. He resigned, and the kingly party blundered on without him.

The King read, with his usual plainness of manner, the speech composed for him. He spoke the despotic language that came so strangely from his lips. He censured the conduct of the Assembly, regarding it only as the order of the Third Estate. He annulled its decrees, enjoined the continuance of the orders, imposed reforms, and determined their limits ; then he enumerated the benefits that kingly condescension allowed.

These were publicity for finance, voting of taxes, and regulation of the expenditure. For this the States will indicate the means, and his Majesty ' would adopt them, if they were compatible with the kingly dignity, and the despatch of the public service.' Having gone so far, the King further condescended to sanction the equality of taxation when the Clergy and the Nobility should be willing to renounce their pecuniary privileges. The dues of property were to be respected, especially tithes, feudal rights, and duties. The King invited the States to seek for and to propose to him means for reconciling the abolition of the lettres de cachet, with the precautions necessary either for protecting the honour of families, or for repressing the commencement of sedition and the like. The States were also to seek the means of reconciling the liberty of the Press with the respect due to religion, the morals, and the honour of the citizens. The King then declared in the most decided manner that he would preserve entire, and without the slightest alteration, the institution of the army. To say that was to say that the plebeian should never attain any grade in the army.

The amiable despot appeared scarcely to appreciate the provoking violence of his speech, for he appeared surprised at the aspect of the Assembly.

When the Nobles ventured to applaud the article consecrating feudal rights, loud voices cried from the Third Estate for silence.

The King, after a moment's pause and astonishment, continued with a grave, intolerable sentence, which flung down the gauntlet to the Assembly, and began the war: 'If you abandon me in so excellent an enterprise, I will, alone, effect the welfare of my people; alone, I shall consider myself as their true representative!' Then he made a bad and foolish ending to a bad and foolish speech: 'I order you, gentlemen, to disperse immediately, and to repair to-morrow morning to the Chambers appropriated to your order, there to resume your sitting.' Having uttered this insane menace, the King left the Chamber, followed by the whole of the Courtly party. The deputies remained alone, looking at each other in a brief composed silence: But the silence was soon broken.

Mirabeau, who with the instinct of the true leader had been more and more asserting himself, rose and said: 'Gentlemen, I admit that what you have just heard might be for the welfare of the country, were it not that the presents of despotism are always dangerous. What is this insulting dictatorship? The pomp of arms, the violation of the national temple are resorted to—to command you to be happy! Who gives this command? Your mandatary. Who makes these imperious laws for you? Your mandatary; he who should rather receive them from you, gentlemen—from us, who are invested with a political and inviolable priesthood; from us, in a word, to whom alone twenty-five millions of men are looking for certain happiness, because it is to be consented to, and given and received by all. But the liberty of your discussions is enchained; a military force surrounds the Assembly! Where are the enemies of the nation? Is Catiline at our gates? I demand, investing yourselves with your dignity, with your legislative power, you enclose yourselves within the religion of your oath. It does not permit you to separate till you have formed a constitution.'

Mirabeau had scarcely ended when the Master of the Ceremonies, de Brézé, entered, and said to the President in a low tone, 'Sir, you heard the King's order!' Bailly seems hardly to have risen to the importance of the occasion. He replied, 'The Assembly adjourned after the royal meeting; I cannot dismiss it till it has deliberated.' Then turning towards his colleagues near him: 'It seems to me that the assembled nation cannot receive any orders.'

That sentence was admirably taken up by Mirabeau, who addressed himself to the Master of the Ceremonies. But if Bailly was weak, Mirabeau was strong. Though he was not in the least entitled to make himself the spokesman of the Assembly, he seized upon the new opportunity. With his powerful and imposing voice, and with terrible dignity, he hurled back these words: 'We have heard the intentions suggested to the King; and you, sir, who can never be his organ to the National Assembly; you, who have here neither place, voice, nor right to speak, you are not a man to remind us of his discourse. Go and tell those who send you, that we are here by the will of the people, and are to be driven hence only by the power of bayonets.'

Brézé was disconcerted, thunderstruck; he felt the power of that new royalty, and, rendering to the one what etiquette commanded for the other, he retired walking backwards, as was the custom before the King. The Court had imagined another way to disperse the States-General—merely to have the hall dismantled, to demolish the amphitheatre and the King's estrade. Workmen accordingly entered, but at one word from the President they stopped, laid down their tools, contemplated with surprise the calm dignity of the Assembly, and became attentive and respectful auditors of a momentous discussion.

A deputy proposed to discuss the King's resolutions on the morrow. He was not listened to. Barnave, the young member for Dauphiné, laid down forcibly the heroic doctrine: 'You have declared what you are; you need no sanction.' Gleizen, the Breton, asked if the sovereign spoke as a master, where he ought to consult. Pétion, Buzot, Garat, Grégoire, spoke with equal energy. 'You are to-day,' added Sieyès calmly, 'what you were yesterday. Let us deliberate.' The Assembly, full of resolution and dignity, began the debate accordingly. On the motion of Camus it was declared: 'That the sitting was but a ministerial act, and that the Assembly persisted in its decrees.' The Assembly next declared, on Mirabeau's proposal, that its members were inviolable; that whoever laid hands on a deputy was a traitor, infamous, and worthy of death.

The battle between the Court and the people had definitely begun. The King was wholly unequal to the occasion. He talked daggers, but he used none. When de Brézé, who came and informed him that the deputies of the Third Estate remained sitting, asked for orders, he walked about for a few minutes, and said at last, in the tone of one tired to death, 'Very well; leave them alone.' That was all he could think of. He had denounced them; had met their resolutions with a formal and autocratic dissolution, and when they still persisted in their course he could only say, with a weary shrug of his shoulders, 'Very well; leave them alone.' But the Queen and the Court were not willing to let them alone, and the next few days witnessed the growth, on the one hand of the Assembly, and on the other of a plot to put that Assembly out of the way for ever.

On June 24 the Clerical Order broke into two. The hundred and forty-nine who sympathized with the Third Estate went from their Hall to the

Commons Hall, while the remainder by a vote of 132 to 118 declared themselves the 'active Assembly of the Clerical Order at the States-General.' They might have as well declared themselves Emperors of the East for all the good it did them. In the Noble Order faction was also at work. Clermont-Tonnerre, the gallant cavalry colonel, the advanced young noble who little dreamed that he would one day vote for veto, support the dictatorship of the King, and die ignominiously by the hands of the crowd, urged the Nobles to join the Third Estate and the dissentient Clergy. Lally Tollendal urged the same thing; but he and those who thought with him were outvoted. In the Commons little happened. The Assembly decreed the establishment of a printing-house at Versailles for the service of the Assembly, and named Baudoin, the Paris deputy, as their printer. Bailly read a letter from Necker thanking the Third Estate for their marks of interest on the previous day. A nominal verification of the powers of the dissentient Clergy took place on the motion of the Archbishop of Vienne, 'in order that they might deliberate in the general assembly of the representatives of the nation.' On the 25th more ecclesiastics came over to the Third Estate, and, more significant still, so did some forty-five of the Nobles, including de Beauharnais, happy in a fair wife from Martinique, who shall yet be an empress; the Duke de la Rochefoucauld, whose coffin shall be broken by a revengeful monarchy more than a generation later; the Duke d'Aiguillon, and, most conspicuous of all, the Duke d'Orleans.

The prince's man, Sillery, the convenient husband of Madame de Genlis, as Mirabeau calls him, pronounced, in the name of all, an inappropriate discourse, such as might have been made by a mediator, an accepted arbiter between the King and the people: 'Let us never lose sight of the respect that we owe to the best of kings. He offers us peace; can we refuse to accept it?' But d'Orleans was rapidly drifting from compromise of the Sillery kind. He was now playing the part, or being made to play the part, of a regular leader. He had a party who regarded him as a head or a figurehead, it is hard to say which, and who had a distinct and defined programme. They wished to bring about the abdication of Louis XVI., and the elevation of the Duke d'Orleans to the throne. The Duke himself, according to some evidence, had no such vaulting ambition, whatever the pushing Saint-Huruge and the pushing Choderlos de Laclos might design for their pleasure-loving puppet.

'The Duke was a man of pleasure,' writes Mrs. Elliott, 'who never could bear trouble or business of any kind, who never read or did anything but amuse himself. I am certain that he never at that time had an idea of mounting the throne, whatever the views of his factious friends might have been. If they could have placed him on the throne of

France, I suppose they hoped to govern him and the country.' Others too besides Mrs. Elliott saw in him only a dissipated weak creature, the tool of daring and desperate men—and women. But he was something more than that.

With such strange allies about him and behind him, d'Orleans was drifting to his doom. His tired bloodshot eyes were fixed, it would seem, upon the crown. They were not far-sighted enough to see what lay beyond. Just at this moment, however, his advent was of great value to the Third Estate. His popularity, however gained, however factitious, was an arm against that menace of armed force which still threatened the Assembly. On this very June 25, after d'Orleans' arrival, Barnave proposed and formed a deputation to the King, to protest against the troops that surrounded the States-General, to ask for their recall, and the free entry of the people to the sittings. It was a timely move on Barnave's part. The people outside were growing fiercely excited at the sight of the soldiers and at the shutting of the doors against them. They might have proceeded to some desperate extremity to try and force an entrance, when Bailly, Clermont-Tonnerre, and the Archbishop of Vienne came to them, and calmed them with the news of Barnave's deputation.

On the 26th a deputation from the electors of Paris came to cheer the Assembly with a commendation of its virtues. There was better cheer still in the advent of Talleyrand-Périgord, Bishop of Autun, to join the Third Estate. Others followed his example, most notably de Juigné, Archbishop of Paris, whose action, said graceful Bailly, added the only crown yet lacking to his virtue. On the 27th the game was up. The King wrote to the Clerical and the Noble Orders, bidding them join their colleagues of the Third Estate. Under protest, the minority of the Clergy and the majority of the Nobles obeyed the royal order. Even in the Commons hall the Nobles still for a while persisted in sitting apart as a special order, with the Duke de Luxembourg at their head; but after a time the distinct seats became confounded, and 'the futile pre-eminences of rank vanished before national authority.' One dogged gentleman indeed, the Baron de Lupé, Noble deputy for Auch, scornful of all compromise, refused to come over. He sat in stubborn and solitary grandeur all by himself in the Chamber of the Nobility, until at last the Court officials shut its doors, and deprived him of his gloomy joy. Even then, however, he was not to be beaten; he made a point of coming daily and walking up and down the corridor outside the Chamber for a certain time each day, an incarnation of the insane obstinacy of his order.

The Duke de Luxembourg made a stately little speech, in which he set forth his sense of duty to his King. Bailly, ever graceful, expressed his joy at the event, and declared that an hour so happy should not be troubled with any work. 'Our sitting should end now.' The sitting did end accordingly, with cries of 'Long live the King,' genuine enough still from all those lips, royalist still, if we except the lips of the Orleanist faction. The Assembly adjourned. The great battle had been fought and won; the three orders were united according to the will of the Third Estate. A careless onlooker might imagine that the struggle was over; that the Saturnian age, long looked for, had arrived. The careless observer would be wrong, as careless observers usually are. The Court had apparently given way, but had only given way to mask its deep revenge; while suspicion, irritation, and triumph had done the one thing that of all others was most deadly to the Courtly party—had alarmed and aroused Paris.

CHAPTER XLI

PARIS AND VERSAILLES

PARIS and Versailles were wild with excitement. Bonfires blazed in the streets, and an enthusiastic populace indulged in wild dances round them, incapable of confining their exultation within more sober limits. In Paris especially the enthusiasm was at its hottest and maddest. Paris had been suspicious, alarmed, almost desperate; it seemed now to have won the day, and gave itself over to a very carnival of exhilaration. It is difficult to form a comprehensive idea of the passion which animated the city. Even those who were present and well able to judge misunderstood the force of events. Gouverneur Morris seemed to think that all was practically at an end. It only remained, he thought, 'to form a constitution, and as the King is extremely timid he will of course surrender at discretion. The existence of the monarchy therefore depends on the moderation of the Assembly. For the rest I think they will soon establish their credit, which, among other things, will bring the exchange between France and foreign nations to be more favourable. If the money of this country is brought into free circulation it, I think, will lower interest everywhere. The sum is immense, and its effects must be commensurate to its activity and mass. At present it lies dead and is poorly supplied by the paper Caisse d'Escompte.'

There was an even keener observer than Morris in Paris. Arthur Young gives a living picture of the activity and excitement of the hour: 'The business going forward at present in the pamphlet shops of Paris is incredible. I went to the Palais Royal to see what new things were published, and to procure a catalogue of all. Every hour produces something new. Thirteen came out to-day, sixteen yesterday, and ninety-two last week. We think sometimes that Debrett's or Stockdale's shops in London are crowded, but they are mere deserts compared to Desein's and some others here, in which one can scarcely squeeze from the door to the counter. The price of printing two years ago was from twenty-seven livres to thirty livres per sheet, but now it is from sixty livres to eighty livres. This spirit of reading political tracts, they say, spreads into the provinces, so that all the presses of France are equally employed. Nineteen-twentieths of these productions are in favour of liberty, and commonly violent against the Clergy and Nobility; I have to-day bespoken many of this description, that have reputation; but inquiring for such as had appeared on the other side of the question, to my astonishment I find there are but two or three that have merit enough to be known. Is it not wonderful, that while the press teems with the most levelling and even seditious principles, that if put into execution would overturn the monarchy, nothing in reply appears, not the least step is taken by the Court to restrain this extreme licentiousness of publication? It is easy to conceive the spirit that must thus be raised among the people. But the coffee-houses in the Palais Royal present yet more singular and astonishing spectacles; they are not only crowded within, but other expectant crowds are at the doors and windows, listening à gorge déployée to certain orators, who from chairs or tables harangue each his little audience : the eagerness with which they are heard, and the thunder of applause they receive for every sentiment of more than common hardiness or violence against the present Government, cannot easily be imagined. I am all amazement at the Ministry permitting such nests and hotbeds of sedition and revolt, which disseminate amongst the people, every hour, principles that by and by must be opposed with vigour, and therefore it seems little short of madness to allow the propagation at present.'

Again he writes : ' The ferment at Paris is beyond conception; ten thousand people have been all this day in the Palais Royal; a full detail of yesterday's proceedings was brought this morning, and read by many apparent readers of little parties, with comments to the people. To my surprise, the King's propositions are received with universal disgust.' He said nothing explicit on the periodical meeting of the States; he declared all the old feudal rights to be retained as property. These, and the change in the balance of representation in the Provincial Assemblies, are the articles that give the greatest offence. But, instead of looking to or hoping for further concessions on these points, in order to make them more consonant to the general wishes, the people seem, with a sort of frenzy, to reject all idea of compromise, and to insist on the necessity of the orders uniting. .... Every hour that passes seems to give the people fresh spirit: the meetings at the Palais Royal are more numerous, more violent, and more assured; and in the Assembly of Electors, chosen for the purpose of sending a deputation to the National Assembly, the language that was talked, by all ranks of people, was nothing less than a revolution in the Government, and the establishment of a free constitution. What they mean by a free constitution is easily understood—a republic; for the doctrine of the times runs every day more and more to that point; yet they profess that the kingdom ought to be a monarchy too, or, at least, that there ought to be a king. In the streets one is stunned by the hawkers of seditious pamphlets, and descriptions of pretended events, that all tend to keep the people equally ignorant and alarmed. The supineness and even stupidity of the Court is without example: the moment demands the greatest decision; and yesterday, while it was actually a question whether he should be a Doge of Venice or a King of France, the King went a-hunting!'

This keen-eyed, keen-witted observer tells us that in these most interesting discussions he found a general ignorance of the principles of government. There was a strange and unaccountable appeal, on the one side, to ideal and visionary rights of nature; and on the other there was no settled plan that could give security to the people for being in future in a much better situation than hitherto—a security absolutely necessary. All the nobility, with the principles of great lords, that he conversed with, he found most disgustingly tenacious of all old rights, however hard they might bear on the people. They would not hear of giving way in the least to the spirit of liberty, beyond the point of paying equal land taxes; which they hold to be all that can with reason be demanded. He weighed the argument on both sides calmly. On the side of the people, it was to be urged that the vices of the old Government made a new system necessary, and that the people could only be put in possession of the blessings of a free government by the firmest measures. But he thought that it could be replied, on the other hand, that the personal character of the King was a just foundation for relying that no measures of actual violence were to be seriously feared. The state of the finances, under any possible regimen, whether of faith or bankruptcy, must secure their existence, at least for time sufficient to secure by negotiation what might be hazarded by violence. ' By driving things to extremities the patriots risk a union between all the other orders of the state, with the parliaments, army, and a great body even of the people, who must disapprove of all extremities : and when to this is added the possibility of involving the kingdom in a civil war, now so familiarly talked of that it is upon the lips of all the world, we must confess that the Commons, if they steadily refuse what is now held out to them, put immense and certain benefits to the chance of fortune, to that hazard which may make posterity curse instead of bless their memories as real patriots, who had nothing in view but the happiness of their country.'

Already the temper of the mob was beginning to grow dangerous. There is a story, perhaps rather a legend, of an unlucky lady, a countess it is said, who ventured to express too audibly in the fermenting regions of the Palais Royal, her disapproval of the Third Estate. Angry hands, chiefly, it is to be hoped, feminine, seized upon the perturbed and protesting countess, a table was sought for eagerly, and found easily—there are always plenty of tables in the Palais Royal—and on this table the unlucky lady was extended, and promptly and publicly whipped. Thus early the national spirit showed itself paternal, or rather maternal, in its chastisement of offenders. This was the first, but not the last, time that aristocratic bodies had to undergo humiliating punishment from the new masters. In another case an old officer was made to go down on his knees humbly in the mud of the Palais Royal, and apologize for some offence against the democratic spirit. Young courtiers who ventured in, thinking that they could swagger it off with high looks and hands on sword-hilts, were soon compelled to beat ignominious retreat, lest worse should come of it. A man suspected of being a spy was literally hounded to death by the mob. All these signs were significant enough of the rising temper of Paris, but their full significance was not appreciated by the Court.

The Courtly party, chafing at their temporary defeat—for temporary they only considered it to be —were raging for revenge. They insisted in their secret conclaves that the only thing to do was to suppress the Assembly, that the Assembly was only to be suppressed by military force, and that the sooner military force was employed the better. If Paris protested, then why not treat Paris as a hostile city, turn against it the swords, the bayonets, the cannon, and the muskets that should have already blotted out the Assembly, and blot out factious opposition in its turn in Paris with a few cavalry charges and a few rounds of cannon shot? That was clearly the thing to do: wear a more or less civil front for the moment, mass troops upon Versailles and Paris, and when the moment came then to work with a will.

The Court was not without means for the perfection of this precious plan. Albert Duruy, in his admirable study of the royal army in 1789, with infinite pains and patience has reconstructed the military machinery of the kingdom at the moment of the revolutionary outbreak. M. Albert Babeau has added to his 'Studies of Social Life under the Old Order' a valuable volume on 'La Vie Militaire'; and M. Ch. L. Chassin's 'L'Armée et la Révolution' contains much information. Much, too, is to be found in the writings of the Bibliophile Jacob. On January 1, 1789, the royal army consisted of three kinds of troops. It is not easy to ascertain precisely the numerical strength of the standing army in 1789. According to the 'État Militaire de la France pour l'Année 1789,' military force comprising the picked men of the Royal Household, the regular troops, and the militia amounted to two hundred and thirty-six thousand men on a peace footing, and two hundred and ninety-five thousand on a war footing; a very respectable muster. On the other hand, Grimoard, in his 'Tableau Historique de la Guerre de la Révolution,' estimates the army of the line at one hundred and sixty-three thousand four hundred and eighty-three men, including the household troops; and Baron Poisson, in his 'L'Armée et la Garde Nationale,' puts forward the round number of one hundred and sixty thousand. That is to say, these two authorities estimate the military strength of France at the eve of the Revolution at a figure very amazingly smaller than the total of the official statistics. At the same time Guibert, in his memoir upon the operations of the council of war, which was published in 1789, estimates the strength of the army on a peace footing at nearly one hundred and eighty thousand men. There is very considerable discrepancy between these figures. The Vicomte de Broc, in his 'Study of France in the Ancien Régime,' adds a further variation by estimating the strength of the regular army in 1789 at one hundred and seventy thousand men, composed of one hundred and twenty-seven thousand infantry, thirty-five thousand cavalry, and eighty-five thousand artillery. But, however these figures disagree, they at least are sufficient to prove that the French Monarchy, at the very moment before the Revolution, was, nominally at least, backed by a decidedly imposing military force. But it was not imposing when contrasted with the military strength of other European states. France had to some degree stood still, while other states were advancing, and now in 1789, Russia, Prussia, and England were more formidable as military powers than the country which in the days of the Sun King had claimed the distinction of being the first military power in Europe. At the same time the situation of France was from a diplomatic point of view exceedingly strong in 1789. The treaty of 1756 enabled her to count on the alliance of Austria, and in consequence Tuscany, of which the Emperor was grand duke; the family compact assured her the support of Spain, Parma, and Naples; the marriages of the two princes of the blood royal, the Count of Provence, and the Count d'Artois, assured her of the sympathy of Sardinia.

The Court party had a man after their own heart to do for them the little business of blotting out the Assembly and, if necessary, of blotting out Paris. This was Victor François, second Duke de Broglie. He was of Italian descent—the family name was Broglio—he had been a gallant soldier of the old school in his day: he was now some seventy years old, obstinate, old-fashioned, wholly unaware that the world had wagged at all since the days of his youth. A soldier was still to him a human machine, able to drill, to march, to shoot and be shot; but with no capacity for thinking, for looking upon the world with critical eyes, for committing the terrible crime of considering whether after all he was bound under all conceivable conditions to obey. Broglie felt sure that the troops were to be relied upon. He had every confidence in himself. D'Artois had every confidence in him. The Queen, unhappily, had every confidence in both. There were plenty of foreign troops coming, daily drawing nearer. Royal-Cravate was at Charenton, Reinach and Diesbach at Sèvres, Nassau at Versailles, Salis-Samade at Issy, the hussars of Bercheny at the Military School; at other stations were Château-vieux, Esterhazy, Rœmer. There were plenty of cannon; the plot was ripening to perfection; all that was to be done was to dismiss Necker, form a good Courtly Ministry, clap the Assembly under lock and key, and shoot down everyone who objected. In vain did Besenval point out to bull-headed Broglie that Paris was dangerously excited. Broglie would listen to no advice. The Parisians were pitiful citizens; Royal-Cravate and the like should teach them a lesson.

Necker himself seems not to have participated at all in this new and extraordinary change in the counsels of the King. He declared positively that he knew nothing of these military movements till it was impossible that they could be concealed from anyone. 'The War Minister,' he says, 'talked of necessary precaution, in consequence of the late seditious appearance at Paris and Versailles, and the explication was natural enough, but could no longer be admitted when Marshal Broglio was called to Court. I could never ascertain,' he adds, 'to what lengths their projects really went. There were secrets upon secrets; and I believe that even the King himself was far from being acquainted with all of them. What was intended was probably to draw the monarch on, as circumstances admitted, to measures of which they durst not at first have spoken to him. Time,' he continues, 'can alone unveil the mystery; with me, above all others, a reserve was maintained, and reasonably, for my indisposition to everything of the kind was decided.'

Necker must have been somewhat easily impressed by the lack of necessary precautions. 'The road,' says Perry, 'between Paris and Versailles at this time resembled a defile through which a vast army was marching. Columns of troops, trains of artillery, baggage waggons, and couriers with despatches, occupied every foot of the way. If Paris resembled a besieged city, Versailles did not less picture a martial camp, in which the palace might be compared to the tent of Darius. The parole and countersign were changed sometimes twice or thrice a day, by way of keeping the soldiers on the alert, and all this time the National Assembly had upon its hand the most important labours of any legislators in any nation.'

It was scarcely surprising if the people, and those who represented or who led the people, began to look with suspicion upon the way in which the Court party were massing troops around Versailles and anigh to Paris. They may well have guessed that the desperate idea had entered into the minds of the Polignacs and Broglies and Besenvals and Vermonts, who represented the royal as opposed to the popular party, to sweep with one wild stroke the new democratic opposition out of existence before the bayonets and the grapeshot of royal troops. Even the democratic leaders had no idea of the way in which the troops were honeycombed by indifference—by disaffection; how little the Court party could really rely upon the one arm to which they trusted for relief from the growing ascendency of the Third Estate.

Yet there were signs too, and significant signs, that all was not well for the Court in the temper of the troops. The soldiers who were in Paris had mixed much with the crowd, had been well treated, talked to, influenced. The Gardes Françaises were more and more in sympathy with the people daily. Châtelet had sent eleven of the guards to prison in the Abbaye for what he considered mutinous conduct. The Palais Royal heard of it; the Palais Royal rose, broke open the Abbaye, and took the prisoners out in triumph. Triumphant Palais Royal then sent a deputation to the National Assembly. The Assembly, sorely puzzled by the turbulence of Paris, discussed the matter for a long time, at last appealed to the King's clemency, and the King, prudently, was clement. The guards, after returning to prison as a formal sign of submission to the law, were set at liberty by the King's order. This was the first popular triumph; it ought to have taught the Court, but could not.

The troops meantime arrived in great numbers: Versailles assumed the aspect of a camp. Paris was encompassed by various bodies of the army, ready to besiege or blockade it as the occasion might require. These vast military preparations, announcing sinister projects, aroused the wrath of Mirabeau. When every deputy feared to speak, in a raised voice, of the concentration of troops, Mirabeau startled them by asking, why were these troops assembled in the vicinity of the National Assembly, and whether the majesty of the people was to be attacked? He demanded that one hundred deputies should instantly bear a petition to the King, requesting the withdrawal of the soldiers. 'What,' said Mirabeau in the course of his speech, 'has been the issue of those declarations and of our respectful behaviour? Already we are surrounded by a multitude of soldiers. More have arrived, are arriving every day. They are hastening hither from all quarters. Thirty-five thousand men are already cantoned in Paris and Versailles, twenty thousand more are expected; they are followed by trains of artillery; spots are marked out for batteries; every communication is secured, every pass is blocked up; our streets, our bridges, our public walks are converted into military stations. Secret orders, precipitate counter-orders are events of public notoriety. In a word, preparations for war strike every eye, and fill every heart with indignation.'

Louis XVI. answered the Assembly roundly and royally, as he conceived royalty. He declared that he alone had to judge the necessity of assembling or dismissing troops. He assured the Assembly that those assembled formed only a precautionary army to prevent disturbances and protect the Assembly. No person could be ignorant, the King declared, of the disorders and the scandalous scenes which had been acted and repeated at Paris and Versailles, before his eyes and before the eyes of the States-General. It was necessary that he should make use of the means which were in his power to restore and maintain order in the capital and the environs. It was one of his principal duties to watch over the public safety. These were the motives which determined him to assemble the troops round Paris. If, however, he artfully suggested, the needful presence of the troops in the neighbourhood of Paris still gave umbrage, he was ready, at the desire of the Assembly, to transfer the States-General to Noyon or to Soissons. In this case he promised to go to Compiègne, in order to maintain the communication which ought to subsist between the Assembly and its king.

Paris was in the greatest excitement; but the Assembly did not seem to understand fully the danger. Guillotin went to Paris to impart a comfortable sense of tranquillity to the assembly of the electors. He assured them that everything was going on excellently, and that Necker was stronger than ever. It would be difficult to find a more fantastic instance of false confidence. That very day, whilst Guillotin was speaking, the Court had struck the stroke which was to herald its victory.

CHAPTER XLII

CAMILLE DESMOULINS

ON July 11, at three o'clock in the afternoon, Necker was seated at table with some guests, when a messenger arrived with a letter from the King. Necker broke the seals, and read to himself with an unmoved countenance the royal order that he should at once, and with all possible secrecy, leave Paris and France. Necker put the letter in his pocket and continued his conversation as if nothing had happened, but as soon as the dinner was over he took his wife aside and told her of his banishment. No thought of disobeying the royal order seems for a moment to have flashed across the mind of Necker. He quietly ordered his carriage, and he and his wife, without a single leave-taking, without even delaying to change their clothes or make any preparations for their journey, without telling their daughter what had happened, set off at once on their flight towards the frontier. Next morning all Paris knew that Necker was disgraced, banished, gone.

The exile of Necker coincides with the first

political appearance of one of the most famous of the revolutionary heroes. Necker's disgrace was Camille Desmoulins' opportunity. All Paris was raging with excitement, at once furious and fearful, longing to do something and not knowing what to do. The Palais Royal was as usual the chief centre of public and political excitement. That day the human hive was thronged and noisy with the hum and buzz of angry voices. All the material for a popular movement raged and fumed there under the tranquil July sky, under the leafy summer of the trees, but there seemed to be no one to turn the moment to account. A mob is a strange helpless, desperate thing, vacillating between the poles of do and do not, waiting for some voice to sum up its secret meaning and direct it in its course. So in the summer heat that great crowd weltered, flowing and eddying, waiting for its voice and hearing none, or rather hearing a babel of voices with no unison in them. Suddenly the crowd found a centre of attraction. A young man, nerved to a kind of prophetic fury by the agitations of the hour, had leaped upon one of the tables of the Café Foy, and was shouting something at the top of his voice. A man who had something definite to say was worth listening to, and the great crowd listened to the lean dark-haired young man, who, with his black eyes blazing with excitement, was shrieking forth a flood of passionate, impetuous speech, and conquering in his fury the stammer which was slightly habitual to his tongue. 'Citizens,' he yelled, sending his voice as far as he could over the sea of staring faces, 'Citizens, you know that the whole nation desired to keep its Necker. Well, I have come from Versailles, Necker is dismissed. That dismissal is the St. Bartholomew's bell of patriots. This evening all the Swiss and German battalions will sally from the Champ de Mars to slaughter us. There is not a moment to lose. We have but one resource—to rush to arms and to wear cockades whereby we may know each other.' So Camille Desmoulins shouted, bubbling with revolutionary thoughts, almost choking with the torrent of his words, wildly incoherent, but pregnant with purpose. The answering yell with which the crowd greeted his proposal told him that he had struck the popular thought. 'What colours shall we wear to rally by?' he went on. 'Will you wear green, the colour of hope, or the blue of Cincinnatus, colour of the liberty of America, and of democracy?' 'Green, green,' the crowd shout uproariously. Camille pinned a green riband to his hat, and a thousand hands tearing at the boughs of the trees fashioned the symbols of cockades from their green leaves. Then Camille, still standing on his table, still dominating with his wild genius the swaying mass, green now with the livery of spring, produced two pistols and held them high in the air. 'My friends,' he cried, 'the police are here, they are watching me, they are playing the spy on me. Very well, it is I,

I, who call my brothers to liberty. But I will not fall living into their power. Let all good citizens do as I do. To arms!' A deafening shout of 'To arms' answered this appeal. Camille, the hero of the hour, the leader of the mob, leaped from his table and led his little army into the streets. Like a living sea the mob of the Palais Royal rushed through the Boulevards, growing larger at every street, at every corner, at every house. Paris was in their hands. They forced the theatres to close as a tribute to the banished Necker; they seized all the busts of Necker and of Orleans that they could find in the shop of sculptor Curtius, and carried them, veiled in black, in Roman triumph through the streets. Camille Desmoulins had made his first bid for fame.

The little Picard town of Guise in the kindly Vermandois was a pleasant place enough for an eager, impressionable boy to be born in, to remember as the cradle of his youth. The undulating plains of the Aisne department are fat and fruitful; in the richer lands along the Oise the farmers of Vervins raise good crops of wheat and rye and barley, of oats and hemp, of flax and hops. The little river Aisne, the larger Somme, water its green meadows, reflect the milky blueness of its skies. It may please us, as it pleases M. Jules Claretie in his charming volume, to imagine the boy Camille wandering by Aisne's waters, a book in his hands, reading and dreaming; or climbing the slope which led to the citadel, pausing for a moment to hearken to some burst of music coming from the church, reciting some verses of Voltaire in front of the chapel, murmuring some mighty lines of Tacitus in the stern face of the citadel.

Guise itself was a fortified town of the third class, with frowning walls that still seemed formidable in the days of Camille Desmoulins' boyhood, but which would be as useful as so much brown paper against modern artillery. The town itself has an old-world air about it, not indeed the old world of the fifteenth or sixteenth century, but the old world of the days when the Revolution was dawning. It was a hard-working, patient, industrious, dignified little town, and it never bore a stranger child than Camille Desmoulins, the 'gamin de génie,' the 'corner-boy of genius' as we may perhaps best translate the term. He was born in the Street of the Great Bridge, hard by the Place of Arms, on March 2, 1760. His father, Jean Benoist Nicolas Desmoulins, was a country lawyer, by no means wealthy, who had risen to the office of 'lieutenant-général civil et criminel au bailliage de Guise'; his mother was Marie Magdeleine Godart, of Wiege village. Camille was the eldest son; there were two other brothers who entered the army, and two sisters, of whom one entered the church and the other lived on until 1838. It is curious to think of a sister of our strange, gifted, wild Camille living on tranquilly into an epoch so different from that in which her brother for a while buffeted so stoutly with destiny.

It was the elder Desmoulins' ambition to educate his son largely, to make him a famous lawyer, to see in him the realization of the dream that old Desmoulins had long ago put aside for himself, the dream of being an advocate at the Parliament of Paris. It did not at first appear as if this revived dream were any too likely to be realized. The studies essential for such a scheme, for the desired success, were not for all comers; they cost money, and the elder Desmoulins had very little money. But luckily—or unluckily, it is hard to say which— one of those useful relatives who seem most appropriate in the domain of comedy came to the rescue. M. de Viefville des Essarts, who had formerly been an advocate of the Paris Parliament, and who was yet in the fulness of time to be Vermandois deputy to the States-General, obtained for Camille a purse at the College of Louis le Grand. Here Camille first fed that extraordinary love for knowledge which was the master passion of his youth; here he first tasted the triumphs of success; here he first sucked the milk of an ideal republicanism; here he first met, and made his friend of, Maximilien Robespierre.

The lovers of an amusing and not perhaps wholly profitless speculation might please their thoughts by fancying what our wild Camille's future might have been if only that useful relative, Viefville des Essarts, had not turned up in the nick of time with his purse at Louis le Grand. Would the wild humours which at times hung about him, as the fogs hung about the marshy places of the Vermandois where he was born, have got the better of him; would he have shocked the little tranquil town more than he did, or served as a soldier like his kin, or settled down after the solid patient pattern of his sire, and made an excellent citizen? Sluggish he could scarcely have ever been; the wild blood that burned in him would have ever and ever said nay to that; but he might have tempered it more to the grave Guise Music. He might—but Viefville des Essarts did turn up; Camille went to Paris, and there is an end to the speculations.

In Paris Camille worked hard, spurred by his indefatigable thirst for knowledge. Every healthy child, says Emerson, is a Greek or a Roman. This young student Camille was devoutly, desperately Roman. The glory of the Roman Republic possessed his spirit with a kind of sibylline enthusiasm. The mighty figures of a high antique republicanism haunted his days and nights. The sonorous periods of Cicero whipped his hot blood to fury; in the gloomy grandeur of Tacitus, in the epic irony of Lucan, he found his hatred of tyranny interpreted for him with the eloquence of the gods. As dear to him as the writings of the classic authors themselves was a book now well-nigh forgotten, then very famous, the 'Révolutions Romaines' of the Abbé

Vertot. In its pages he looked upon the pale phantom of stern Roman virtues, and seemed to enter into spiritual brotherhood with a Brutus or a Gracchus, a Marius or a Cato.

Camille Desmoulins lives for us in the wonderful portrait by Rouillard in the Versailles museum. The dark skin, the dark hair, the dark burning eyes give something almost of a gipsy aspect to the face. It is the face of a child of genius, wayward, erring, brilliant, fantastic, the face of an artist, a visionary, a dreamer of dreams. No more attractive face looks out upon us from the gallery of the past, no more attractive personality passes across the stage of the Revolution. His love for the beautiful Lucile is one of the most romantic stories in history that is so often romantic; among all the women of the revolutionary period her gracious figure is the fondest and the fairest.

CHAPTER XLIII

TWELFTH AND THIRTEENTH OF JULY

ON that same day a serious collision occurred between the people and the troops. According to a picturesque contemporary account the Prince de Lambesc, with a body of German cavalry, rode into the Place Louis Quinze, a spacious square, and, with a menacing attitude, announced by the mouth of two of his trumpeters that he had orders to disperse all groups of citizens who might be assembled on the place, or in the gardens of the Tuileries. An elderly man answered one of the heralds, in a manner which occasioned the trumpeter to ride back to the prince, to tell him that he had been insulted by a citizen to whom he had communicated his highness's pleasure. On this, the prince, in a passion, galloped up to the offending, but unarmed old man, riding over a woman, and striking the object of his revenge with his drawn sword. The circumstance, slight as it may appear in itself, was regarded as an attack upon the citizens of Paris by the military; and the cry of, To arms! To arms! reverberated from street to street, like the repeated claps of thunder amid surrounding hills and woods.

The whole city was in confusion in an instant; a mixture of rage and dismay was on every countenance. A blow had been struck, which was considered as an incentive to a quarrel, that coercive measures of the military might be better justified. A battle must be fought. The play-houses, the churches, and even the shops, were all shut up; workmen ran out of their manufactories with their tools and implements of trade in their hands as weapons of attack or defence, as exigence might require.

It is not easy to be sure of the events of that strange day. It seems pretty certain, however, that the first serious struggle took place on the Place Vendôme, where the bust-bearing mob came against a detachment of Royal-Allemand and a detachment of Dragons-Lorraine. The soldiers charged the crowd, killing and wounding; the crowd, instead of flying, held its own, and forced the troops back to the Place Louis Quinze. It is said that in the scuffle a Savoyard who was carrying the bust of Orleans was wounded by a bayonet-thrust, and a young man who was carrying the bust of Necker was shot dead. The sight of the retreating soldiers startled the Prince de Lambesc. With some confused idea of securing a better military position he charged into the Tuileries Gardens, upsetting in his wild ride a peaceful citizen. The boom of cannon was heard. Startled citizens declared that this was the signal to the legionaries massed round Paris to fall upon the city. The alarm spread in all directions and awoke the most warlike spirit. The Court had expected some such disturbance to arise ; had even counted upon it for the furtherance of the Courtly plan. There were troops massed in the Champ de Mars, waiting for just such an excuse of revolt as this to do their work. But the Courtly plan did not succeed. Those soldiers in the Champ de Mars were as valueless as the painted monsters of a Chinese army.

The French Guards now made their momentous irruption in history. They had been showing a mutinous spirit for some time. They were as bitterly dissatisfied with their present commander, Châtelet, as they had been devoted to his predecessor, Marshal Biron, who had managed them with great skill, and had much increased their efficiency. Châtelet was a man of a martinet spirit, who made himself very unpopular with the men under his command, altering and meddling where alteration and meddling had best been left alone. But even their dislike did not on this very day on which they renounced their allegiance prevent them from saving Châtelet's life from the fury of the mob. The fury of the mob, the courage of the mob, the success of the mob were largely aided by the action that the French Guards took on this memorable day. They now broke loose, advanced at quick time and with fixed bayonets to the Place Louis Quinze, and took their stand between the Tuileries and the Champs Elysées, and drew up in order of battle against the German regiment of the Royal-Allemand. Now was the time to make use of those forces stationed in the Champ de Mars. But somehow those forces showed an unexpected languor, an unexpected dilatoriness. The hours were driving on: evening was beginning to fall before the Swiss could be fairly got to the scene of disturbance. As they came up they were confronted by the Guards in the Champs Elysées with levelled muskets. The Swiss halted, and refused to fire. The officers had no other alternative but to lead their soldiers back to the Champ de Mars.

While all this wild work was going on, Paris was not entirely left without guidance. The pale phantoms of municipal power had indeed no influence, but the electors were still an existing organized body, and in this moment of trial they took the helm judiciously. Very difficult it was to take the helm. The position of the electors was exceedingly perplexing. The Hôtel de Ville, where they assembled, was flooded by a tumultuous mob, shrieking for arms, vociferating wild counsels, raging with incoherent threats. It was a trying time for the electors, into whose hands a power to which they made no pretence was suddenly thrust. Loyal subjects of their King, they naturally hesitated to commit themselves to acts the end of which seemed so uncertain, or to assume an authority to which they had no legal right. When they did decide to take up the authority, it was not so easy to get it either recognised or obeyed. They had to deal not only with an insurgent patriotism; they had to deal too with those who, caring nothing for patriotism, saw in the general disturbance their chance to profit. All the rogues, the vagabonds, the destitute, the desperate, the evilly-disposed from inclination and the evilly-disposed from despair, were out and abroad, and the electors were at their wits' end to keep them in check and preserve the order of the city.

Moleville paints a moving picture of the disorder, fermentation, and alarm that prevailed in the capital during this fearful day. A city taken by storm and delivered up to the soldiers' fury could not present a more dreadful sight. Detachments of cavalry and dragoons made their way through different parts of the town at full gallop to the posts assigned them. Trains of artillery rolled over the pavement with a monstrous noise. Bands of ill-armed ruffians and women, drunk with brandy, ran through the streets like furies, breaking the shops open, and spreading terror everywhere by their howlings, mingled with frequent reports from guns or pistols fired in the air. Many of the barriers were on fire. Thousands of smugglers took advantage of the tumult to hurry in their goods. The alarm bell was ringing in almost all the churches. A great part of the citizens shut themselves up at home, loading their guns, and burying their money, papers, and valuable effects in cellars and gardens. During the night the town was paraded by numerous patrols of citizens of every class, and even of both sexes; for many women were seen on that mad night with muskets or pikes upon their shoulders. Such was Paris, without courts of justice, without police, without a guard, at the mercy of one hundred thousand men, who were wandering wildly in the middle of the night, and for the most part wanting bread. It believed itself on the point of being besieged from without and pillaged from within. It believed that twenty-five thousand soldiers were posted around to blockade it and cut off all supplies of provisions, and that it would be a prey to a starving populace.

If the departure of Necker threw the capital into this state of excitement, it had no less effect at Versailles and in the Assembly. The deputies went early in the morning of July 13 to the Hall of the States. Mounier spoke against the dismissal of the ministers. Lally-Tollendal delivered a lengthy eulogy upon Necker, and joined Mounier in calling upon the King to recall the displaced ministers. A deputy of the nobles, M. de Virieu, even proposed to confirm the resolutions of June 17 by a new oath. M. de Clermont-Tonnerre opposed this as useless; and recalling the obligations already taken by the Assembly, exclaimed, 'We will have the constitution or we will perish!' The discussion had already lasted long, when Guillotin arrived from Paris with a petition entreating the Assembly to aid in establishing a citizen guard. Guillotin gave a terrible description of the crisis in Paris. The Assembly voted two deputations, one to the King, the other to the city. That to the King represented to him the disturbances of the capital, and begged him to direct the removal of the troops, and authorize the establishment of civic guards. The deputation to Paris was only to be sent if the King consented to the request of the Assembly.

The King replied that he could make no alterations in the measures he had taken, that he could not sanction a civic guard, that he was the only judge of what should be done, and that the presence of the deputies at Paris could do no good. The indignant Assembly replied to the royal refusal by a series of stout-hearted and significant declarations. It announced that M. Necker bore with him the regret of the nation. It insisted on the removal of the troops. It reiterated its assertion that no intermediary could exist between the King and the National Assembly. It declared that the ministers and the civil and military agents of authority were responsible for any act contrary to the rights of the nation and the decrees of the Assembly. It maintained that not only the ministers, but the King's counsellors, of whatever rank they might be, were personally responsible for the present misfortunes. It declared that, as the public debt had been placed under the safeguard of the honour and the loyalty of the French people, and as the nation did not refuse to pay the interest thereon, that no power had the right to pronounce the infamous word 'bankruptcy,' and no power had the right to be wanting to the public faith under whatever form and denomination it might be.

After these strong and prudent measures, the Assembly, to preserve its members from all personal violence, declared itself permanent, and named M. de Lafayette vice-president, in order to relieve the respected Archbishop of Vienne, whose age incapacitated him from sitting day and night. The Assembly greatly feared that the Court might seize upon its archives. On the preceding Sunday evening Grégoire, one of the secretaries, had folded up, sealed, and hidden all the papers in a house at Versailles. On Monday he presided for the time, and sustained by his courage the weak-hearted, by reminding them of the Tennis Court, and the words of the Roman, ' Fearless amid the crash of worlds.'

When the morning of July 13 dawned Paris was seething in excitement. The electors in permanent committee formally called upon Flesselles, the Provost of the Merchants, to organize the Paris militia, and the permanent committee rapidly drew up a proclamation, which was posted upon the door of the Hôtel de Ville, authorizing the establishment of a militia. Many of the provincial towns possessed a militia, and the democratic leaders had been eagerly desirous of establishing one in Paris, where it might prove of the most inestimable service to them The militia was to consist of forty-eight thousand citizens, called up by registry of two hundred men each day for three or four days in each of the sixty districts of Paris. These sixty districts were to form sixteen legions, twelve of which were to form four battalions, and the other four three battalions only, named after the quarters of the city from which they were raised. Each battalion was to consist of four companies. Each company was to consist of two hundred men. Every member of the new force was to wear a cockade composed of the colours of the city—red and blue. The staff officers were to have a seat in the permanent committee. The arms given to each man were to be returned to the officers at the end of the service. In default of this the officers were to be answerable for the weapons. The officers were to be appointed by the permanent committee.

The city certainly responded nobly to the demand of the permanent committee. It has been said that the militia was formed almost as soon as the fable described the army of Cadmus to assemble. From all the ends of Paris honest burgesses streamed to the various centres of the sixty districts. It is written that at noon about eighteen thousand had been mustered, and called over on the Place de Grève, before the town-house, with at least three times their number of less regular armed citizens at their backs, who seemed ready to hazard, or even lose, their lives at the first word of command. There were, moreover, a choice band of volunteers, clothed and paid by a society of patriots, on whom the greatest dependence was placed. Thousands of citizens, totally unaccustomed to arms, were soon seen armed at all points, and wearing the red and blue cockade of the new army. The mass of the people now showed themselves the enemies of pillage. They respected property, only took arms, and themselves checked robbery. Some mischief, indeed, took place. The priests of the House of the congregation of St. Lazarus were found by the arms-seeking mob to have corn in their granaries. The mob, with some queer angry memory of famine in their minds, raged over the discovery, ravaged the place, and stupefied themselves with the wine in the cellars. But, on the whole, order was fairly well maintained. Small groups of thieves committing robberies on their own account were promptly haled to the Place de Grève, the common place of execution, and hanged by the ropes which were used to fasten the lanterns. It was this wild justice which first found voice for that terrible cry of 'À la lanterne!' which was yet to ring so often and so ominously through the streets of the transformed city.

It was high time for Paris to arm itself. Every moment during the early hours of that dreadful day Paris expected to see the troops of the King enter the menaced city. Everyone was shrieking for arms, everyone was eager to shoulder a musket or brandish a pike, or, for that matter, to handle some mace, some battle-axe, or two-handed sword, long out of fashion, the rusted property of vanished knights whose bones were dust and whose souls are with the saints, we trust. It was easier to shriek for arms than to get arms. The bewildered committee in the Hôtel de Ville, badgered for arms, were at a loss what to answer. They could only say that if the town had any they could only be obtained through the Provost. The mob replied by bidding them send for the Provost immediately.

The Provost, Flesselles, was on that day summoned to Versailles by the King, and to the Hôtel de Ville by the people. He was a new man, who had only received the office some few weeks before. He was a weak man, wholly unequal to the gravity of the situation. He seems to have thought that a revolution could be allayed with rose-water; that glib phrases, unctuous manners, could soothe down the difficulty. It would have been better for himself if he had gone to Versailles. Possibly he was afraid to refuse the summons of the crowd. Possibly he thought he could better serve the King at Paris. He went to the Hôtel de Ville, and made liberal promises; so many thousand muskets that day; so many more hereafter. He said he had got a promise from a Charleville gunsmith. In the evening Flesselles' chests of arms were delivered at the Hôtel de Ville. When they were opened, however, they were found to be filled with old rags. Naturally the multitude raged with a great rage with the provost. Flesselles declared that he had been himself deceived. To quiet the mob, he sent them to the Carthusian monastery, promising them that they would find arms there. The astounded monks received the raging crowd, took them all over the monastery, and satisfied them that they had not as much as a gun to shoot a crow with.

The people, more irritated than ever, returned with cries of treachery. To pacify them, the electors authorised the districts to manufacture fifty thousand pikes. They were forged with amazing rapidity, but the greatest speed seemed too slow for such an hour. The impatient masses thought of the Garde Meuble on the Place Louis Quinze. There were weapons there indeed, but of a venerable type—old swords, old halberts, old cuirasses. Such as they were, they served the turn of the impatient mob, who speedily distributed to hundreds of eager hands weapons that belonged to the history of France, weapons that were now to play a part in more momentous history. Powder destined for Versailles was coming down the Seine in boats; this was taken possession of, and distributed by an elector, at the grave risk of his life. The cannoneers of the Gardes Françaises brought into the city to swell the general armament a train of their artillery which they had taken from the Gros Caillou Hospital. The people then bethought them of the grand store of guns at the Invalides. The deputies of one district went, the same evening, to Besenval, the commandant, and Sombreuil, the governor of the Hôtel. Besenval promised to write to Versailles about it. Write he did to de Broglie, but he received no answer. Next morning at seven o'clock the mob, headed by Ethis de Corny, of the permanent committee, made a more decided demand, swept into the place, and seized the store of weapons. Paris was bristling with steel.

That night of July 13 was one of the strangest Paris had ever seen. All night long its streets echoed to the tramping of feet of patrols; all night the air rang with the clink of hammer on anvil, where men were forging pikes. All night citizen soldiers, eccentrically armed and eccentrically drilled, held themselves in readiness to fight. All night the permanent committee held the sceptre of authority at the Hôtel de Ville, where Moreau de Saint Méry had once to threaten menacing rapscallions with a blowing up of the whole building with gunpowder before he could reduce them to quiet. All night the Place de Grève was choked with cannon and piles of arms. All night good patriots helped the feeble civic illumination by hanging lamps from their windows. The strangest night Paris had ever seen came and went and heralded the strangest day.

CHAPTER XLIV

THE BASTILLE

WHEN the morning of July 14 dawned, probably nobody in all that distracted, desperately heroic Paris, dreamed that the light of one of the most famous days in the history of mankind was being shed upon the world. Nobody probably dreamed that the Fourteenth of July would be remembered through generation after generation as a sacred day of liberty. Not even fiery young Camille Desmoulins, with his stutter and his patriotism, who occupied himself on July 14 by arming himself with a musket and bayonet, 'quite new,' at the captured Invalides. Not Doctor Marat, concerned no longer with light and electricity, but busy with graver things, and revolving like the pious Æneas many cares in his mind. Not the Sieur Santerre, first of French brewers to employ coke in the roasting of malt, and of whom it shall yet be said, inaccurately, that he ordered drums to beat, to drown the dying speech of a king. There were plenty of men in Paris that day who were prepared to make a bold stand for freedom, and to die with arms in their hands rather than submit to the menaces of a Court prompted by Polignacs, and buttressed by Royal Allemands; but there was no prophet to see that this particular day was to prove the day of days, and all through the fall of a prison.

The mind's eye, cleared and strengthened by much study of old prints, can construct for itself a sufficient picture of the Bastille as it was. When the mob came surging up from Saint-Antoine on that memorable day, they saw for almost the last time the sight which had been familiar to Saint-Antoine for generations and generations. The grey, gaunt, oblong block, with its eight tall towers or buttresses, one at each angle, and two between on each of the longer sides, had cast its daily shadow over Paris for nigh four hundred years. Etienne Marcel, Provost of the Merchants, started it in 1357, when France was still reeling from the defeat at Poictiers, and luckless John lay in the hands of his enemies. In those days it consisted only of a fortified gate. It was made into a fortress by Hugues Aubriot, Provost of Paris, in 1370, under Charles V. Hugues Aubriot was one of the first to experience the capabilities of his Bastille as a prison. He was accused of being overmuch inclined to the Jews, of being overmuch inclined to Jewesses, of being at once a roysterer and a heretic. He was condemned to be burnt alive, but the King's clemency saved him, and substituted imprisonment on bread and water for life. Within the solid walls of his own Bastille the Provost of the

Merchants was first confined. His story is the first chapter in the long chronicle of injustice which had linked itself through the centuries with the name of the Bastille. The last chapter was now reached, and was being read with amazing rapidity by Saint-Antoine.

The story of Hugues Aubriot's career has all the materials in it for melodrama. Aubriot had a standing quarrel with the University of Paris, and with Etienne Guidomare. Guidomare seems to have been a typical student of the time. There was something of Panurge, something of François Villon, something of Abelard, and something of the Admirable Crichton in his composition. Provost Aubriot offended the university on the day of the feast of Lendit in 1377, in September, by interrupting them on their parchment-buying procession to the Plain of St. Denis with a procession of his own, in which a luckless lady of bad character, Agnes Piedeleu by name, was being convoyed through the streets of Paris stark naked to the pillory. The woman, shivering and ashamed, denounced the provost at every street turn as the abettor of the crime for which she was suffering—she was accused of causing the ruin of a young girl—and she called on the students to rescue her. There was very near being a free fight, which was only averted by the discretion of the rector of the university. Hugues Aubriot had student Guidomare arrested on a trumped-up charge of seducing a young girl named Julienne Brulefer, and the student only escaped through King Charles V.'s intercession and clemency. The feud between Aubriot and the university, between the provost and the student, straggled on into the next reign, Charles VI.'s, when Aubriot again arrested Guidomare upon the old charge. Guidomare retaliated by accusing Aubriot of keeping a Jewish mistress. The Jewess gave testimony against Aubriot, and killed herself in open court. Provost Aubriot was doomed to die the death, but the royal mercy changed the sentence to perpetual imprisonment in the Bastille, of which he had laid the first stone, and of which he was the first prisoner. Shortly after he had been clapped into gaol there was a kind of twopenny-halfpenny insurrection in Paris; the mob broke open the Bastille—this was its first siege—and sought to make the ex-provost a captain over them. The released prisoner affected great gratitude, promised to do wonders for them on the morrow, but when the morrow dawned, dismayed insurrection found that it had lost its leader. Aubriot, sufficiently thankful to breathe the free air again without putting his head in peril for his liberators, had slipped out of Paris in the night. He made his way to Dijon in Burgundy, where he was born, and where a little while later he died, and was more or less forgotten. Such is the story: historical or legendary, it is a good story, and inaugurates with sufficient effect the career of the Bastille.

Many strange inmates that Bastille had from the

days of Hugues Aubriot to the days of de Launay. Illustrious and obscure, base and noble, famous throughout the world, or destined to remain for ever a mystery, the denizens of the great keep pass like shadows before us. Larivière and Noviant, ministers of the mad King Charles VI., knew the Bastille, and narrowly escaped death for their supposed share in the burning of the 'Savages.' The two hermits of the order of St. Augustin, who came to Paris to cure the mad king, were lodged in the Bastille for a while as guests until they failed, when they were beheaded. Montagu, convicted of plotting against Charles, went to his death from the Bastille. Pierre des Essarts, his enemy, who died on the scaffold in his turn, held the Bastille when it was besieged by the Burgundians, led by the butcher Caboche. Then came the influence of the English in 1415. The Armagnacs in the Bastille were massacred in 1418. When Henry V. was made regent of France he made his brother Clarence captain of Paris, and put English garrisons in the Bastille, Louvre, and Vincennes. Stout English soldiers lounged at ease in that Bastille which Englishmen afterwards were to help to take. When the French factions united against England, and traitor Michel Laillier opened the gates to Richemont, the English garrison were allowed to march out and embark behind the Louvre. The Duke of Exeter, who succeeded Clarence, killed at Baugy, as Governor of Paris, made Sir John Falstaff governor of the Bastille. Falstaff was succeeded by Lord Willoughby d'Eresby, under whom it was evacuated. Under Louis XI. the Bastille did not want for tenants. It knew d'Haraucourt, Bishop of Verdun; probably Cardinal Balue; certainly Antoine de Chabannes, Count of Dammartin, who actually escaped. It knew Louis de Luxembourg, Count of St. Pol, and Armagnac, Duke of Nemours, who were both executed. Under Francis I. it held Admiral Chabot and his enemy Chancellor Poyet. Under Henry II., Anne du Bourg and Dufaure were imprisoned for Protestantism, and du Bourg was executed. Montgomery and Montmorency were Bastilled by Catherine de' Medici. Under Henry III. the Bastille greeted the monk Poncet, the Archdeacon Rossiers, and our old friend Bussy d'Amboise. Laurent Têtu held the Bastille during the 'Battle of the Barricades,' and surrendered it to de Guise, who handed it over to Bussy Leclerc. Madame de Thou was the first woman imprisoned in the Bastille. It does not seem quite certain whether Brisson the President, whom Bussy Leclerc hanged, and who asked, like Lavoisier, to be allowed to live till he had finished the work he was engaged upon, was in the Bastille. Mayenne compelled Leclerc to surrender the Bastille; he retired to Brussels, and there tranquilly died. Du Bourg l'Espinasse, the successor to Leclerc, refused at first to surrender the Bastille to Henry IV. 'If the King be master of Paris, I am master of the

Bastille,' he asserted sturdily. He was allowed to march out with the honours of war, and Henry entered accompanied by Biron—poor Biron, actually the hero of 'Love's Labour's Lost,' whom grim fate carried there again to his death. The Count of Auvergne's long imprisonment is one of the features of Bastille history.

Jean de Saulx, Viscount of Tavannes, was imprisoned in the Bastille, was exchanged against four ladies, imprisoned again, and finally escaped. Sully threw himself into the Bastille at the death of Henry IV. Condé was imprisoned in the Bastille. La Galigai, wife of the murdered Concini, knew the Bastille. Under Richelieu the place had ever so many prisoners, including old Bassompierre, and ex-governors Vitry and Luxembourg. The Bastille was besieged in 1649 under the Fronde by d'Elbœuf, and surrendered by du Tremblay. De Retz smiled at some talk there was of pulling down the fortress. Mademoiselle was at the Bastille in 1652, firing on the enemy. Danish Rantzau lay his term in the Bastille, and died of dropsy soon after his release. Under Louis XIV., the false Christ Morin was bastilled and burnt. Then came the wild time of the poisoners and sorcerers. Madame de Montespan was accused of attending a mass when naked. People talked much then of indecent masses, of naked women used for altars, black candles burned, and mass said and gospel read backwards, and other nonsense, which, however, helped to keep the Bastille going. M. de Bragelonne was sent to the Bastille in 1663 for gambling in an unprivileged house. Fouquet lay in the Bastille guarded by famous d'Artagnan and his musketeers. Bussy Rabutin in 1665 was imprisoned for the second time for writing the 'Histoire Amoureuse.' Lauzun was clapped in the Bastille for jealousy of Mme. de Monaco. The Bastille knew Marsilly, the English agent, Maupeou, de Rohan. It knew the Man in the Iron Mask, whom Colonel Jung considers to have been one Marcheuille, the chief of a plot against Louis XIV., arrested on the banks of Somme in 1673. A quarrel between Count d'Armagnac and the Duc de Gramont over a horse-race ended in a blow and one night's imprisonment. In 1686 a young Englishwoman was imprisoned for aiding the escape of Protestant children. She escaped herself, we learn, somehow. It would almost seem as if our English dramatist Vanbrugh was in the Bastille for a season. An Englishman named Nelson knew of its hospitality. So like shadows come and go the heroes of the Bastille history: the fanciful may imagine that their grey ghosts flitted on the air on that July 14, and surveyed with ironical satisfaction—if, indeed, as Lamb doubts, ghosts can be ironical—the destruction of their old-time prison-house.

Carlyle, writing at a time when the taking of the Bastille was as recent as the 'Year of Revolution,' 1848, is to us, complains despairingly of the difficulty of his task. 'Could one but, after infinite reading, get to understand so much as the plan of the building.' No such difficulty lies in the student's way to-day. There is a little library of books in existence upon the Bastille; the ambitious scholar can study it in plan and section, and in the Arab phrase know it as well as he knows his own horse. In the year of centenary, and for a twelvemonth before, Paris was amused and entertained by the erection of a sham Bastille, which recalled, though in a changed locality, the terrors and the triumphs of 1789. Perhaps to the imaginative mind that mimic reconstruction of old Paris may bring a little closer the conception of the old Rue Saint-Antoine, and the old Bastille with the little houses and the little shops nestling at its base. It is a picture in little indeed; the lath and plaster and cardboard have not the proportions of the antique stones, so many of which now withstand the wash of the Seine on the Concord Bridge. But we must remember, too, that the Bastille was not really so portentous as it looks in the pictures and engravings of the time. In those pictures, in those engravings, the proportions of the Bastille are amazingly exaggerated—no doubt, as has been suggested, for the sake of enhancing the merit of the victors. The Bastille was in reality not quite so high as the Louvre, and was not half so long as the Louvre colonnade. Its walls were ninety-six French feet high on the exterior, and seventy-three feet internally, and nine feet thick. Its ditches were twenty-three feet lower than the level of the interior courts.

It is sufficiently easy for the revolutionary student to reconstruct the scene of the greatest and shortest siege in history. The grounds of the Bastille lay in the angle formed by the Place Saint-Antoine and the Rue de la Contrescarpe, and extended all along the Rue Saint-Antoine to the point where the Rue des Tournelles abutted on it. This was the point at which the attack took place. The spectator standing at the opening of the Rue des Tournelles saw the two end and three side towers rising high and sullen in front of him. Below to the right, and at right angle to the fortress, was the entrance to the Bastille. Immediately adjoining this gate, and nestling to the outer wall of the Bastille, was a small cluster of shops, and shops continued with intervals all along this low outer wall well down the Rue Saint-Antoine to the Saint-Antoine gate.

Every one of the eight grim towers bore its own name, and its own terror. On the side which looked towards the city were ranged the Tower of the Well, the Tower of Liberty—surely the most ironical baptism—the Tower of La Berthaudière, and the Tower of La Basinière. On the side which flanked the Faubourg of Saint-Antoine were the towers of the Corner, of the Chapel, of the Treasure, and of the Compté. Sully in the spacious days of the fourth Henry had joined the grand arsenal to the

Bastille, which was thus a perfect storehouse of arms, a fact familiar to the popular mind, and much ruminated upon at a moment when arms became essential.

Who first thought of the Bastille; across whose adventurous mind on that July morning did the idea flash of directing the strength of insurgent Paris against the ancient prison? We shall probably never know. The people wanted arms. Wild incoherent schemes of battle with the royal troops in the Champ de Mars, of triumphant march upon Versailles, seethed in unreasoning brains. Cooler and more logical minds thought of defending Paris against possible, against almost inevitable assault, and of arming awakened patriotism as speedily as possible. Under these conditions it was natural that the minds of men should turn to the two great storehouses, or to what they believed to be the two great storehouses, of arms in the city, the Hôtel des Invalides and the Bastille fortress. No man's mind on the morning of July 14 cherished the thought of capturing the Bastille as a great act of patriotic protest. When Saint-Antoine turned to march upon the prison, it had no notion that it was inaugurating a new epoch in history. Saint-Antoine wanted weapons, so did its brother, Saint-Marceau. Saint-Marceau knew that arms were stored in the Invalides. Saint-Antoine believed that arms were stored behind the grey familiar walls of the Bastille. Saint-Marceau naturally and simply went to the

Invalides. Saint-Antoine no less naturally and simply went to the Bastille.

But the determination of Saint-Antoine and others to march upon the Bastille was causing the wildest excitement in the Hôtel de Ville, where the committee of electors were desperately, well-nigh despairingly, deliberating. What, they asked themselves piteously, could an ill-armed, ill-disciplined rabble do against the impregnable Bastille? What could come of any such business but swift, inevitable retribution from the armies that were gathering like eagles around Paris? Still, Bastillism was in the air. Everyone's thoughts turned to the Bastille, inside the Electoral Committee as outside of it. The wildest schemes for its capture were solemnly submitted to the storm-tossed assemblage. One worthy locksmith had the brilliant idea that it was to be taken by the good old Roman plan of the catapult, which by dashing enormous blocks of stone at the Bastille should batter a breach in its wall through which patriotism might rush. The classically-minded locksmith was elbowed aside by M. de la Caussidière, major-general of Parisian militia, who insisted that the Bastille, like all other fortresses, was only to be taken according to the regular and formal rules of military warfare. Ideas as wild, if not wilder, were agitating elsewhere heads as frenzied. Certain of the men of Saint-Antoine had set a captain over them in the person of that brewer Santerre, who had first of Frenchmen employed coke in the roasting of malt, the brewer Santerre whom Johnson had met and talked with when he travelled with the Thrales in Paris in 1775. He was now engaged in turning the scientific side of his mind upon the question of the moment. Scientific Santerre thought that an ingenious blend of oil of turpentine and phosphorus might be forced through the pumps of fire-engines and so set fire to the accursed place. Scientific Santerre had the pumps actually carried to the space before the Bastille. As the oil and phosphorus notion was soon abandoned, the pumps were used later in an endeavour to send a stream of water upon the touchstones of the Bastille cannon. This ingenious purpose was baulked by the fact that the pumps refused to carry their stream of water anything like high enough.

What was an indignant populace, what was a storm-tossed Electoral Committee, to do in the face of that grim, grey, unconquerable fortress? Neither populace nor committee knew that by some curious blundering de Launay, governor of the Bastille, had little means of holding out long. There was powder enough and to spare indeed, but a grave lack of provisions. He had only two sacks of flour, it seems, and a little rice wherewith to feed his garrison. The garrison was small enough too—thirty-two Swiss with their commander, Louis La Flue, eighty-two Invalides, Major de Losme-Salbray, and the Governor himself. A grim position, though there were fifteen good cannon on the platforms of the towers, and though it needed no great number of men to handle fifteen cannon. But the crowd outside the Bastille, and the crowd outside and inside the Hôtel de Ville, knew little or nothing of the bad garrisoning and worse victualling of the Bastille. They only saw before them their old familiar enemy holding its head high, and they wasted their wild energies in desperate devices such as those of the classical locksmith and the scientific Santerre. The Electoral Committee in its perplexity sent at eight o'clock a deputation, Bellon, Billefod, and Chaton, military men all of them. These actually breakfasted with de Launay, spent some three hours with him, and came back to say that de Launay had drawn back his cannon and would only use them in self-defence. This was not what the crowd outside the Bastille wanted. Not for three hours' parley did they come together, did they now wait clamouring under the grey walls. All Paris seemed to be marching on the place.

For, once set in motion, the popular movement became irresistible. As the wild mob tramped its way through the faubourg, it grew and grew in volume. Every street, every alley, every shop, hovel, garret, and cellar, yielded some recruit for the wild ranks, some man who could brandish a knife or shoulder a musketoon, or wield some improvised pike of his own making. Out of the slums and the blind-alleys ran rivulets of squalid ferocious humanity to swell the roaring tide that was sweeping, wave upon wave, against the Bastille. Those who had first arrived before the fortress found themselves compelled to abide at their post. Every avenue of approach to the Bastille was choked with men. Every moment the pressure from afar grew greater. What had been the extreme outer rank and fringe of the crowd a second since, was now in its turn cinctured by fresh contingents, all swaying, shouting, pushing towards the Bastille. Whatever those who were nearest to the Bastille may have felt as they gazed upon its apparently impregnable towers, they had to go on with their task. Retreat was impossible. Before them lay the prison, behind them the most fantastic multitude that ever came together for the assault of mortal fortress before. Poor wretches more ragged than the beggars of Callot's fancy, smug citizens in sober browns and hodden greys, National Guards in vivid uniforms, lean men of the law in funereal black, strangers from all the ends of the earth in odd foreign habiliments, gentlemen in coats that would not have shamed a court ceremonial, all were blended together in one inconceivable raving medley.

At ten of the clock that inconceivable, raving medley found an ambassador in the person of Thuriot de la Rosière, deputed by the district of Saint Louis de la Culture, and accompanied by Dourlier and Toulouse and a number of the crowd. Thuriot de la Rosière demanded speech of the Governor, and so became for the moment famous, unwitting of a Ninth of Thermidor yet to come when he shall help to refuse speech to a Robespierre, and so become for the moment again famous. Speech was at first denied, afterwards granted, and Thuriot de la Rosière, unaccompanied, was permitted to enter and to interview the Governor. Thuriot de la Rosière seems to have conducted his interview with de Launay in imperious fashion. He harangued the soldiers. The Swiss did not understand a syllable, but the Invalides, it is said, understood and trembled at their stern significance. 'I come,' he said to de Launay, 'in the name of the nation to tell you that your levelled cannon disturb the people, and to call upon you to remove them.' De Launay declared that he could only remove them in obedience to a direct order from the King himself. Still he had, he declared, withdrawn them from the apertures so that they were invisible from outside. De Launay seems to have definitely promised not to make any use of his cannon unless attacked in the first instance. While the interview was going on, it is said that the people outside began to grow alarmed at Thuriot's long absence, and to cry out for him, and that to pacify their demands de Launay led Thuriot to the platform of the tower that the people might see him. Perhaps Thuriot only came on the platform of the tower to see that the cannon were indeed withdrawn from the embrasures according to promise. Anyhow he appeared on one of the towers, and was greeted with a wild cry of joy from the crowd below.

If one could only conjure up some picture of the sight of that crowd, of the sea of faces which stared up at those Bastille turrets, and watched for the figure of Thuriot de la Rosière, black against the sky. To Thuriot, looking down, a sea of indistinguishable faces, stretching far as the eye could reach down every avenue, lost itself at last in mere blackness of packed heads in the distant streets. The faces were mostly French faces, ferocious faces, the faces that the Old Order had so zealously driven down out of sight, the faces of a rabble whom famine and despair held shut for so long in the shadow of death, and who had now crept out into the July sunlight to look about them a little with blinking, bloodshot eyes. If there was much that was wolfish, much that was obscene, much that was ominous in those haggard faces, it was the fault of the Old Order which made them what they were. It made them into beasts of prey, and now the beasts of prey were free, and would fain rend their masters. But the faces were not all such nightmare visions. There were faces there of men made to lead, of men who were to be famous or infamous by and by. The French Guards, with the qualities of training impressed upon their grave soldierly faces, lent a solid dignity to the mad scene. Other faces too, besides French faces, were discernible in the throng. One spectator sees the Tartar face of a Turk among the assailants. What brought the child of Islam there? There was probably at least one British face there, the eager Scotch face of William Playfair of Edinburgh; indeed if he were not there it is hard to see how he avoided it. While his brother John Playfair was quietly making himself a quiet name as a mathematician and geologist in Edinburgh wandering William had drifted into France, and drifted into the Revolution. He was a member of the Saint-Antoine militia, which had been enrolled on the night before this Bastille morning, and it is scarcely likely that he would be found missing from the ranks of his new fellowship. As we here probably see the first of him, we may as well see the last of him. It was his destiny to rescue d'Éprémesnil from popular fury in the Palais Royal, in the February of 1791—a kindly courageous deed which has been inaccurately ascribed to Pétion—to be threatened by the fulminations of Barère, to escape by way of Holland to London, and ruminate a scheme for destroying the Revolution which he had served by means of a system of forged assignats; to return to Paris after Waterloo and edit 'Galignani's Messenger,' which still goes on while poor Playfair is forgotten; and to die in London at the age of sixty-four.

There is another face of English mould visible to the mind's eye among the besiegers of the Bastille—the face of John Stone of Tiverton. We may meet and part with him too at once. It was his destiny to bring together the 'gallant and seditious Geraldine,' young Lord Edward Fitzgerald, and the beautiful Pamela, daughter of Madame de Genlis and of Equality Orleans. It was his destiny to share the suspicion with which the Revolution regarded all Englishmen after the affair of Toulon, and to taste the fare of French prisons. It was his destiny to adore the Girondists, and to glorify Charlotte Corday. It was his destiny to die peacefully in Paris after his stormy life, and to sleep in Père la Chaise, by the side, no doubt, of Helen Maria Williams, whom he loved, not wisely, but too well.

Such are some of the faces we may note while the crowd grows and gathers in the space about the Bastille. Thuriot de la Rosière, having seen and been seen by the multitude from the summit of the prison, came down again to address a vain appeal to the soldiers under de Launay's command, and to assure the mob without that de Launay would not surrender. At this news the clamour and the confusion grew louder and more bewildering. The angry sea still tossed, but as yet the signs were not entirely menacing. A number of persons came forward asking for arms, asking for peace. As they appeared to be well intentioned, M. de Launay was not unwilling to receive them, and allowed the first drawbridge to be lowered. On this drawbridge the new deputation rushed, but was followed in its rush by a number of the crowd without. The Governor appears to have feared an attack upon his little garrison, the order to fire was given, was obeyed, the crowd was driven back with bloodshed, and the drawbridge hurriedly pulled up again amidst the wild cries of those outside, who considered themselves the victims of treachery. Fire and bloodshed had begun; fire and bloodshed was to be from that moment the order of the day.

If it were only not so astonishingly hard to unravel the story of this famous siege! The very multiplicity of existing accounts only renders the task more difficult. The different descriptions of the day's deeds vary in the most essential particulars, conflict and clash upon points which are absolutely essential to the proper comprehension of the story. Never perhaps has the difficulty of sifting historical testimony, and winnowing satisfactory grain from the monstrosity of chaff, been more fantastically illustrated. On the most vital points, one apparently perfectly credible witness will say one thing, and another witness, apparently no less credible, apparently testifying in no less good faith, will roundly assert diametrically the opposite. We have on record the statements of men who were outside the prison; we have also the statement of one man who was inside the prison during the whole siege; and it is beyond expression perplexing to find that the accounts refuse to tally. That two accounts of such a wild, tumultuous affair should differ in some degree is inevitable; that they should differ as widely as they do is almost inexplicable. But they do differ, and all that the amazed student can do is to weigh as best he can, and decide as best he can, and so make the best or worst of it. The actual truth is apparently unknowable; each of us must read by the gloss of the law of probability as best he can.

Thus, for example, it would appear from some accounts that after Thuriot de la Rosière's interview with de Launay there was another deputation, another interview between the Governor and a deputy of the people, M. de Corny. Between the Corny interview and the Thuriot interview much confusion seems to have arisen, and some writers attribute to Corny what others attribute to Thuriot de la Rosière. Again, as regards the firing upon the deputation for whom de Launay had lowered the first drawbridge, it is stated in the memoir of one of the besieged soldiers that the firing only began in self-defence when the armed mob came rushing towards them shouting demands for the Bastille and imprecations upon the troops, and began cutting the chains of the drawbridge. Some say that de Launay's men only fired powder in order to alarm the somewhat disorderly invaders of the drawbridge. However, from whatever cause, firing had taken place, and the regular siege of the Bastille had now begun. Two soldiers, Louis Tournay of the Dauphin Regiment and Aubin Bonnemère of the Royal Comptois regiment, mounted on the bridge which closed the Court of the Government, aided perhaps by bayonets stuck between the stones, and, climbing on the roof of the guard-house, they succeeded in getting inside the first enclosure. De Launay had only left one Invalide to guard the drawbridge here. He had given orders to the soldiers at the second gates not to fire upon the assailants before first calling upon them to retire, which could not now be done in consequence of the distance between besiegers and besieged. Comparatively at their ease, Louis Tournay and Aubin Bonnemère hacked away at the chains of the drawbridge, apparently under no 'fiery hail.' The bridge at last fell, crushing some of the assailants underneath it. The crowd foamed over and the first court was won.

But the winning of that first court was not everything, was not even much, seemed, indeed, almost nothing to the invaders. It is difficult to form a clear idea of the swift succession of events during the early hours of that July noon. From the Cour de Gouvernement, from adjoining roofs, from behind the shelter of convenient walls, the besiegers blazed away desperately and wholly unavailingly at the walls, the towers, the turrets. From the platforms the besieged answered back, firing at random into the crowd below, and with more effect. Accounts clash here as at all points of this momentous siege. If we were to accept the authority of certain highly-wrought engravings of the time, we should conjure up a picture of a mighty keep, its ramparts bristling with legions of defenders, and assailed by a desperate populace, who are boldly attacking it in front, and who in some representations are actually endeavouring to take it by assault by means of scaling ladders and the like. Anti-revolutionary historians on the other hand have made light of the whole business, have sneered at the famous siege as a theatrical sham from beginning to end, have declared that the Bastille never would have been taken, never in fact was taken, but was only surrendered by a humane governor who was barbarously betrayed. What is certain is that the Bastille was surrounded through all the early morn and afternoon of that summer day, by an hourly swelling crowd ; that all the streets in the immediate neighbourhood were black with an excited throng, starred here and there by spots of colour where soldiers in brilliant royal uniforms and men of the Gardes Françaises mingled with the assailants. After firing began—however firing did begin—it kept on for hours, shots spitting from the black earth, from the yawning windows, from the tiled roofs upon the keep, and having about as much effect upon its rugged walls as so many cheap fireworks. From the Bastille itself, occasionally but not too regularly, rolled down an answering peal. Once and once only was a Bastille cannon fired. It has been asked in wonder why de Launay did not use his cannon save this one time, why he did not play with his artillery upon the concourse beneath, and sweep, as he easily could have swept, the streets for the time being clean of enemies. It is hard to find an answer. De Launay was perhaps unnerved. He seems to have been a man capable of conceiving strenuous deeds, but little capable of carrying them into execution. Perhaps he put confidence in those assuring orders of Besenval's, and looked for hourly relief. Perhaps he began to fear that the Bastille must fall, and deemed it as well not to put himself beyond the pale of pity with that wild mob, who might be soon his masters. Perhaps he felt that he could not count on the obedience of his soldiery. Whatever the reason may have been, it is certain that the Bastille cannon were with one exception not used on that wild day; their last chance of shooting forth flame and iron upon a rebellious Paris was happily denied to them.

In all that seething mass of besiegers certain men make themselves especially conspicuous, certain names have passed into history enveloped with a kind of legendary fame, much akin to that which belongs to the heroes of heroic epics, to the Four Sons of Aymon, and the Peers of Charlemagne. Especially conspicuous, especially dear to Saint-Antoine, was Santerre—then thinking nothing of the advantages of coke in the roasting of malt, thinking only of blended oil and phosphorus, or of any other blend that would serve to roast the Bastille. Santerre got wounded in that siege, but not to the death; he was fated to outlive the Revolution, and mourn the ruin of an excellent brewing business.

Another conspicuous figure was young Élie, officer in a regiment of the Queen, who came to the siege in citizen's attire, and went away to invest himself in his military garb to command the more respect, and was back again and in the thick of it as soon as might be. Near to him was another young man, some thirty years of age, Pierre Auguste Hulin, who had been many things in his span— waiter, working clock-maker, chasseur to the Marquis de Conflans, and now Bastille besieger. Another soldier was close at hand, Arné, 'Brave Arné,' Joseph Arné, only twenty-six years old, a native of Dole in Franche Comté, a grenadier of the company of Resuvelles, and a good-looking, impetuous, soldierly youth, as his face survives to us in portraits. A wine merchant named Cholat was near too, playing a cannonier's part. In the thick of the press was an active young man in the sober suit of a Châtelet usher, Stanislas-Marie Maillard, whose fame was not to be limited like that of Élie and of Hulin to the one brave day. Marceau was here beginning his 'brief, brave, and glorious' career. Hérault de Séchelles, the young president of the Paris Parliament, good-looking and gallant, the son of a gallant soldier sire, was in the hottest of it all. Many tales have grown up around these names, or some of these names. It is hard to say, in this siege of the Bastille, what is legend and what unadorned truth. It would seem as if we had to abandon the highly picturesque legend of Mademoiselle de Monsigny, the young beautiful girl whom the mob took for de Launay's daughter, and incontinently proposed to burn there and then as an expiatory victim for the sins of the father, and who was only rescued by the bravery of Aubin Bonnemère, while the real father, who was on guard in the Bastille, was brought to the parapet by his daughter's cries, and immediately shot dead. Aubin Bonnemère got a sabre of honour in 1790, but it is said that this deed of his is very doubtful.

Through the crowd, as we have seen, deputations made from time to time their way with drums beating and flags of truce. One of these deputations came from the Hôtel de Ville after excited individuals had come rushing in with the still hot grape-shot from the fire of de Launay's solitary cannon. It called upon de Launay solemnly, by order of the permanent committee of the Paris militia, to allow the Bastille to be occupied by the militia in common with his own troops, who were from that moment to be under the civic authority. This order was signed by de Flesselles, the pale doomed Provost, as president of the committee. Luckless de Flesselles, he sat in the grand hall of Saint-Jean surrounded with papers, letters, and people who came, the envoys of the different districts, to accuse him of treachery to his face. Through all the din he still strove hard to soothe the mob with affability, to face calmly the terrors that threatened him. Some of the electors, finding themselves compromised with the people, turned round and attacked him. Dussaulx, the translator of Juvenal, and Fauchet endeavoured to defend him, innocent or guilty, and to save him from death. Under such terrible conditions did he try to give orders such as this which was now carried to the Bastille. It was conveyed by a deputation which included M. de la Vigne, president of the electors, and the Abbé Fauchet, who has left on record a glowing account of the attempt to get speech with de Launay. According to this account the deputation tried three several times to approach and present their order; and each time were fired upon and forced to retire. On the other hand, the besieged story is that the deputation were called upon from within to come forward, that they hung back for some ten minutes in the Cour de l'Orme without venturing forward, and that de Launay thereupon declared to his soldiers that the deputation was evidently only a snare, as a genuine deputation would not have hesitated to approach. The hesitation of the deputies, if hesitation there were, was due no doubt to the cries of the people behind them who kept shouting to them to beware of the treachery of the Governor. It is easy to see how between besiegers and besieged, each desperately suspicious of the intended treason of the other, any chance of coming to any possible understanding was exceedingly unlikely. No understanding was arrived at, and the fight, if fight it can be called, raved along its course, leaving in its wake great waves of excitement that eddied back to the Hôtel de Ville and kept all there in passion and panic.

All through the long hours the fight went on, panic and passion at the Hôtel de Ville sending its electric thrills of panic and passion to the Bastille, and the Bastille sending back its electric thrills of panic and passion to the Hôtel de Ville. The pale Provost Flesselles still kept up a determined air of patriotism, although patriotism at large was growing hourly more suspicious of him. 'I saw him,' says Dussaulx, 'chewing his last mouthful of bread; it stuck in his teeth, and he kept it in his mouth two hours before he could swallow it.' The pale Governor de Launay grew more and more undetermined as the minutes stretched into hours and no hint came of Besenval's promised aid, of the great deeds that the Court party were going to do. Still Saint-Antoine, far as eye could reach, was black with raging humanity, still the fearful gaze beheld only tossing pikes and the light on musket barrels pointed to the walls as to the heavens and almost as vainly, and vomiting fire. Over that wild welter a banner, even banners, floated—mysterious banners which have puzzled and shall puzzle historians of the Bastille doomsday ever since. What was the banner, what were the banners, used on that day? Maillard and others carried flags; but these may have been white in sign of pacific intent. They certainly were not red. The red flag was then only the emblem of martial law, and did not become the symbol of revolution till 1792. Little Saint-Antoine seems to have carried a green flag. Republicanism is anxious to prove that some sort of banner was borne on that great day which was regarded as in some degree a national banner; but the thing seems hard to prove. It is more than likely that, very much as men on July 12 wandered about Paris with the tilting helmets of the Valois Princes upon their heads, and the swords perhaps of Merovingian monarchs in their hands—very much as Georget from Brest handled the King of Siam's cannon—so the banners that flapped on the wind of that wild fight may have been royal standards of all hues and ages conveniently lifted from wherever patriotism with a taste for the picturesque could lay hands upon them. Indeed in certain of the engravings which represent episodes in this new Titanomachia the curious may discern on certain of the banners therein displayed signs which look exceedingly like the insignia of royal rule, the lilies of the Bourbon line. It is difficult to believe that patriotism had on July 14 sufficiently formulated its existence, sufficiently solidified itself to be ready equipped with a patriotic banner all complete. Cockades indeed it had got—whether Flesselles strove to amuse it with such toys or no. They were no longer the green cockades of Cincinnatus and Camille Desmoulins. These had been dismissed with contumely for suggesting the green of the d'Artois livery. The new cockades were red, white, and blue. Over their origin authorities have long wrangled and shall long wrangle. But the tricolour banner had hardly sprung into existence on that day. The gules and argent and azure of its heraldry did not vex the feverish eyes of de Launay looking carefully over at the madness with a method in it beneath him. It was perhaps lucky for that madness with a method in it that de Launay was not the man of the whiff of grapeshot. A whiff of grapeshot, a succession of whiffs of grapeshot, would have held the Bastille a little longer; would have beaten back Saint-Antoine for the time being, in spite of those cannon that the Gardes Françaises brought up and trained into position against the Bastille; might have altered the course of history. But de Launay was not the man of the whiff of grapeshot.

For a moment, however, it seemed as if de Launay might be the man of the whiff of gunpowder. He had talked big before to Thuriot de la Rosière about what he would do at a push; he would blow the Bastille and all Saint-Antoine too into the July heaven. Now in this hour of gravest pressure, when all Paris seemed to be raving around the Bastille, when cannon were being brought to bear upon its gates, when the guard-house was vanishing in a sheet of flame into the air, and the flame was being briskly fed by cartloads of straw; when no help whatever came from de Besenval on the other side of the river, or from those courtly legions massed about Versailles—why then it seemed to de Launay that he would try the last, that he would be as good as his word, and do his best to blow the Bastille and its enemies out of existence together. But with de Launay apparently conception and execution were two widely different things. He caught up a fuse and made for the powder store of the Sainte-Barbe. But there a soldier, Jacques Ferrand, who did not share the heroic mood of the Governor, met him with the point of the bayonet and kept him back. One may imagine that a more determined man would not have been so kept back. He might have beaten down that bayonet. He might have found a pistol somewhere instead of that fuse. He might have either shot the mutinous soldier, or shot into the barrel of powder nearest to him, and so carried out his purpose, and caused the Bastille to disappear on the wings of the afternoon. But no. Baulked at the Sainte-Barbe powder store, de Launay still clutching his fuse ran with all speed to the Liberty Tower, where another store of powder was kept. There he again endeavoured to fire the powder. There he was prevented again by soldier Bequart, who by doing so saved the Bastille—for some few days, and saved his own life and the life of the Governor—for some few minutes. Then de Launay seems to have given up, and the end approached. The discouraged garrison were determined to capitulate, were eager to escape with their lives if they could make no better terms. They tried at first to make better terms. They beat a drum, they hoisted a white flag on the Tower of the Basinière. The assailants saw only new treason in these signs of peace, and continued furiously to advance, furiously to fire. The Swiss officer La Flue, speaking through a grating by the drawbridge, shrieked for permission to be allowed to march out with the honours of war. It is difficult to understand how any human voice could be heard, no matter how loudly it shouted, over all that infernal din. But the Two Friends of Liberty say that he was heard, and answered with savage cries of refusal. Then La Flue, after a pause for some hurried writing by de Launay, held out through the aperture a paper and cried out that they were willing to surrender if the assailants promised not to massacre the troops. All eyes were fixed on that fluttering piece of paper, all minds were speculating as to the words it might contain. But between that paper thrust through the grating by the outstretched hand of the Swiss officer, and the wild mob who were eager to read it, there was truly a great gulf fixed. The deep and yawning ditch of the moat lay between assailants and assailed, and how was that ditch to be bridged over? An unknown, courageous individual brought a plank, which was laid on the parapet and stretched across the ditch to within touch of the drawbridge, and held in its place at the other end by the weight of many patriot bodies. Then the unknown courageous individual advanced along this perilous bridge, stretched out his hand for the paper, almost had it, when he reeled, either because he lost his balance, or struck by a shot from above—or perhaps behind, for the assailants were reckless in their shooting—and so fell into the ditch, and lay there, shattered. But another volunteer for the perilous plank was not wanting. Stanislas-Marie Maillard—or was it la Réole? for accounts differ—advanced on the extemporized bridge. We see him in a picture of the time, poised over the dangerous place with legs well stretched out, with sword held well behind him in his left hand, perhaps for balance, with right hand extended to seize the offered paper. As a proof of the difficulty of deciding any point in this perplexing siege, it may be curious to mention that M. Gustave Bord in his 'Prise de la Bastille' authoritatively states that la Réole was the first to attempt the plank and to fall into the ditch; while M. Georges Lecocq in his volume says that there is no doubt that Maillard was the man to make the first attempt and fail, and fall into the fosse, and that Élie was the man to successfully secure the paper handed out by La Flue. After all, it matters very little. Malliard or another bore back the paper, gave it to Élie or to Hulin, who read it aloud. It contained these words:—'We have twenty tons of powder; we will blow up the garrison and the whole quarter if you do not accept the capitulation.' 'We accept on the faith of an officer,' answered Élie, speaking too rashly—for the wild world behind him resented all idea of capitulation—'lower your bridge.' Perhaps even then they would not have obeyed if the sight of three cannon levelled at the large drawbridge had not prompted their decision. The small drawbridge at the side of the large one was lowered, and in a moment was leaped upon by Élie, Hulin, Maillard, la Réole, and the others, who bolted it down. The Gardes Françaises, executing a dexterous manœuvre, formed in front of the bridge, and prevented the wild mob behind from flinging themselves into the ditch and meeting death in their desire to crowd on to the narrow drawbridge. The door behind this lower drawbridge was then opened by an Invalide, who seems to have asked a needlessly foolish question as to what Élie, Hulin, and the others wanted. 'We want the Bastille' was the natural answer, and with that word they entered—and took it. Immediately they rushed to the great drawbridge and lowered it, Arné leaping on it to prevent any possible attempt to raise it again. It was close upon six o'clock of the July evening. The mob surged in ; the inevitable hour had come ; the Bastille was taken.

If only that fair triumph had been quite unstained ! Still, although not wholly stainless, it remains one of the greatest triumphs ever won in the name of liberty. A hundred years have come and gone as I write. It is Sunday, July 14, 1889. The still summer air is soft with recent rain, the late summer roses hang their tinted heads, a faint mist clings about the near woods, and a grey sky, broken with hopeful gleams of silver light, canopies the companionable river. All is rest, and peace, and beauty in this fair river corner of the world that seems almost as far from the London of to-day as from the Paris of this day one hundred years ago, when the Bastille and all that the Bastille meant, and all that the Bastille represented, met its fate. From this river-land of rosebush and poplar-tree, of greenest grass and silver sky, a place almost as fair and peaceful as the Earthly Paradise of the poet's dream, it is strangely fascinating, strangely surprising, to project the mind back to that July 14, just one century ago, when Paris was fierce with flame and red with blood, and hoarse with strange cries of triumph and revenge, and the grimmest shadows fell over the darkling Seine. There would be less peace here by the Thames, or yonder by the Seine, or indeed by any river in the world to-day, were it not for the deed of that other day, that day dead a hundred years, which beat down the barriers of the Bastille and gave freedom her freshest laurels.

CHAPTER XLV

AFTERMATH

IF only that fair triumph had been quite unstained! If only that embracing of the conquered by the conquerors had been kept up! If only there had been no killing of Swiss, no killing of Invalides! One Swiss was killed at once; one luckless Invalide was killed at once; it was, of all the victims that passion-driven mob could have chosen, none other than Bequart, whose hand held back de Launay's hand from firing the powder at the Liberty Tower, and who it is said had fired no single shot during all that wild day. The hand that saved the Bastille and saved Saint-Antoine was savagely hewn off with a sabre-stroke; Bequart's body was pierced with two sword-thrusts and then dragged off to be hanged with another victim, Asselin, at the Place de la Grève, while the bleeding hand was borne aloft and ahead in triumph. The masses of men now rushing over the Bastille were wild beyond control. They were goaded, it is said, by some last shots fired from the higher platforms by soldiers who were unaware of the capitulation and who thought themselves still free to carry on the fight. The firing became so reckless on the part of the victors that some of their own party fell victims to it. Humbert was wounded, and Arné only succeeded in stopping it at the peril of his life. De Launay, conspicuous in his grey coat and red ribbon, formed one more valiant determination and once more failed to carry it out. When the place fell, and triumphant Saint-Antoine swarmed into it, a Roman thought seems to have struck him, and he attempted to kill himself with the sword-blade concealed in his cane. He did not succeed in this any more than he had succeeded in firing the powder. Maillard, Cholat, Arné and many another, lynx-eyed, strong-handed, were upon him. Arné snatched the sword-blade away from de Launay's uncertain hold. The crowd gathered around raving at him, howling for that death which he had striven to inflict upon himself. Hulin, Élie, and the other leaders closed around him; they wished to keep their word and bring him away from the Bastille in safety. But it was easier to take the Bastille than to keep de Launay alive. Élie might have promised, but Saint-Antoine had not promised, would not be bound by any promise. Saint-Antoine wanted de Launay's blood, and now encircled the little knot of men who stood around de Launay endeavouring to protect him, and urging with pale, earnest faces that the prisoners should be carried to the Hôtel de Ville and duly tried there for their offences in resisting Saint-Antoine. With the greatest difficulty, Élie, Hulin, Arné, Maillard, and the others got de Launay out of the Bastille. Saint-Antoine was snatching at him with its hundred hands, pouring imprecations upon him from its hundred throats. Saint-Antoine wanted de Launay's blood and meant to have it. Already it had dragged, nearly dead, poor Registrar Clouet, captured near the Saltpetre arsenal, to the Hôtel de Ville. Clouet's blue and gold uniform had made him seem suspiciously like Governor de Launay to insurgent patriotism. He was with difficulty released from their reluctant hands on the assurance of the Committee that Clouet was not de Launay, and by the determined courage of the Marquis de la Salle and the Chevalier de Saudry. De Launay's thin face, sharp nose, wrinkled forehead, furrowed cheeks, sunken eyes, and hard mouth, were the centre of attraction for all that furious crowd. In vain the unhappy man, with the terrors of death upon him, pleaded to Hulin, pleaded to Élie, for the protection they had promised. They had promised and they did their best to perform, but they could not perform the impossible. The wrath of the mob began to extend from de Launay to his protectors. One, L'Épine, was struck down, was nearly killed. Hulin observed that the mob seemed only to know de Launay by the fact that he was bare-headed. He conceived the heroic idea of putting his own hat upon de Launay's head; and from that moment he received the blows intended for the Governor. The royalist tradition of which

M. Ch. d'Héricault is chief champion, insists, perhaps with truth, that de Launay, still more heroic than Hulin, gave him his hat back again, wishing rather to die than endanger him. At last Hulin, in spite of his great strength, was forced aside at the Place de la Grève. Then Saint-Antoine closed upon its victim. The last words of de Launay as his murderers fell upon him stabbing and striking was, 'Friends, kill me quickly, do not let me languish.' They did kill him quickly. His head was swiftly hewn off and held aloft on the point of a pike. This was the first time of the many times that heads were so stricken off and carried on pike-point through Paris. Everyone knows or should know the ghastly sketch by Girodet of de Launay's head on the pike, with its grim expression of startled horror. That expression of startled horror on dead uplifted faces soon became familiar enough to Parisian eyes. A fearful fashion had been set. De Launay had a companion in his death in a far better man than himself, Major de Losme-Salbray, who had always been exceedingly gentle to the Bastille prisoners, and whom now, at the Place de la Grève, Saint-Antoine began to kill. The young Marquis de Pelleport, who had known five years' imprisonment in the Bastille for libels written in England, made a determined effort to save de Losme and came very near to sharing his fate. De Losme's head was cut off and thrust, too, upon a pike. Of the other prisoners, de Miray was killed in the Rue des Tournelles, and M. de Persan, lieutenant of the Invalides, by the Port au Blé. As for the rank and file, the smock-frocks of the Swiss led the mob to think that they were prisoners, and so saved them from the first fury of the attack. The Invalides came very near to perishing to a man. But the Gardes Françaises protected them, succeeded in shielding them and carrying them off to barracks. The murders could not be prevented, but the wholesale massacre of the Bastille defenders was averted.

But the vengeance of Saint-Antoine was not sated. All through that day it had been nursing its wrath against de Flesselles, till that wrath had swollen to blood-madness. Was it not said now by de Flesselles' enemies that a letter from the Provost had been found in the pockets of dead de Launay, and did not that letter bid him hold good and hope for succour till even while he, de Flesselles, amused the Parisians with cockades and promises? Saint-Antoine had got its hand in at killing now. Raging, with the heads and hands of the Bastille victims on pikes, it foamed now into the Hôtel de Ville, where Flesselles sat, pale, patient, and weary, and shouted wild accusations, wild condemnations at him. De Flesselles behaved composedly. 'Since my fellow-citizens suspect me,' he said, 'I will withdraw.' Saint-Antoine yelled to him to go to the Palais Royal. 'Very well, sirs,' he answered quietly, 'let us go to the Palais Royal.' His composure seems to have impressed the crowd, for though they pressed about him as he descended the stair they followed him without doing him any harm across the Place de la Grève. He might even have got off, but a young man suddenly sprang forward, presented a pistol at him with the words, 'Traitor, you shall go no farther,' fired, and shot him dead. Then Saint-Antoine swooped upon the prone body and hewed off its head, which in another moment was lifted high on a pike-point by the side of the head of de Launay. So through the Paris streets those ghastly trophies were paraded in terrifying procession with the beatings of drums, the shouting of strange cries, the waving of banners. Patriotism was awake and was doing grim work.

A more agreeable procession was formed a little later when the prisoners in the Bastille, who had been forgotten in the first wild excitement of victory, were unearthed, set free, and escorted in triumph through the streets. The actual number of prisoners did not keep up the popular character of the Bastille for horrors. Only seven prisoners were found in the dungeons. Four of these were imprisoned as forgers. Another, the Count de Solages, was imprisoned by his father's wish to curb his riotousness and extravagance. The two others were old men who had gone mad in prison and had been kept in prison because the authorities did not very well know what else to do with them. One was Tavernier, natural son of Pâris-Duvernay, who had been in the prison since 1759. The other was James Francis Xavier Whyte, who had been incarcerated for mental derangement since 1781. These two prisoners were afterwards placed in the Charenton madhouse.

The seven prisoners were solemnly conducted from the Bastille to the house of Santerre, where the wounded brewer entertained them sumptuously. Then they were led along the Rue Saint-Antoine to the Palais Royal by the Gardes Françaises with drums beating and banners waving. An excited populace thronged eagerly to behold these victims of tyranny and might perhaps have crushed them to death in their sympathetic enthusiasm if it had not been for the butt-ends of the escort's muskets. One person we might have expected to find among the occupants, but history so far as we have searched yields no trace of him. Réveillon the paper-manufacturer, the unwilling hero of the famous riot which had proved so momentous in its consequences, had fled for safety to the Bastille and therein vanished from knowledge. Mr. Stephens in his account of the Bastille on the morning of July 14 says, 'At present it contained but seven prisoners, together with poor Réveillon, the paper-manufacturer'; but he forgets all about poor Réveillon when he comes to the release of the prisoners, and I have striven in vain to find any trace of him. It does not seem likely that if he had been in the Bastille at the time of its capture his name would have escaped public notice. Wherever he was he certainly has vanished from knowledge. There were more important matters going than the fate of a paper-manufacturer, and yet it is curious that, considering how inevitably his name will be associated with the early hours of the Revolution, it is seemingly impossible to follow his fortunes farther than the threshold of the Bastille.

The news of the liberation of the Bastille prisoners soon spread to the other prisons and prompted a keen desire for like liberty in the breasts of the inmates. The poor prisoners imprisoned for debt at La Force and the Châtelet broke out, took the key of the fields, and rejoiced to find themselves free. Amongst them was an Irish peer, the Earl of Massareene, who had been nineteen years a prisoner. Irish peers had a way of turning up in the most unexpected places—witness that pair, father and son, who were slaves to the barbarous Turk, and played their curious part in the history of Morocco. But no one perhaps is hero of a stranger story than this indebted gentleman, who passed his life very pleasantly within the four walls of a gaol and who owed his liberty at last to a revolution. The mighty cause that threw down the Bastille and destroyed the Old Order prompted Lord Massareene to force his way out of his prison at the head of his fellow-prisoners. So the wind that uproots the oak may release the acorn.

Paris as a whole did not disgrace itself on the

night of July 14. The murders, horrible as they were, were but the work of a few persons, and were regarded at the time, rightly or wrongly, as the acts of a wild justice. But there was practically no pillaging, no disorder, no repetition of the unworthy acts of July 12. The great city had done a great work and was perhaps calmer in its victory than it had been in its expectation. It had had its victims and its martyrs; it had its heroes. It had Élie, with his battered sword. It had sleepless Moreau de Saint-Méry. It had Fauchet and Marceau and Hulin and many another man. These were unlike in all things else, but alike in their determination to keep for the people the Paris they had won? The Parisians showed a determination worthy of their leaders. In the full flush of victory they did not forget prudence. An attack seemed inevitable. They prepared to receive it. Everyone helped in the task of protecting the town. Barricades were made, entrenchments dug, weapons distributed. The militia kept watch and ward. The night of victory was passed under arms. Paris was ready to face the uttermost.

CHAPTER XLVI

THE STONES OF THE BASTILLE

So the Bastille stands, much as it stood once before now, four centuries ago, gaunt, gutted, the imperfect shell of a prison house. Then, those four centuries earlier, busy Parisian hands laid stone upon stone with infinite care, thinking to build till doomsday. Now busy Parisian hands were pulling stone from stone in fierce impatience. Poor Aubriot, who was kind to Jews and Jewesses, if his ghost might revisit the glimpses of the waning July moon, would think that doomsday had indeed come. So it had in a sense, the doomsday of that whole system which Aubriot thought as enduring as the firmament. Paris, waking up next morning and staring at the abandoned walls, knew its strength at last. It is impossible, perhaps unprofitable, to speculate upon what might have happened if de Launay had surrendered at once, and if the first heralds of insurgent Saint-Antoine had been permitted to walk their free way through its corridors and lay their patriotic hands upon whatever weapons they could find. Perhaps the lease of life of the house of Capet might have been a little further prolonged. But with that desperate struggle, that wild, astonishing triumph, the sudden conquest of the long unconquerable, the rising revolution received the revelation of its power. The Bastille was an unimportant place enough. But being taken, and taken in such a way, it became the symbol and the inspiration of a new world.

A contemporary writer declares that if the towers of this edifice, of which there were many, had been giants, instead of inanimate masses of mortar and stone, they could not have more effectually kept alive the indignation of the people against them. The mob appeared to be resolved not to allow one particle to stand beside another. That such may be the fate of all similar burying places for living virtue must, says the observer piously, be the wish of every man who is not a monster at heart. A piece of one of the stones of this so detestably celebrated building soon became scarce. Everyone gathered what he could, and converted it into tablets and ornaments. Even rings and ciphers were engraved from pieces, and made into patriotic presents. That which a short time before had been hideous to look on, now was esteemed as a precious relic. In this form, the philosopher meditates, the traditional history of the disgraceful and abject condition of man in the eighteenth century will be best handed down to future ages. It is said that, on the morrow after the taking of the Bastille, the crowds of people which came from all parts to see it were so great, that five hundred of the militia could not keep them at a distance whilst the walls were being thrown down. Everything that could be found in the doomed prison-house, from rusty iron chains to mouldering archives, was eagerly dragged into the daylight, subjected to an eager scrutiny.

One hundred times since that day has the fourteenth of July come round again; one hundred times the civilized world has had good reason to rejoice that a Parisian mob stormed and destroyed a worthless fortress. As we look back over the lapsed century we can see that with the passage of every year the importance and the dignity of the taking of the Bastille has grown and strengthened. Men have not been wanting, we have seen, who try to minimize its importance, to diminish its historic dignity. They urge that the Bastille at the time of its fall was a place of no importance. They say that it had ceased to be the terror-house of political prisoners. They maintain that it was not in any military sense taken at all. They protest that the whole episode was an absurd blunder which attached to the Bastille an importance that it had long out-dated, and which gave its captors a burlesque air of pseudo-heroism. They even assert that it was a crime, the herald of a long catalogue of crimes. There is little or nothing to be said for such arguments. It was not the captors of the Bastille who were responsible for the blunders and the bloodshed of the Revolution. It was the condition of things which made the capture of the Bastille so momentous. The very fact that at the time people of all parties thought its fall so momentous is enough to prove the case. Even if the Bastille itself had ceased to terrify, it still represented the old terrific idea. It was a very strong argument in stone in favour of the feudal system, and all that the feudal system meant. It had long been the dread and the curse of Paris, the merciless answer to all freedom of thought, of word, of deed. If the first wave of the rising tide of democracy beat against it and overwhelmed it, it was not for nothing. Its mighty keep, its eight portentous towers were the solid visible presentment of all that was worst in the Old Order of things. It was a symbol, and symbols are the most potent influences in the struggles of political forces. But it was not merely a symbol. It still held prisoners; it was still ready to hold prisoners; its guns were a standing menace to Paris. If we were to imagine a London mob of to-day besieging the Tower of London the event would certainly have little historic dignity or importance. Long generations have gone by since the Tower of London represented any despotic system, or had any political significance or symbolism whatever. But every man who attacked that Bastille upon that midsummer day one hundred years ago, looked upon the Bastille as the petrifaction of the Old Order and the old despotism. The youngest could remember how it had been used for the basest political purposes, how it had been employed to stifle freedom. It was hated, it was justly hated ; it was natural and significant that the first popular stroke should be levelled against it ; its fall is an event of moment in the history of man, a day of thanksgiving in the history of civilization.

The first fury of popular success conceived of nothing better to do with the Bastille than to destroy it utterly, to blow it as far as possible from the face of the earth. It would send its key across the Atlantic to Washington to lie on his table at Mount Vernon. It would destroy all the rest. The thought was not unhappy if it had been but confined to the mere bricks and mortar of the famous keep and eight terrible towers. But this was not so. General de Gribeauval had collected together within the walls of the Bastille quite a little museum of models, and of objects connected with sling instruments of war. The luckless Gribeauval collection was scarcely likely to be sacred in the eyes of irritable Parisians seeking arms. Whatever was serviceable, whatever was weaponable among the specimens of an antique warfare, was seized upon eagerly and converted to new uses. The rest was pulled apart, scattered abroad, thrown aside, dispersed, a mere wreck, the despair of military archæologists. Unhappily, too, patriotism, inspired by a kind of Omar-like passion, conceived the idea that the archives of the Bastille, all the vast mass of papers it contained, were as detestable as the rest, and as deserving of destruction. The ground about the Bastille was littered for days with a wealth of documents. Much of the mass was wantonly destroyed. Much went into the prudent hands of the butterman and the trunk-maker. A small part was rescued by collectors. Some portion went to Russia. Some portion of it passed into the hands of the State, which suddenly awoke to the importance of these papers before it was all too late. These have since in various ways at least partially seen the light. Beaumarchais, like the adventurous, intelligent man he was, guessed that there were good gleanings to be gathered from this harvest of flying paper, and laid burglarious hands on a considerable quantity. Either less fortunate envy or purer patriotism, however, noted and denounced him, and Beaumarchais had, somewhat reluctantly, to disgorge his treasure, which, as he gracefully explained, he had gathered from under the feet of the people on July 15, while he was visiting the Bastille at the head of a party of armed men.

If it is hard to forgive the destruction of so much precious historical matter, it is easier to forgive and easy to understand the spirit which prompted the total annihilation of the Bastille itself. On July 16 it was decided by the Assembly of Electors that the building should be obliterated, and a committee was formed to see that the determination was carried out. The Committee found a zealous and a faithful servant in the patriot Palloy. Out of the ruins of the Bastille a curious figure rises, the figure of the patriot Palloy. The patriot Palloy, who weathered the Revolution better than many a better man, was, at the time of the taking of the Bastille, a master mason of some five and thirty years. He had prospered and made money by his trade. He was associated with the royal hunting buildings. He had always a keen eye to the main chance, and a kind of half-humorous, half-buffoon insight into the popular temper which guided him with sufficient shrewdness to serve his turn. He took a part in the attack upon the Bastille, but his real attack was reserved for the days succeeding its fall. Under the directions of the committee of demolition he fell upon the Bastille at the head of a large body of workmen, and set to work with a will. His quick and crafty wit saw a way of turning the Bastille to good account. It was not enough for him, he said, merely to throw down the walls of the hated fortress, he wished to perpetuate the horror of its memory. So he set to work at once to turn every possible fragment of the Bastille to ingenious account. Out of its stones he constructed eighty-three little models of the Bastille, which he sent, one each, to each of eighty-three departments. What, we may wonder, have become of all of those eighty-three miniature Bastilles now? Some are lodged securely in local museums. With the bars and bolts he fabricated swords, and struck any quantity of medal. Every dismembered morsel of the Bastille was turned to account to make statuettes of Liberty, patriotic busts, snuff-boxes, paper-weights, and all manner of toys and trinkets for true patriotism to wear around its neck or at its watch chain. It became promptly the fashionable thing to carry some souvenir of the Bastille on one's person, thanks to the enterprise of Palloy, and the patronage of the Orleanist princes who set the example. The larger stones were employed, many of them, to help in the construction of the Bridge of the Revolution, that the people of Paris might for ever tread beneath their feet the stones of the hated building. Even private individuals had staircases constructed of the same materials and for the same patriotic purpose. Perhaps the grimmest fact in connection with all this wholesale distribution of the Bastille was the present which Palloy made to the Dauphin of a set of dominoes which had been made from the marble of the chimney of the Governor of the Bastille. Rumour has inaccurately reported that the dominoes were constructed from the bones of prisoners found in the Bastille. It does not need that additional touch to make the thing more tragic. It is infinitely, ironically pathetic to think of the poor little lad playing, or being asked to play, with the fragments of the great fortress which had for so long represented the power and terror of his race, and which now, reduced to a mass of trinkets and rubbish, was but the helpless herald of his own destruction and the destruction of his house. That the King, Louis XVI. himself, should have accepted and made use of a Bastille paper-weight with his own portrait engraved thereon, which was presented to him, is less pathetic and not at all surprising.

Palloy was consumed by a very high sense of his own importance. He organized the workmen under his control into a kind of solemn and apostolic guild ; he called the emissaries whom he despatched with the models of the Bastille to the different departments, Apostles of Liberty. Palloy and his workmen were bound together by solemn oaths of fidelity and mutual assistance, and their organization held together for some years, and figured often in connection with the conquerors of the Bastille, who formed a sort of armed and official corporation, in many ceremonies and functions of the early revolutionary years. When the Bastille was finally made up into models and medals, Palloy's fertile mind conceived the notion of a column to stand upon its site. But that conception was not destined to be carried out for many a long year—not until the reign of Louis Philippe, when the absurd plaster elephant which Napoleon set up, and in which Victor Hugo's Gavroche used to hide, was in its turn abolished.

Palloy himself, as we have said, weathered the Revolution and many rules beside, but we may part company with him here, after casting a prophetic glance over his grotesque career. He proved to be the most perfect French parallel to our illustrious Vicar of Bray. To him whatever was, in the way of government, was right. A fairly good craftsman, a wretched writer and rhymer, he employed his talents and his half-crazy wits in turn for the benefit of every party. At first a constitutional royalist, he took the revolutionary fever in all its various stages, and became in turn Girondist, Montagnard, Hébertist, a devotee of Thermidor, a follower of Robespierre, a partisan of the Directory. The moment Napoleon came to power our Palloy became a furious Bonapartist, but his fury faded with the return of the Bourbons, and the loyal royalism which had long lain dormant reasserted itself. Forgetting the clumsy caricatures with which he had insulted the agony of Louis XVI. and Marie Antoinette, he took to writing royalist songs of a sufficiently ridiculous and despicable nature; but he veered again to zealous Orleanism the moment that Louis Philippe came to the throne. He died at last in 1835, the weathercock of that wild period, the picture in little of every successive phase of the political events of his life. It may be fairly said that the Revolution did not produce a more ridiculous figure. His tergiversations, his impudence, his crack-brained self-conceit rank him at least amongst the most remarkable caricatures of history.

Palloy's mean, foolish, cunning countenance may still be familiar to the curious in the engravings of the day. That porcine face grinned its pitiful approval of all powers that be; those fish-shaped eyes saw with servile indifference so many good and gallant things go down into the dust. A fulsome epigram composed or prompted by himself, and inscribed at the foot of his likeness, informed the world that a future age, impressed by the greatness of this good man, would confuse the word 'patriot' with the word 'Palloy.' Well, the term patriot has remained with Palloy, remained as the most curious brand of ignominy that could well be attached to his despicable name.

Such as he was, he helped to set the fashion of what may be called 'Bastillism.' His little effigies, constructed from the veritable stone of the Bastille, were the precursors of all manner of miniature Bastilles. Ingenious potters, commended by Camille Desmoulins, devised large stoves in the shape of the Bastille, wherewith to warm the feet of deputies in the Convention. These served the double purpose of keeping the actual temperature comfortable, and feeding by the sight of their significant shape the patriotic hearts within the legislative bosoms. Plates were fabricated representing, more or less ably according to the capacity of the artist, the taking of the Bastille. It was quite a glorious thing to eat one's food off a platter which served to perpetuate such memories and inspire such heroic aspirations. Those plates were common enough then, but the Bastille has been re-destroyed time and time again in their destruction, and specimens of them are worth their weight in gold now. Which thing is also a sermon.

END OF THE SECOND VOLUME

www.ingramcontent.com/pod-product-compliance
Lightning Source LLC
Chambersburg PA
CBHW022116290426
44112CB00008B/692